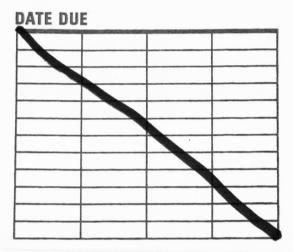
RISM

CS

AMATEURISM
AND
ATHLETICS

Leisure Press
P.O. Box 3
West Point, N.Y. 10996

CONTENTS

Preface

I want to express my appreciation to Professors Donald R. Casady, John M. Burdick, and Louis Alley at the University of Iowa for guidance and constructive criticism during the dissertation phase of this project. I am also indebted to Professors Philip L. Reuschlein, James Keating, and Kenneth Doherty for their encouragement, suggestions, and creative ideas on this subject.

I also want to acknowledge cooperation of the staffs at the International Olympic Committee Headquarters in Lausanne, Switzerland, the British Olympic Committee office, the British Museum Library, Lord's Cricket Ground, The Amateur Rowing Association in London, the Bethel College and Seminary Libraries, the University of Minnesota Library and the University of Iowa Library. Without the assistance of men and women in these offices this book would not have been possible. I also want to express appreciation for the assistance of Robert Lynde in collecting data in Switzerland and London on our way home from the International Olympic Academy in 1971.

I also want to express appreciation to Rachel Sargent Robinson for permission to use quotations from her excellent book entitled *Sources for the History of Greek Athletics*, The Harvard University Press for permission to use quotations from the Loeb Classical Library, The University of Chicago Press for permission to quote James B. Keating's article "Sportsmanship as a Moral Category" published in the October 1964 issue of *Ethics*, The Pennsylvania State University Press for permission to quote from James B. Keating's article "The Heart of the Problem of Amateur Athletics" published in the January 1965 *Journal of Education*, The Athletic Institute for permission to quote from Kenneth Doherty's article entitled "Modern Amateurism" in the volume entitled *Health and Fitness in the Modern World*, The Amateur Athletic Union of the United States for permission to quote extensively from its 1977 *Official Handbook of the AAU Code*, and the University of Colorado, Department of Classics for permission to quote from Clarence A. Forbes' article entitled "Crime and Punishment in Greek Athletics" published in the *Classical Journal* in February 1952. I also want to express appreciation to Kenneth Doherty for permission to quote from personal correspondence from him. Without cooperation with the above individuals and publishers this book would not have been complete.

I am also grateful for the sabbatical leave granted me by the administration of Bethel College which provided the time to complete this project. I am also indebted to Professor Lorraine Eitel for an early proof reading of the manuscript and to Jean Lindblom for excellent work in typing the final manuscript. Special recognition is also due to my wife, Laurene, for her assistance and encouragement during the past ten years of work on this project.

E.G.

CHAPTER I

The Importance of Amateurism As An Issue

INTRODUCTION

The meaning, purposes and values of amateurism in sports, as well as the implications of classifying some competition as amateur, have been subjects of controversy since the development of modern amateurism in the nineteenth century. Sloane, one of the original members of the International Olympic Committee, has said that at the time of the first modern Olympic Games in 1896 "the perennial question of the amateur and the professional (was) the most knotty, elusive, and exasperating of all questions connected with sport."[1] In a study of incidents involved in the past modern Olympic Games, Fuoss observed in 1951 that:

> One of the most persistent problems in connection with the program of competitive sports is that of amateurism. Evidence indicates that Olympic authorities have been more concerned with the problem of amateurism than probably any other aspect of the Olympic Games.[2]

The fact that some aspect of amateurism has been on the agenda for most, if not all, sessions of the International Olympic Committee meetings emphasizes the importance of the issue and the controversial aspect of the problem.[3] Today, for coaches, athletes, administrators, and spectators, amateurism continues to be a confusing and perplexing problem locally, nationally, and internationally.

Further evidence of the problems involved in amateurism is presented in an article by Doherty in which he cited a letter dated February 1, 1966, by Avery Brundage, a former president of the International Olympic Committee: "I have been endeavoring to establish a uniform amateur definition for many years, but when you are dealing with 25 to 30 sports in 120 different countries, in a score or more languages, it is not easy."[4]

Many of the problems surrounding amateurism become apparent even to the casual reader of the eligiblity or amateur codes and official interpretations used for the Olympic Games over the years. For example, this code for many years stated: "anyone awarded a scholarship mainly for his athletic ability"[5] was ineligible for Olympic competition, but it was common knowledge to American college athletes, coaches, and educators that a high percentage of the college varsity athletes in the United States who have participated in the Olympic Games have received financial assistance which was based on their athletic ability and not their scholastic ability.

Another part of the code for years stated that "those who have capitalized in any way on their athletic fame or success, profited commercially therefrom or have accepted special inducements of any kind to participate, or have secured employment or promotion by reason of their sports performances rather than their ability are ineligible for the Olympic Games."[6] These two aspects of the amateur code serve as examples of some of the problems underlying amateurism and as evidence for the accusation that amateurism breeds hypocrisy and deceit. If amateurism does indeed create a situation that breeds excessive hypocrisy and deceit, then possibly amateurism has created a more serious evil than any evils that might result from athletic professionalism.[8]

During the first half of the nineteenth century, being an amateur was primarily a social distinction, and it is argued by some that amateurism is still an aristocratic concept. Because of the aristocratic distinctiveness of some amateur rules perhaps there is a segment of the United States population and the population of other countries that is really no more "free" to participate in the modern Olympics than were the peasants and slaves of ancient Greece during the time of the ancient Olympics because of the time and expense necessary to become a local, national, or international champion. For example, in the United States, which is the richest country in the world, 24.3 percent of the population had incomes of less than $3.999 and an additional 8.0 percent made between $4,000 and $4,999 in 1965.[9] Many would argue that most of the people in these income categories could not attain a level of athletic achievement necessary for national or international competition and fully abide by some of the amateur codes of that year or today.

As the twentieth century progresses, questions are increasingly being asked about the equality of opportunity to participate in athletics, the opportunity for fair competition, and the general justice and ethics of amateurism, which Brundage claimed is a "philosophy of life."[10] Some of these questions stem from the position of athletes in military organizations, on industrial teams, in colleges and universities and in nations with various types of government. For example, it is obvious that the position of an athlete under a communistic form of government or in a society with a guaranteed annual wage has implications for amateurism.

As a graduate student in physical education, with an interest in history and philosophy, I became intrigued with the questions and concerns expressed about amateurism and the Olympic Games during the 1960's. As I began to study the issues involved, I became aware of the confusion and lack of understanding that existed on the subject; therefore, I began to consider researching the topic for my doctoral dissertation.

In order to determine if there really needed to be a study of amateurism, I wrote to three respected leaders in the field of amateur sports. All three — Donald Hull,[11] former executive director of the Amateur Athletic Union of the United States; Avery Brundage,[12] former president of the International Olympic Committee; and Kenneth Doherty,[13] author and former executive director of the Pennsylvania Relays — said there was a need for additional research on amateurism. Doherty summarized this need with the following statement: "In my opinion no problem in the entire area of competitive sports is so crucial and timely as that of amateurism. Like so many problems of our time, development has occurred with increasing rapidity until one feels that each day or each action may be the critical one."[14]

My awareness of the problems surrounding amateurism and the recognition of this concern by international sports leaders ultimately led me to research the subject for my doctoral dissertation which was titled "A Study of Amateurism in Sports."[15] Since completing my dissertation in 1970, I have continued to study the issues involved and to collect information on the subject. Part of the continued research has meant attending the International Olympic Academy in Greece, and collecting information at the International Olympic Committee headquarters in Lausanne, Switzerland and in London during 1971.

Since 1971 some major changes in amateurism have evolved, especially related to the Olympic Games, but there are still many views on the various issues. I believe that some of the confusion stems from a lack of understanding of athletics in ancient Greece, and how sports and amateurism evolved during the nineteenth century. Because athletics and the subject of amateurism continues to be of worldwide concern, I decided to revise and update my doctoral dissertation in hopes of adding light to the subjects.

Some of the common questions about amateurism are: How did amateurism evolve? What are the values involved in amateurism? What makes one a professional? Is professional inherently evil?

APPROACH TO THE STUDY

In my research I have sought to 1) identify the practices and principles of athletics in ancient Greece that have implications for the controversy surrounding contemporary sports and amateurism, 2) identify the basic purposes and distinctions of amateurism as espoused in the nineteenth and twentieth centuries, 3) identify some problems in applying different definitions of amateurism to societies during various eras, and 4) suggest some solutions to the problems of amateurism thus identified.

In order to understand adequately contemporary amateurism and its associated problems, it is my opinion that one must understand the historical development of amateurism and sports and the circumstances in which amateurism evolved. Therefore, the basic approach of this study of amateurism in sports is historical. The views expressed are based on the belief that amateurism is a by-product of developments in sports, and that developments in sports and amateurism are closely associated with technological and social advances and changes in society.

Much of the material in this study is related to the modern Olympic Games, because since 1894, the modern Olympic Games and the International Olympic Committee have been important factors in the development of amateurism. This has been true for primarily two reasons: 1) the modern Olympic Games have become the highest level of competition in many sports, and as a result, participation in the Olympic Games is the goal of most athletes who desire the highest level of competition in such sports, and 2) the amateur or Eligibility Code of the Olympic Games has become the standard of amateurism to which all individuals must conform if they desire to participate in the Olympic Games and to which national and international organizations must conform if they are to be given some authority by the International Olympic Committee in conducting the modern Olympic Games. However, the Olympic games *per se* are not being studied. Instead, it is amateurism in general and amateurism as defined and advocated by the International Olympic Committee and other organizations that is being studied.

In Chapter II, I shall identify the major purposes of amateurism, define the meaning of the key terms, and discuss some of the reasons why amateurism has been difficult to define. The material in the chapter identifies some of the aspects of amateurism which make the next four chapters clearer and more meaningful.

The historical background of this study on amateurism begins in Chapter III with a review of athletic practices in ancient Greece. Included in this review is a survey of the nature of the awards given, the opportunities to compete, the motives for participating, the rules for various events and festivals, and other facts that have played a part in modern amateurism. This review is included because the modern Olympic Games are a revival of the ancient Olympic Games and because advocates of contemporary amateurism have often referred to athletics in ancient Greece as the model to be emulated.[16] [17]

Chapter IV deals primarily with the historical development of sports and some technological and social developments in the nineteenth century. Chapter V describes the development of amateurism during the nineteenth and early twentieth century in more detail. The major emphasis of these chapters is on sports in Great Britain and the United States since contemporary amateurism evolved primarily from the events and cultures in these two countries.

The development and the influence of the modern Olympic movement on amateurism is presented in Chapter VI. In order to convey the changing meaning of amateurism in sports, I have included numerous definitions of amateurism in both Chapters V and VI.

After the establishment of a historical perspective, the basic issues and problems involved in contemporary amateurism are discussed in reference to certain basic principles, which, in my opinion, should govern a system or framework of athletic competition for the general public.

FOOTNOTES

1 William M. Sloane, "The Olympic Idea, Its Origin, Foundation, and Progress," *The Century Magazine*, (June 1912), p. 410.

2 Donald E. Fuoss, "An Analysis of the Incidents in the Olympic Games from 1924 to 1948. with Reference to the Contribution of the Games to International Goodwill and Understanding" (unpublished, D. Ed. Type C Project; Columbia University, 1951), p. 251.

3 Nadejda LeKarska, "An Extraordinary Record," *Bulletin of the Bulgarian Olympic Committee* (Circa, 1966), p. 18.

4 J. Kenneth Doherty, " A Better Future for United States Track and Field," *Quarterly Review* (June 1966), p. 39.

5 *The Olympic Games* (Lausanne, Switzerland: International Olympic Committee, 1967), p. 44.

6 Ibid.

7 John C. Kofoed, "Sport and Snobbery," *The American Mercury,* 15 (December 1928), p. 432.

8   Howard J. Savage, *et al. American College Athletics,* Bulletin No. 23 (New York: The Carnegie Foundation for the Advancement of Teaching, 1929), p. 302.

9   Bureau of the Census, *Statistical Abstract of the United States, 1967* (Washington, D. C.: Government Printing Office, 1967), p. 333.

10   Avery Brundage, " Principles of the Olympic Movement," *Journal of the American Association for Health, Physical Education and Recreation* (November 1959), p. 26.

11   Donald Hull, Executive Director of the Amateur Athletic Union of the United States, personal correspondence to the writer on October 2, 1967.

12   Avery Brundage, President of the International Olympic Committee, personal correspondence to the writer on October 19, 1967.

13   Kenneth Doherty, personal correspondence to the writer on October 19, 1967.

14   Ibid.

15   Eugene A. Glader, "A Study of Amateurism in Sports" (unpublished Ph.D. dissertation, University of Iowa, 1970).

16   *Addresses of President Avery Brundage at Solemn Openings of I.O.C. Sessions Between 1952 and 1968* (Lausanne, Switzerland: International Olympic Committee [n. d.]). pp. 11-13.

17   Tait McKenzie, "The Chronicale of the Amateur Spirit," *Proceedings of the Fifth Annual Convention* (The National Collegiate Athletic Association, 1910), pp. 40-41.

CHAPTER II

Amateurism and Sports

INTRODUCTION

In the first section of this Chapter, I shall discuss the major purposes of amateurism as a category of competitive sports. These purposes are 1) a social distinction, 2) a special advantage distinction, and 3) a motivational distinction. Most of the historical documentation for the purposes of amateurism is included in Chapter V and VI, which review the development of amateurism, rather than in this chapter in order to present these distinctions more succinctly here. In the second section of this chapter, I shall discuss the basic characteristics and distinctions of the terms "professionalism," "sport," and "athletics." In the last section of this chapter, I list some of the reasons why amateurism has been difficult to define.

MAJOR PURPOSES OF AMATEURISM

Social Distinction

One of the primary and original purposes of amateurism as a category of sports was social distinction, that is, to separate the so-called gentleman amateur from the lower classes of society. The "mechanics clause" in some definitions was an obvious indication of the social distinction of amateurism during the nineteenth century. The "mechanics clause" in these definitions eliminated mechanics, artisans, and labourers from the amateur ranks.

Associated with the exclusive attitude of the upper class people was the low regard with which the professional athlete, who competed for money, came to be viewed during the nineteenth century. Involved in the social distinction was the view, which emerged during the second half of the nine-teenth century, that any person who competed for money was not only basically inferior, but also a person of questionable character.[1] [2] Prior to about 1860, competing for a prize was common in amateur sports and was not viewed with disdain by gentlemen. In fact, money prizes had been awarded to winners in the Amateur Rowing Championship in England until 1861.[3] But when professional athletes who were deceitful and dishonest became identified with the practice of competing for prizes, the custom came under suspicion by the gentleman class. However, many of the prob-lems that emerged were due to the absence of uniform rules and governing agencies for controlling sports and not just the practice of competing for a prize.

The social distinction of amateurism was also associated with the aristo-cratic attitude prevalent in England during the nineteenth century and early twentieth century, which was described by Whigham in 1909.

> Now there are certain attributes that are supposed to belong to those of high birth. The fact that a man is born into [the] society of gentlemen imposes upon him certain duties and, to some extent the ideas of his class. He is expected to have a broad education, catholic tastes, and a multiplicity of pursuits. He must not do any-thing for pecuniary gain; and it can easily be seen that he must not specialize. It is essentially the mark of a bourgeois mind to specialize.[4]

In England this lofty view toward life and snobbish attitude toward spe-cialization became part of the amateur spirit in athletics.* Related to the class consciousness of the people in England and the development of athlet-ics, Griffin, writing in 1891, said:

> The 'gentlemen' part of the clause, although 'sour grapes' to numbers, was not only absolutely necessary, but proved the savior of athleticism. But for confining athletics to the select side of soci-ety, the better class of men would not, they could not, under the then existing state of affairs, have gone in for sports, which would, therefore, never have reached its present high estate.[6]

This statement leads to the conclusion that a restrictive category of sports was considered necessary by some people in order to attract the upper classes to sports. The assumption was that the sports movement would grow more rapidly when the upper classes became interested in sports.

As a means of bringing order to athletics and implementing the social dis-tinction of the classes, athletic or sports clubs were founded and closed

---

*This view of life in England is described in Broderick's article "A Nation of Amateurs."[5]

competition within a club or among clubs was held. One of the first means used by clubs to provide some assurance of honest competition was the requirement that made it difficult, if not impossible, for athletes to compete under false names. This was often accomplished by restricting competition to club members or persons introduced by club members.

Special Advantage Distinction

Beginning in the 1820's, competitors who had a special advantage because of the skill and strength developed in their regular occupation were declared ineligible for amateur competition. For example, during the early part of the nineteenth century it was believed that laboring people had an advantage in athletics, as originally was the case in rowing, because the nature of their work made them physically stronger and sometimes more skillful than the gentleman amateurs.[7] Thus, it was concluded that it was unfair for a gentleman to compete with a laborer because of the physical advantage of the laborer.[8] As a result, the laborer was automatically classed as a professional. This resulted in a category of competition restricted on the basis of ability and social position and not on the basis of money earned from athletic competition.

In more recent years this special advantage distinction has been used to declare ineligible for amateur competition athletes who have profited from their athletic skills or have neglected their usual vocation. The assumption is that people who earn money from their athletic abilities and who can neglect their regular jobs will be able to train harder and longer than persons who must work for a living, and as a result, such persons will have a special advantage in competition. This view was clearly reflected in the Eligibility Code for the Olympic Games of 1964, 1968, and 1972 by statements which declared that participants in the Games 1) must have a basic occupation, 2) cannot neglect their usual vocation or employment, and 3) cannot, by special training in a camp, interrupt their occupation for more than four weeks in a calendar year.[9] These specific restrictions by the International Olympic Committee were eliminated in October, 1974.[10]

Motivational Distinction

A third purpose for the development of amateurism related to the motive for which a person participated in athletic competition. Perry, an American writing in 1904, described the "true amateur athlete, the true sportsman...[as] one who takes up his sport for the fun of it and love of it, and to whom success or defeat is a secondary matter so long as the play is good."[11] Perry later described an amateur as one who "is unskillful because untrained; desultory because incessant devotion to his hobby is unnecessary and wearisome; ineffective because, after all, it is not a vital matter whether he succeed or fail."[12]

According to many definitions, an amateur was a person who competed "solely for the love of sport"[13] or solely for the pleasure and physical, mental, and social benefit that could be derived from athletics.[14] Stemming from this emphasis of love for the game was the requirement that participants in the Olympic Games in 1948 through 1960[15] [16] had to sign a statement containing the pledge,

> I...declare on my honor...that I have participated in sports solely for pleasure and for the physical, mental, and social benefits I derive, therefrom; that sport to me is nothing more than a recreation without material gain of any kind, direct or indirect...[17]

Such motives for engaging in competition have usually been considered to be worthy by advocates of contemporary amateurism. In contrast to these positive motives for engaging in competition are the motives implied by the many definitions of an amateur which state that a person who receives any pecuniary reward for participation in sports is a professional. The implication is that any person who competes for some financial reward has engaged in competition with unworthy, or at least questionable, motives.

Related to the above purposes of amateurism as a category of sports is the objective of promoting "fair and equal competition" by means of amateurism. In some respects this could be looked upon as a fourth purpose, but it is really a facet of the purposes of the special advantage distinction and the motivational distinction discussed in the preceding pages. "Fair and equal competition" as an objective of amateurism could also be thought of as an aspect of the social distinction.

In a similar manner, many of the rules of various amateur sports organizations help achieve more than one of the purposes of amateurism. For example, the restriction on the amount of time that may be spent in training, the prohibitions against competing for money, and the requirement that a person have an occupation help to achieve both the purposes of the special advantage distinction and the motivational distinction. Rules such as the one preventing "broken-time" payments* and limits on the amount of money that may be earned from competition or be allowed for expenses could be considered as meeting all three of the distinctions discussed in the preceding pages.

Most likely no leader in amateur organizations today would admit that

---

*The term broken-time or broken-payment refers to the practice of paying the athlete for time away from his usual job when he is involved in practice for competition or competition itself or travelling to or from competition or practice.

social distinctions are still a consideration in amateur sports, but it is never-theless true that eligibility rules of the Olympic Games until October, 1974 did discriminate against some people on the basis of the type of job they held.

The preceding statements lead to the conclusion that an amateur in sports may be considered as one who participates in his leisure without ex-tensive training, and without financial, social or other significance attached to winning or losing. When viewed in these terms amateur sports is a type of play or recreation. This view of amateurism in sports fits the definition of sports given in A New English Dictionary of Historical Principles which, in 1888, described sport as a "pleasant pastime, entertainment, or amusement; recreation or diversion."[18]

Underlying these aspects or characteristics of amateurism in sports are certain fundamental principles which were inherent in the common view of amateurism in the past century. These principles include the idea that sports should develop physical and moral qualities in the participants. This empha-sis is perhaps best expressed by the leaders of the modern Olympic move-ment. For example, de Coubertin, the founder of the Olympic Games stated that he intended that "Olympism be a school of moral nobility and purity, as well as of physical endurance and energy."[19] [20]

Brundage, the immediate past president of the International Olympic Committee, stated that in 1969:

> ...the Olympic movement is far more than a quadrennial sport fes-tival. It is a philosophy of education and life itself, the develop-ment of the complete man, mentally, physically, morally, with the idea that character is more important than knowledge—the com-plete man inbred with the amateur spirit—the seeking for perfec-tion in whatever field he may be interested—the devotion to the task is the secret of success in any enterprise.[21]

The emphasis on "seeking for perfection" that Brundage mentions is an aspect of contemporary amateur sports which conflicts with the recrea-tional emphasis of amateurism discussed earlier in the chapter.

BASIC CHARACTERISTICS OF SOME KEY TERMS

Characteristics of Professionalism

In contrast to the view of an amateur given in the first section of this chapter is the view held by many people of the professional in sports. The professional is viewed as a person to whom winning is important because athletics is his business—his means of livelihood.

Traditionally, the professional athlete is considered to be a person who earns a pecuniary reward for participating in sport and is a more skillful player than those identified as amateurs. The professional athlete also normally trains and practices harder and longer than an amateur because the pecuniary reward serves as an incentive and makes it possible for the professional to spend more time practicing. The additional time spent practicing obviously helps the professional become a more skillful player than the amateur. Thus, a cyclic effect results.

In 1909 a committee that had been appointed to study the problems of amateurism defined a professional athlete as

> one who enters or takes part in any athletic contest for any other motive than satisfaction of pure play impulses or for the exercise, training, and social pleasure derived, or one who desires or secures from his skill or who accepts of spectators partisan or other interest, any material or economic advantage or reward.[22]

In 1885 Hartwell expressed an extreme view of professionalism by defining professionalism as "the purpose to win a game by any means, fair or foul."[23] This extreme view toward professionals is due to the opinion that pecuniary rewards are such a great source of motivation that a person will inevitably use corrupt practices to win games and the rewards.

A similar view was expressed in 1919 by Hetherington, who was chairman of a committee on amateur law of the Athletic Research Society. Hetherington listed the following evils of professionalism:

> The tendencies 1) to physical injury through accident, 2) to overindulgence, 3) to specialization, 4) to bad manners at play and bad spirit in defeat or victory, 5) to evasion of rules of the game, 6) to violations of the classification necessary for fairness in competition (eligibility), 7) to develop as a spectacle for the amusement of the public. The first three of these tendencies to evil reduce or destroy the physical value of play; the fourth and fifth moral values; the sixth and seventh the social organization and the respect for athletics as an educational influence.[24]

Another reason that earning a reward for participation in athletics was considered bad by some advocates of amateurism was expressed by de Coubertin. He believed people who earned money from participating in athletics would tend to "give up their whole existence to one particular sport, grow rich by practicing it, and thus deprive it [the sport] of all nobility, and destroy the just equilibrium of man by making the muscles preponderate over the mind."[25]

Related to this attitude about professionalism was the development during the nineteenth century of the view that professionals were a corrupting influence on others. This viewpoint led many to believe that in order to purify sports, a category of sports called amateur was necessary in order to keep professionals from mixing with non-professionals.[26]

As a result of these views, amateurism and professionalism have been traditionally viewed as opposites. However, this view is not completely accurate. A more accurate method of viewing the two terms would be to think of them as a continuum. The extreme of the amateur end of the continuum would represent people who engage in athletics or sports *solely* for love or pleasure and for *no* other purposes, and who do not care whether they win or lose. The other extreme of the continuum, the professional end, would represent people who engage in athletic competition solely for motives such as pecuniary rewards and fame. In between these extremes would be people who participate in athletics or sport for numerous motives. The multi-faceted reasons these people compete in sports deserves serious attention. The following statement by Keating, a professor of philosophy, explains the complexity of man's motives for competing.

> We would be guilty of inexcusable psychological over-simplification were we to assume that, if a man does not compete for money, then he must be doing so solely from the love of the activity itself. To omit fame, social preferment, ego-satisfaction, and so on, would be to betray an ignorance and superficial view of athletic motivation that is appalling. Likewise, it would be a serious error to conclude that because a man gets paid for competing that he cannot love the activity in its own right.[27]

Differences Between Sport and Athletics

Another aspect of the problem of amateurism is the failure to understand the differences between the meaning of the terms "sport" and "athletics." This failure has been and continues to be the cause of considerable confusion concerning the difference between an amateur and a professional athlete. One of the basic factors involved in this confusion is the ambiguity associated with the motives of the amateur and the professional athlete. Underlying this ambiguity about motives is a basic distinction between sport and athletics which Keating refers to as "the heart of the problem of amateur athletics."[28] Although the terms "sport" and "athletics" are often used interchangeably in contemporary English, the historical meaning of the two words conveys an important distinction, which is vital to a proper understanding of amateurism in sports. The word "sport" means a "pleasant pastime; entertainment or amusement; recreation, diversion."[29] Historically, the word "sport" comes from the Middle English and French words *desport* and *disport* which mean "to carry away from work." In contrast, the root meaning of the word "athlete" is derived from the Greek verb *athlein,* which means "to compete for a prize," or the noun *athlos* which means contest, or *athlon* which means "a prize rewarded for successful completion of a contest."[30] Thus, by definition it is quite evident that historically the emphasis on the two words was quite different. Regarding the difference, Keating stated that:

> *In essence, sport is a kind of diversion which has for its direct and immediate end, fun, pleasure, and delight and which is dominated by a spirit of moderation and generosity. Athletics, on the other hand, is essentially a competitive activity, which has for its end victory and which is characterized by a spirit of dedication, sacrifice, and intensity.*[31]

It is this distinction that is involved in the current usage of the words "amateur" and "professional" in sports. Thus the goal of sport or amateurism as defined above is "joy in the activity itself and anything—any word, action or attitude—which makes the game [or the contest] less enjoyable should be eliminated."[32] This same emphasis is expressed in the following statement by de Coubertin: "The important thing in the Olympic Games is not to win, but to take part."[33] This same emphasis was noted in 1910 by Hetherington, a member of a research committee that studied amateurism, who wrote: "In its broader meaning amateurism is identical with the play spirit; in its technical meaning it is contrasted with the professional spirit."[34]

Another expression that conveys this attitude of sport is: "It's not whether you won or lost that counts, but how you played the game." Keating's suggestion of changing the word "played" to "enjoyed" in this statement conveys more clearly the proper meaning of the expression.[35] Participating with this emphasis and attitude, a person will tend to be self-sacrificing, generous and will try to do whatever will contribute to the pleasure and joy that can be derived from the activity. This may mean playing very hard to provide an enjoyable experience for the opponent.[36] It may also mean playing one's weakness and an opponent's strength or vice versa, if that will increase the joy of the activity,[37] because it is assumed that reasonably commensurate competition is usually the most enjoyable for both contestants or sides. This aspect of competitive sport involves a "cooperative endeavor to maximize pleasure and joy."[38]

In contrast to the emphasis in sport and amateurism expounded in the preceding paragraphs is the nature of athletics. The objective of an athlete by definition and by nature is "one who contends for a prize" and who "seeks to demonstrate his excellence in a contest governed by rules."[39] The very nature and goal of the athlete is to strive for excellence to win, to train, and to sacrifice for the attainment of these goals.[40] As a result the athlete, in contrast to the sportsman or amateur, is confronted with what Keating refers to as an "inexorable law."

> *Excellence, he will find is a jealous mistress whose favors are granted only after evidence of complete dedication. But, such dedication requires great expenditure of time and effort which, in truth, are very expensive commodities. Unless the young athlete is independently wealthy he will come to see that if he is going to dedicate himself fully to a given activity, then it will be necessary to earn his living in the process. Thus, the pursuit of excellence in athletics tends naturally and inevitably to some form of profes-sionalism.*[41]

WHY AMATEURISM HAS BEEN SO DIFFICULT TO DEFINE

The problem of defining amateurism has been one of the most difficult issues in sports for more than a century. This difficulty has been caused by a few basic factors. One has been a failure by growing bodies in sports to understand the difference between the terms "sports" and "athletics." A second factor has been that the objectives and goals of sports clubs and organizations have often been unclear and/or not acceptable to large segments of the population. For example, separating "workers, artisans, and mechanics" from the upper middle and upper classes, which was one of the objectives of amateurism during the nineteenth century, has not been ac-ceptable to the laboring classes for decades. The degree to which this is still an objective of some individuals and sports organizations is a moot ques-tion. This "snobbish" attitude would obviously not be accepted today by the general public, although this restriction received few protests when the laboring class worked six ten-hour days each week and when organized sports on Sunday was not generally accepted because of religious beliefs. Another example of this lack of clarity in the objectives of amateurism in-volves the question of what is actually meant by the statement of the Inter-national Olympic Committee which states that one of the fundamental prin-ciples is to "assemble amateurs of all nations in fair and equal competi-tion."[42] Is it fair and equal competition for all nonprofessionals that is the primary goal of the Committee, or is it fair and equal competition for amateurs *as defined* by the International Olympic Committee? Would it be unfair and unequal to assemble the best athletes, amateur and professional, for competition? Does the current Eligibility Code of the International Olympic Committee really make for fair and equal competition for all peo-ple from various cultures and countries?

A third reason why defining amateurism has been difficult in recent years is in part due to an improper understanding of the historical development of sports and sports organizations during the nineteenth century. Because there was no governing body during each sport's early years, the usual rules and regulations for conducting the sports were lacking. This absence of uniform rules for sports and the absence of regional, national, and international sports-governing bodies for the various sports during the nineteenth century left a void that led to many of the abuses and problems that came to be identified with professionalism in sports. From this chaotic background, sports clubs and organizations emerged which established rules and regulations for governing sports.

In England and the United States, the private sports clubs and private schools and colleges were primarily responsible for bringing order to sports. On the international level, the founding of the modern Olympic Games was the major force in creating order in sports during the nineteenth and early twentieth centuries. Because of the many worthy accomplishments of these amateur organizations, many people have associated amateurism with what is positive and good in sports and professionalism with what is bad in sports. However, because problems associated with professionalism arose in areas where there were no agreed-upon rules and no controlling organizations does not mean that professionalism in sports was the cause of problems, nor does it mean that amateurism was or is the cure.

As a result of the association made between amateurism and the order that early sports organizations brought to sport, some people and organizations seem to have come to a position that implies that amateurism is an end in itself, rather than a means to an end. The following statement by Brundage implies this idea:

> The felicitous phrase 'religion of sport' used by de [sic] Coubertin...was well chosen for the chivalrous amateur code of fair play and good sportsmanship [which] embraces the highest moral laws. It is a humanitarian religion — it, like the golden rule, stands for the right against wrong. No philosophy, no religion preaches loftier sentiments. [43]

In spite of what Brundage says, amateurism in itself is not sacred. Fair play, high moral standards and sportsmanship are certainly desirable in competitive athletics, but to equate amateurism with these qualities is confusing and inaccurate. Nevertheless, Brundage's statement does not serve to illustrate the fact that the meaning of amateurism has not always been clearly understood.

SUMMARY

In this chapter the major purposes and characteristics of amateurism as a category in competition in sports were described. One of the purposes,

24

especially during the nineteenth century, was the social distinctiveness or exclusiveness of amateurism, which separated the lower classes of society from the so-called "gentleman class." A second purpose of amateurism has been to provide a method of declaring ineligible for amateur competition people with special advantages. A third basic purpose of amateurism has been to declare ineligible competitors whose motives for competition were personal gain. Interrelated with these purposes has been the desire to conduct "fair and equal competition" in sports.

In the second part of this chapter an explanation was given for the meaning of the terms "professionalism," "sports," and "athletics." In essence, athletics and professionalism are characterized by seriousness of purpose and a desire to win. In contrast to this emphasis, sport is characterized as an activity in which a person engages solely for the pleasure and physical, mental, and social benefits that may be derived from the activity. In the last part of the chapter some comments were made concerning why amateurism has been difficult to define. Unfortunately, amateurism has often been associated with problems in sports due to the absence of governing organizations. As a result, the purposes of organizations and the meaning of terms have often been confused. Consequently, numerous problems with amateurism have arisen. These problems are discussed in Chapter VII. The next chapter is a review of some facets of athletics in ancient Greece which are significant to a thorough study of amateurism.

FOOTNOTES

1   Archie Hohn, ed., *How to Sprint,* Spalding Athletic Library, No. 500B. (New York: American Sports Publishing Company, 1929), pp. 189-97.

2   H. Hewitt Griffin, *Athletics* (London: George Bell and Sons, 1891), pp. 7-9.

3   Edwin Daupier Brickwood, writing under the name "Argonaut," *The Arts of Rowing and Training* (London: Horace Cox, 1866), p. 151.

4   H. J. Whigham, "American Sport from an English Point of View," *Outlook,* 93 (November 1909), p. 740.

5   George C. Brodrick, "A Nation of Amateurs," *The Nineteenth Century,* 284 (October 1900), pp. 521-35.

6   Griffin, *Athletics,* p. 9.

7   R. C. Lehman, *The Complete Oarsman* (London: Methuen and Co., 1908), p. 255.

8   Griffin, *Athletics,* p. 9.

9   *The Olympic Games* (Lausanne, Switzerland: International Olympic Committee, 1967), pp. 43-45.

10   "New Rules," *Olympic Review,* 85-86 (November-December 1974), pp. 585-586 .

11   Bliss Perry, *The Amateur Spirit* (New York: Houghton, Mifflin and Company, 1904), pp. 8-9.

12   Ibid., p. 11.

13   Howard J. Savage, *et al., American College Athletics,* Bulletin No. 23 (New York: The Carnegie Foundation for the Advancement of Teaching, 1929), p. 35.

14   Bill Henry, *An Approved History of the Olympic Games* (New York: G. P. Putnam's Sons, 1948), p. 323.

15   Ibid.

16   Kenneth Doherty, "Modern Amateurism," *Health and Fitness in the Modern World* (Chicago: Athletics Institute, 1961), pp. 231-232.

17   Henry, *An Approved History of the Olympic Games,* p. 317.

18   *A New English Dictionary on Historical Principles,* ed. by James A. H. Murray, IA (Oxford: The Clarendon Press, 1888), p . 665.

19   Avery Brundage, "Address at 68th Session of the International Olympic Committee in Warsaw," *Newsletter* (Lausanne, Switzerland: International Olympic Committee, No. 22, July 1969), p. 362.

20   John Apostal Lucas, "Baron Pierre de Coubertin and the Formative Years of the Modern International Olympic Movement 1883-1896" (unpublished D.Ed. Dissertation, University of Maryland, 1962), p. 141.

21   Brundage, "Address at the 68th Session of the International Olympic Committee in Warsaw," p. 362.

22   Clark W. Hetherington, C. A. Waldo and William L. Dudley, "Report of Committee on an Amateur Law," *American Physical Education Review,* 15 (March 1910), p. 178.

23   Edward Mussey Hartwell, *Physical Training in American Colleges and Universities,* United States Bureau of Education, Circular of Information No. 5 (Washington, D. C.: Government Printing Office, 1886), p. 124.

24   "The Athletic Research Society," *Mind and Body,* 17 (February 1911), p. 363.

25   Pierre de Coubertin, "The Redemption of Athletics," *Mind and Body,* 5 (October 1898), p. 167.

26   Ibid.

27   James W. Keating, "The Heart of the Problem of Amateur Athletes," *Journal of General Education,* 16 (January 1965), p. 265.

28   Ibid., pp. 261-62.

29   *A New English Dictionary on Historical Principles,* p. 665.

30   James W. Keating, "Sportsmanship as a Moral Category," *Ethics* 75 (October 1964) pp. 27-28.

31   Ibid., p. 28.

32   Ibid., p. 30.

33   *The Olympic Games,* p. 2.

34   "The Athletic Research Society," p. 362.

35   Keating, "Sportsmanship as a Moral Category," p. 31.

36   Ibid., p. 30.

37   Keating, "The Heart of the Problem of Amateur Athletics," p. 269.

38   Keating, "Sportsmanship as a Moral Category," p. 30.

39   Ibid., p. 31.

40   Keating, "The Heart of the Problem of Amateur Athletics,"p. 267.

41   Ibid.

42   *The Olympic Games,* p. 11.

43   Brundage, "Address at the 68th Session of the International Olympic Committee in Warsaw," p. 362.

CHAPTER III

Athletics In Ancient Greece

INTRODUCTION

The development of contemporary amateurism has some roots in athletics in ancient Greece. One of these roots involves the modern Olympic Movement which was founded in 1894 with the goal of reviving the ancient Olympic Games. This fact is important because since 1894 the International Olympic Committee, which governs the modern Olympic Games, has become the standard bearer and leading advocate of amateurism in sports. In addition, from the beginning of the modern Olympic movement, many aspects of athletics in ancient Greece have been held up as ideals by the founders of the modern Olympic Games and the twentieth century advocates of the Olympic concept of amateurism. Furthermore, many lessons can be learned from studying athletics in ancient Greece. This study is of value in the search for a system or framework of athletic competition that is appropriate for the general public in contemporary society. Consequently, a review of the various aspects of athletics in ancient Greece is important to any comprehensive study of amateurism.

These aspects of athletics in ancient Greece are especially significant in terms of their implications for contemporary amateurism: the nature of awards for winning, the motives for participating in athletics, the extent of participation in athletics by the total population, and the causes of problems and corruption in athletics.

The basic values of twentieth century amateurism as defined at various times by the International Olympic Committee and other amateur sports organizations have not always been in total harmony with athletics in ancient Greece. These differences are of special interest in this chapter. One of the values of amateurism clearly stated by the International Olympic Committee in the eligibility rules for the Olympic Games from 1962 to 1974 was that competitors "must always have participated in sport as an avocation without material gain of any kind."[1] Another distinction of twentieth century amateurism of significance has been defining an amateur as "one who engages in sport solely for the pleasure and physical, mental or social benefits he derives therefrom and to whom sport is nothing more than recreation."[2] These values and rules stand in contrast to athletic practices in ancient Greece.

The first section of this chapter briefly surveys the history of athletics in ancient Greece from about the fourteenth century B.C. to about the sixth century A.D. The second section of this chapter discusses various aspects of life and athletics in Greece which are especially pertinent to contemporary amateurism in sports. Within various sub-sections special attention has been given to factors that contributed to the development and the decline of athletics in Greece.

ATHLETICS IN ANCIENT GREECE FROM
THEIR BEGINNING TO THEIR FINAL YEARS

Athletics Before 440 B.C.

The ancient Olympic Games are traditionally believed to have lasted for a total of 1,169 years from 776 B.C. to A.D. 393.[3]* The actual beginning date of athletic games at Olympia may extend back as far as 1370 B.C. This secondary literary evidence in English translation has been cited by R.S. Robinson. It hints at the beginning of Olympic Games in 1370 B.C. Whatever the actual dates of the Olympic festivals prior to their recorded history, evidence such as found in Homer's *Iliad* and *Odyssey* does indicate that the Greek public was apparently familiar with athletics long before 776 B.C.[4] Scholars have estimated the date for Homer's works as between "the tenth and sixth centuries B.C. — but whatever the century, it is clear that Homer was narrating his story for a public that was already athletic-minded."[5]** Homer's description of the funeral games in honor of Patroclus is the best

---

*For perhaps the most complete and accurate list of all ancient Olympic victors and dates in print, the interested reader may refer to Luigi Moretti, "Olympionikai, I Vinitori Negli Antichi Agoni Olimpici," Atti. Roma: Accademia Nazionale Dei Lincie. Series VIII, Vol. 8. 1957, pp. 53-198.

**Marrou [1964] holds the view that Homer wrote the *Iliad* and the *Odyssey* about 850-750 B.C., and that the *Iliad* and the *Odyssey* are apparently not about Homer's own time, but deal primarily with the period of 1180-1000 B.C. with some references to events centuries earlier.[6]

known account of the athletics in Greece prior to 776 B.C.[7]*

It is generally agreed that the athletic games of this period were of an informal nature restricted to members of the aristocracy which consisted of the kings and chieftans, and perhaps to the warriors that surrounded them.[14] There is no evidence of any formal athletic training associated with the games. The warrior during this era was trained for battle and the athletic games consisted of events associated with military skill and prowess. The typical events at these funeral games were foot races, wrestling, boxing, throwing the javelin, throwing a stone (discus), archery and chariot races.

From this period of informal and impromptu athletic competition referred to in Homer's writing, athletics in Greece gradually developed into a fairly well-organized system. Some evidence of the growth of athletics is indicated by the addition of events at the Olympic Games. In 724 B.C. a race twice the length of the stadium was added, and in 720 B.C. a long-distance race of twenty-four stadium lengths was added. In 648 B.C. horse races and the Pancration were added. In 632 B.C. an important step was taken at the games with the addition of a separate competition for youth.[15] During this period of athletics in ancient Greece, participation was basically limited to the aristocratic class.

During the sixth century, three other major festivals similar to the Olympic Games developed into special prominence. The first two were the Pythian and Isthmian Games, which were reorganized in 582 B.C. The third was the Nemean Games, which was reorganized in 573 B.C.[16]

In the second half of the sixth century B.C. Xenophanes issued one of the first, if not the first, written expression of concern over the growing popularity and emphasis on athletics.[17]** However, Xenophanes' criticism probably

---

*Some other indications of the athletic activities of this period are the account of the after-dinner games of the Phaeacians,[8] the boxing match between Odysseus and Irus,[9] the funeral games for Lord Amarynceus,[10] the games in Elis,[11] the games for Pelias portrayed on the Cypselus chest and described by Pausanias,[12] and the games in honor of Triopian Apollo mentioned by Herodotus.[13] For a discussion of the origin of Greek games see Walter Woodburn Hyde. *Olympic Victor Monuments and Greek Athletic Art.* Washington: The Carnegie Institution of Washington, 1921. pp. 7-14.

**But if't were in swiftness of foot that a man should win the day, in the close of Zeus by Pisa's stream at Olympia, or if't were in the five-events or the wrestling, or he should hold his own in the painful boxing-bout, or the dire contest that they call Pancratium—whatever it were, he would be more honored of the eyes of his fellow-townsmen; he would win the prominent right of sitting at the front in the games and contests, there would be food for him from the city's store and a gift to make him an heirloom. Or if again his victory were with horses, then too all this would fall to him —yet it would not be deserved as't would be were it mine, for the poet's skill is better than the strength of men and horses. 'Tis very unconsidered, the custom of man in this matter; it is not right that strength should be judged worthier than most holy skill. For not though a city had a good boxer, nor a five-event-man, nor a good wrestler, nor yet a good runner—which of all the

had little effect on the athletics in Greece. By the fifth century the spontaneous and informal athletic contest of the earlier centuries had evolved into many local and Panhellenic contests, and regular training under experienced trainers had become a regular part of life in the Greek community. The popularity of athletics in Greece reached a peak during the Persian War[18] in which the decisive battles were at Salamis in 480 B.C. and Plataea in 479 B.C.[19] These victories "not only gave a fresh impulse to the Panhellenic festivals: it [they] raised athletic training into a national duty."[20] The renewed association between military needs and physical training was an important aspect of this era. This was the era in which Greek society came the closest to attaining what late nineteenth century and twentieth century writers have referred to as the "athletic ideal."[21]

Athletics from about 440 B.C. to about A.D. 550

After the height of athletic interest in Greece during the first half of the fifth century, conditions changed, and athletics also changed.[22] The changes in athletic practices brought on critics such as Euripides who wrote that "although there are myriads of evils throughout Greece there is nothing worse than the race of athletes."[23] By about 400 B.C. "the word 'athlete' had become a term applied to a specially-trained group of persons."[24] During this period of decline from the athletic ideal, awards for athletes increased in extravagence.[25]

After 146 B.C. Greece had come under the control and domination of Rome and was no longer truly independent.[26] During the early part of Rome's control of Greece there was a general decline in activities at Olympia and the festival became more of a local celebration.[27] [28]. However, interest in athletics was revived under the Caesars, beginning in about 36 B.C. and lasting until about A.D. 265.[29] During this period the major festivals continued as usual, and some Roman emperors introduced additional festivals. For example, Julius Caesar apparently sponsored games in 45 B.C., and Augustus instituted games at Nicopolis in Northwestern Greece and at Naples, and in A.D. 86 Domitian founded the Capitoline Games at Rome.[30] Augustus' interest in the athletic games is clearly evident from the following statement in his writings: "Twice in my own name I furnished exhibitions of athletes gathered from all parts of the world, and a third time in the name of my grandson."[31] There is considerable evidence of an interest in athletics by the Romans, but the emphasis and spirit of athletics was different for the Romans. For the Romans the festivals tended to be entertainment or amuse-

---

deeds of man's strength hath the greatest honour in the Games — never for that would she be the better ordered; and but little is the joy a town would get in a man's victory beside the banks of Pisa, for a city's treasure-houses are not fattened so.
                          Xenophanes, "Elegiac Poems 2."[17]

ment for spectators, while for the Greeks the games had been opportunities for competition.[32] For the Roman emperors, satisfying the masses was a major concern and the emperors used the chariot races, gladiatorial combats, theatrical performances and athletic contests as "the best means for purchasing popular favor, keeping the masses contented, and making them forget their own insignificance."[33]

During the expansion of the Roman Empire, a class of athletes developed for whom athletics truly became a means of livelihood. By the middle of the first century B.C. athletic unions or guilds were common.[34] By 100 A.D. "nearly every city in the East had its athletic union."[35]

It is traditionally agreed that the Olympics came to an end in 393 A.D., although some evidence indicates that the games may have continued until 426 A.D. Whether the Olympic Games ended in 393 A.D. may be questioned,[36] but traditional Greek athletics were coming to an end. However, "as late as the sixth century [A.D.], we still hear of the athletic games at Antioch."[37] Also, the Code of Justinian, which was issued in 528 A.D., implies that athletic games in mainland Greece still existed at that time.[38]*

The existence of the Olympic Games for 1,169 years is a remarkable achievement, especially when consideration is given to many social, political, and religious changes and other problems in Greece during these years. This long record of the ancient Olympic Games, along with the recorded information of numerous other festivals,[40] serves as a symbol of the importance of athletics to the Greek people of this era. This review of Greek athletics, which ranges from the period of the informal impromptu Games of the Homeric era to the height of the athletic popularity around 480 B.C. and to the demise of athletics in the sixth century A.D., permits numerous observations regarding athletics to be made which are germane to the study of amateurism. For example, by noting the trends in athletics after the middle of the fifth century B.C., the Greek athletic ideal of the early fifth century becomes more evident by contrast in emphases and practices.

ASPECTS OF GREEK ATHLETICS GERMANE TO CONTEMPORARY AMATEURISM

The Greek Athletic Ideal

The views of many nineteenth and twentieth century advocates of con-

---

*The following portion of the Code of Justinian x .53 was translated by R. S. Robinson from Tessot, Les Douze Livres du Code de l'Empereur Justinian de la seconde ed. IV (Paris, 1810) and used with paid permission.

Athletes are by custom excused from civil obligations if they give proof of themselves: that they have competed all of their life; that they have won no fewer than three wreaths at a sacred festival—at least one of them in Rome or in Ancient Greece; that they have won the wreath fairly without bribing or buying off their opponents.[39]

temporary amateurism are based on their understanding, the Greek "athletic ideal." For example, de Coubertin, the founder of the modern Olympic Games, "considered his form of 'pedagogical sport' a 'revival of the Greek ideal.' "[41] De Coubertin also viewed the Olympic Games and amateur athletics as a "cornerstone" of his system of educational philosophy.[42]

This athletic ideal referred to by de Coubertin and others is based on the Greek view of the harmony of the body, mind, and spirit. One aspect of this ideal is the spiritual association the Greeks made between athletics and the gods. Greek gods were truly made in the image of man. "Their gods craved what men desired, and...manly strife was of all things most acceptable."[43] To the Greeks, Heracles, the son of Zeus, who Pindar claimed founded the ancient Olympic Games,[44] was the example of an athlete and god image. The early Greek religious views were not concerned with ideas such as the attainment of Nirvana, the sinfulness of pleasure, or the mortification of the flesh,[45] religious beliefs that for some people have conflicted with physical development.

Another part of the Greek ideal was the balance or all-around training of the body and the harmonious development of the mind and body. These emphases were effectively conveyed by de Coubertin with the expressions "an active mind in an active body" and "nothing in excess."[46]

The balance between mind and body came the closest to being obtained in Athens where the education of young boys consisted primarily of gymnastics, grammar, literature, and music.[47] In Sparta the educational system was basically oriented toward physical training to prepare soldiers for the state.[48] However, the military purposes of athletics in Sparta and in Athens stressed general or broad athletic skills which were consistent with the ideal of a balanced or harmoniously developed body.

The ideal body type of the fifth century is also illustrated in the art work of the period.[49] The sculpture and paintings that remain provide evidence that a well-conditioned body was regarded as beautiful. As a result of this, every Greek citizen took pride in his physical fitness and beauty."[50]

Another aspect of the Greek athletic ideal is what Gardiner calls the athletic ideal of Pindar,[51] which is evident in Pindar's *Eleventh Olympian Ode.*[52]* Pindar viewed athletic ability as a gift from a god "bestowed especially on members of ancient and honourable families."[53] Pindar also praised the "cost and pain" that an athlete endured to achieve victory.**

---

*The following lines (3-12) from the *Eleventh Olympian Ode* convey some of Pindar's views.

But when anyone is victorious by aid of toil, then it is that honey-voiced odes are a foundation for future fame, even a faithful witness to noble exploits.

Far beyond envy is the praise that is thus stored up for victors at Olympia; and such praises my tongue would fain, feed and foster; but by the gift of a god alone doth a man flourish forever, as thou dost, with wisdom of heart.[52]

**Isthmian Ode* i.42.

Another key concept in Pindar's ideal athlete relates to the word *aidos* which Gardiner claims does not adequately translate into English. *Aidos* refers to a spirit of competition that conveys feelings of respect, reverence, modesty, and courtesy and is a direct opposite of the words insolence and contemptuous.[54] Gardiner states, "In sport *aidos* is that scrupulous sense of honour and fairness."[55] Certainly winning by bribery was incompatible with the spirit of *aidos*. *Aidos* is the spirit that Pindar believed was pleasing to the gods, therefore, he believed that the gods rewarded with victory those that trained hard and competed with this spirit.[56]

Thus, it is evident that what nineteenth and twentieth century men have referred to as the athletic ideal of Greece of the fifth and sixth centuries B.C. was an athletic emphasis strongly associated with religious beliefs, educational objectives and military motives.

At the beginning of the fifth century, the opportunity to participate in athletics was extended to citizens not included in the aristocracy and by the end of the century all male citizens were going to the gymnasium. According to Marrou this trend "...caused great disgust to the old aristocrats, who felt that with this 'democratization' of sport everything of importance in the old culture has been degraded."[57] These same aristocrats, who had the leisure time and money to engage in athletics, also began to despise work and workers as conditions changed.[58]

The similarity between this aspect of ancient athletics and nineteenth and twentieth century amateurism is significant. Consequently, these are important factors to consider when thinking of the athletic ideal of ancient Greece and its implications for contemporary amateurism.

Military Motives for Participation

From the days of Homer to the peak of the period of athletic interest following the defeat of Persia at Salamis in 480 B.C., the constant need for citizens to be militarily prepared was a very important motivating factor in the growth and development of physical education and athletics in Greece.[59] At one time, being a citizen warrior from age eighteen to sixty was a normal pattern of life.[60] Lucian, who lived between A.D. 125 and 180,[61] clearly explains the military value of athletics to the Greeks with his dialogue between Solon and Anacharsis, who both lived during the sixth century B.C. In the dialogue Solon states:

> After that, having invented many forms of athletics and appointed teachers for each, we teach one, for instance, boxing, and another the pancratium, in order that they may become accustomed to endure hardships and meet blows, and not recoil for fear of injuries. This helps us by creating in them two effects that are most

useful, since it makes them not only spirited in facing dangers and unmindful of their bodies, but healthy and strong in the bargain.

Those of them who put their bent heads together and wrestle learn to fall safely and get up easily, to push, grip and twist in various ways, to stand being choked, and to lift their opponent high in the air. They too are not engaging in useless exercises; on the contrary, they indisputably acquire one thing, which is first and greatest: their bodies become less susceptible and more vigorous through being exercised thoroughly. There is something else, too, which is not trivial: they become expert as a result of it, in case they should ever come to need what they learned in battle. Clearly such a man, when he closes with an enemy, will trip and throw him more quickly, and when he is done, will know how to get up again most easily. For we make the contest under arms, and we expect to find men thus disciplined far superior, after we have supplied and trained their bodies naked, and so have made them healthier and stronger, light and elastic, and at the same time too heavy for their opponent.

You can imagine, I suppose, the consequences — what they are likely to be with arms in hand when even unarmed they would implant fear in the enemy. They show no white and ineffective corpulence or pallid leanness, as if they were women's bodies bleached out in the shade, quivering and streaming with profuse sweat at once and panting beneath the helmet, especially if the sun, as at present, blazes with the heat of noon. What use could one make of men like that, who get thirsty, who cannot stand dust, who break ranks the moment they catch sight of blood, who lie down and die before they get within a spear's cast and come to grips with the enemy?[62]

In support of the significance of military preparedness on athletics, Plummer writes:

Until the time of Alexander [356-323 B.C.], victory among the Greeks depended upon the muscular power, endurance, and skill of individual warriors. The central and principle feature of early Greek warfare was the hand to hand grapple. Therefore, it was essential in preparing for war that each soldier be made as active and vigorous as possible. That this mode of warfare prevailed until a late date may be seen from the fact that Plutarch attributed the victory of the Thebans over the Spartans at the battle of Leutra, B.C. 371, to the superiority of the former in the art of wrestling.[63]

35

The fact that Plato (427-347 B.C.) also recognized the value of athletics is shown by his preference for the standing style of wrestling as a preparation for war.[64]* However, as the years passed "adults found a hundred ways of escaping military service"[65] according to Durant. By 400 B.C. "war itself had become professionalized by technical complications, and required the full time of specially trained men; citizen soldiers had to be replaced with mercenaries."[66]

During the fourth, third, and second centuries B.C., a trend in Greek education, which parallels the decline of military and physical training can be observed in the curriculum of the ephebia, which was a school for training youths between eighteen and twenty years of age. When the first ephebia was founded in Athens during the fourth century B.C., the educational emphasis was on military and gymnastic training, but by 137 B.C. the orientation had changed to philosophical and literary studies, but physical education always remains as part of the curriculum.[67] In short, "the life of comfort and domesticity, or business and scholarship had replaced the Periclean life of exercise, martial discipline, and public office."[68] At the same time the property class became smaller in number, so that the number of people willing or available to serve in the military, which consisted partially of property class members, also become smaller. For example, the population of male adult citizens in Attica is reported to have been reduced from 43,000 in 431 B.C. to 22,000 in 400 B.C. and to 21,000 in 313 B.C.[69] Two of the reasons for the decline in the population were the long succession of brutal wars which killed many of the most able young men in Greece and plagues such as the Great Plague of 430 B.C.[70]

Following the fall of Greece to the Romans in 146 B.C., the motivation to be physically and militarily prepared to defend one's city-state no longer existed. As a result, the basic reason for physical fitness had vanished. For the Roman conquerors the athletic training and competition of the Greeks had little appeal other than for entertainment. Part of the reason for this attitude was that Roman armies consisted primarily of mercenaries, so the masses saw little need to be physically fit for military purposes.[71] This survey of the changes in military needs and the resulting changes in motivation for participation in athletics makes it evident that evil or corruption in athletics in ancient Greece was only part of the reason for a decline in athletic interests.

The relationship between athletics and the military in ancient Greece is of

---

*As to the devices introduced by Antaeus or Cercyon in the art of wrestling for the sake of empty glory, or in boxing by Epeius or Amycus, since they are useless in the business of war, they merit no eulogy. But the exercises of stand-up wrestling, with the twisting free of neck, hands and sides, when practiced with ardour and with a firm and graceful pose, and directed towards strength and health—these must not be omitted, since they are useful for all purposes."[64]

interest when studying the issue of amateurism because training for athletics and training for military service were identical in many respects during the time of the early ancient Olympic Games. From this discussion one can see that athletic participation in ancient Greece was not actually an avocation as was required of athletes by the International Olympic Committee from 1961[72] to 1974[73]

Religious Motives for Participation

Another factor of special significance to Greek athletics was the association between religion and athletics. Regarding the important connection between the ancient Olympics and the Greek gods, Schobel stated, "that without these gods invented by man it would be impossible to understand Olympia."[74] The relationship between athletics and religion in ancient Greece was clarified by Gardiner who wrote:

> Sports were definitely placed under the patronage of the gods, and the victorious athlete felt that he was well pleasing to the gods and owed his success to them. Further, the athlete felt that any violation of the rules of the games, especially any unfairness or corruption, was an act of sacrilege and displeasing to the gods. This feeling undoubtedly tended to preserve the purity of sport at Olympis even when corruption was rife elsewhere. Religious conservatism too tended to check any innovations and accordingly, though additions were made to the programme, the events remained essentially unchanged for nearly twelve centuries. It was to religion that Greek athletics and Greek athletic festivals owed their vitality.[75]

However, over the years belief in traditional Greek gods began to decline, especially among the educated class.[76] This is evident from the following remark by Plato:

> But nowadays, when, as we say, a certain section of mankind totally disbelieve in gods, and others hold that they pay no regard to us men, while a third party, consisting of the most and worst of men, suppose that in return for small offerings and flatteries the gods lend them aid in committing large robberies, and often set them free from great penalties — under such conditions, for men as they now are, the device of Rhadamanthys would no longer be appropriate in actions at law. Since, therefore, the opinions of men about the gods have changed, so must their laws change.[77]

Included in the group of men who had little use for the traditional Greek gods was the growing alien bourgeoisie in Greece. At approximately the same time that faith in the traditional Greek gods was on the decline, other religions were being imported from areas primarily in or near the Eastern regions of the Roman Empire. Added to this change in religious belief was the emergence of the so-called "mystery religions," which became widespread in the Greco-Roman world prior to the birth of Christ.[78] With these changes emerging in the religious beliefs of the Greeks, the traditional Greek gods became less of a motivating factor in athletics.

Within this religious environment, Christianity appeared and spread rapidly throughout the Greco-Roman world. As Christianity spread, some of the early leaders of Christianity began to condemn the Olympic Games and other festivals honoring pagan gods. Perhaps the best evidence of the conflict between Christianity and the games and festivals is Tertullian's *Spectacles*. To Tertullian, who wrote this around 200 A.D., "the real issue" of the athletic games was that they were a form of idolatry. He said, "For the titles by which games still go today betray the nature of their origin. In these titles there is clearly expressed for what idol and for what superstition of one kind or another they were designed."[79] "What wonder it is then, if the whole paraphernalia of these contests are tainted with idolatry—with unholy crowns, priestly superintendents, assistants from the sacred colleges, and last, but not least, with the blood of bulls?"[80] Tertullian believed that it was not only sinful to participate in various kinds of spectacles, but also wrong to be a spectator at such idolatrous functions.[81] As a result, Christians were exhorted not to attend.[82] Obviously, not all Christians felt as strongly about this matter of idolatry as Tertullian, but it is understandable that Christians who were willing to die for their faith in the Roman arenas were not about to participate in or grant approval to athletic festivals with pagan emphasis and motive.

At least two other religious factors were instrumental in the decline of athletics. One of these was the belief that all flesh and matter were evil. This view was held by many Christians as is evident in the development of asceticism and monasticism. In addition, several cults or groups such as the Gnostics, Marcionites, and Manichaeists held this view.[83] At the same time the Stoics in Greece were preaching a viewpoint in which the body was held to be a detriment to the soul.[84] [85]

A second reason why many early Christians minimized athletics and physical training was a firm belief in the imminent return of Christ.[86] This belief relegated the concern for material things and bodily welfare to a status far below spiritual concerns oriented toward eternal life.

Many factors were responsible for the decline in athletic participation and the athletic festivals in Greece and the Roman Empire[87] Included in these factors was the spread of Christianity. Concerning this point Forbes states:

> *Law, oaths, rules, vigilant officials, traditions, the fear of flog-*
> *ging, the religious setting of the games, a personal sense of*
> *honor—all these contributed to keep Greek athletic contests*
> *clean. And most of the thousands of contests over the centuries*
> *were clean. Though corruption undoubtedly increased with the*
> *growth of professionalism, it was finally Christianity and not cor-*
> *ruption that caused the abolition of Greek athletics. The games*
> *were a powerful survival of paganism, and intrenched Christianity*
> *insisted that they had to go.* [88]

Artistic Appreciation as a Motive for Participation

The close association between art and athletics also had a strong influence on athletics in Greece.[89] To the Greeks "the youthful male figure,
quite undraped, seemed...a thing supremely beautiful."[90] The importance of
a beautiful body is clearly evident in art and sculpture in Greece, especially
during the fourth and fifth centuries. At Olympia alone "there were hundreds of athletic statues."[91]

Related to the art of the Grecians is the custom of athletes to practice and
compete in the nude. Although there is some question as to how universal or
common the practice of exercising and competing in the nude was during
the different historical periods, most Greek historians believe that nudity
was at least common, if not universally practiced, for hundreds of years.*
The practice of competing in the nude apparently began at the fifteenth
Olympiad in 720 B.C. In discussing the relationship of nudity and art, Gardiner states that nudity "must certainly...have been almost universal in the
palaestra of the sixth century."[92] It seems reasonable to assume that the extensive practice of nudity

> *served as a valuable incentive to the youth of Greece to keep*
> *themselves in good physical condition. The Greek with his keen*
> *eye for physical beauty, regarded flabbiness, want of condition,*
> *imperfect development as a disgrace, a sign of neglected educa-*
> *tion, and the ill-trained youth was the laughing stock of his com-*
> *panions. Hence every Greek learnt to take pride in his physical*
> *fitness and beauty.* [93]

However, to the Romans the custom of competing and practicing in the
nude was degrading and slowed their acceptance of Greek athletic
practices.[94]

---

*Concerning the practice of nudity it is interesting to note that in Lucian's dialogue between
Solon and Anacharsis they are discussing athletes training in the nude. *Anacharsis, or Athletics,*
3-69.

Educational Philosophy and System

Interwoven with the military needs, religious beliefs, artistic attitudes and other values, the education of the Greeks, with its stress on physical education, had a profound effect on Greek athletics and physical fitness through the fifth century B.C. because Greek physical education was essentially training in athletic skills. Although the physical education received by the students in school was essentially training in athletic and military skills, this training did not involve the specialization and dietary practices of the professional athletes. Physical education in schools, including the Athenian Ephebia, was taught with broader values and motives than just winning in athletics. Thus, physical education is distinguished from athletic training and professionalism in ancient Greece.[95] [96] As a result, a gap developed between professional athletics and physical education. In the local festivals in which there were various categories in which to compete, the ideal of Greek athletics and physical education probably continued much longer than at the Panhellenic festivals.

Gardiner, describing the Greek educational system, says:

> In most Greek states education was voluntary, but the Greeks were enthusiasts for education, and few who could afford it failed to avail themselves of the service of the schoolmaster and the paidotribes for their sons, at least under the age of fourteen, when the elementary course of education usually ended for the poorer classes. The well-to-do, however, continued their education, attending the lectures of mathematicians, rhetorians, grammarians and practicing in the palaestra or gymnasium till the age of seventeen or eighteen.[97]

Built upon this educational background for younger children emerged the Athenian Ephebia, in 335 B.C., which was originally compulsory for all male citizens for two years between the ages of eighteen and twenty. Originally the training in the ephebia was military and gymnastic, but it later became more philosophical and literary in emphasis.[98]

In the Greek educational system the goals sought were certainly more comprehensive than just victory in athletics. The Greeks were concerned with possessing healthy and strong bodies for the development of the mind and soul, as well as for military defense and the beauty of the properly-proportioned body. To the Greeks of this period physical education was of practical importance as well as of aesthetic and religious value. Lucian attempts to convey some of this idea in his *Anacharsis* when Solon says to Anacharsis:

> But above all and at all hazards we endeavor to insure that the citizens shall be virtuous in soul and strong in body, thinking that such men, joined together in public life, will make good use of

themselves in times of peace, will bring the city safe out of war, and will keep it always free and prosperous. [99]

Another excellent illustration of the high value placed on physical training by the Greeks is Xenophon's account, written about 350 B.C., of a conversation between Socrates* and Epigenes in *Memorabilia:* [100]

On noticing that Epigenes, one of his companions, was in poor condition, for a young man, he said: "You look as though you need exercise, Epigenes." "Well," he replied, "I'm not an athlete, Socrates." "Just as much as the competitors entered for Olympia," he retorted. "Or do you count the life and death struggle with their enemies, upon which, it may be, the Athenians will enter, but a small thing? Why, many, thanks to their bad condition, lose their life in the perils of war or save it disgracefully: many, just for this same cause, are taken prisoners, and then either pass their days, perhaps in slavery of the hardest kind, or, after meeting with cruel sufferings and paying, sometimes, more than they have, live on, destitute and in misery. Many, again, by their bodily weakness earn infamy, being thought cowards. Or do you despise these, the rewards of bad condition and think you can easily endure such things? And yet I suppose that what has to be borne by anyone who takes care to keep his body in good condition healthier and generally more serviceable than good, or do you despise the effects of good condition? And yet the results of physical fitness are the direct opposite of those that follow from unfitness. The fit are healthy and strong; and many, as a consequence, save themselves decorously on the battlefield and escape all the dangers of war; many help friends and do good for their country and for this cause earn gratitude; get great glory and gain very high honours, and for this cause live henceforth a pleasanter and better life, and leave to their children better means of winning a livelihood.

"I tell you, because military training is not publicly recognised by the state, you must not make that an excuse for being a whit less careful in attending to it yourself. For you may rest assured that there is no kind of struggle, apart from war, and no undertaking in which you will be worse off by keeping your body in better fettle. For in everything that men do the body is useful; and in all uses of the body it is of great importance to be in as high a state of physical efficiency as possible. Why, even in the process of thinking, in which the use of the body seems to be reduced to a minimum, it is matter of common knowledge that grave mistakes

*Socrates died in 399 B.C.

41

*may often be traced to bad health. And because the body is in a
bad condition, loss of memory, depression, discontent, insanity
often assail the mind so violently as to drive whatever knowledge
it contains clean out of it. But a sound and healthy body is a
strong protection to a man, and at least there is no danger then of
such a calamity happening to him through physical weakness: on
the contrary, it is likely that his sound condition will serve to produce effects the opposite of those that arise from bad condition.
And surely a man of sense would submit to anything to obtain the
effects that are the opposite of those mentioned in my list.*

*"Besides, it is a disgrace to grow old through sheer carelessness
before seeing what manner of man you may become by developing your bodily strength and beauty to their highest limit. But you
cannot see that, if you are careless; for it will not come of its own
accord."*[101]

Closely associated with the educational system of Greece was the social
and economic structure. The Greeks were enthusiastic about education, but
not everyone could afford to go to school.[102] Originally, an education was
just the privilege of the wealthy aristocrats, and it remained their privilege
well into the fifth century.[103]

Class System and Social Structure

Underlying all the factors that contributed to the development of Greek
athletics and provided the leisure needed for training for and participating in
athletic contests was the class system in the city-states. In Sparta during the
seventh and sixth centuries B.C., the citizens were able to devote themselves
to serving the state by having serfs or *helots,* a type of slave, work for
them.[104] Worth noting is the fact that at times helots were so "...bitterly
dissatisfied and ready to rebel...[that] the state of constant military preparation in which the Spartans lived may have been partly due to the consciousness of this peril perpetually at their doors."[105]

Certainly the slaves and serfs were a vital if not indispensable part of the
social structure and economy of Greece during this time.[106] There appears
to be little doubt that slavery provided part of the labor with which Greece
developed into a prosperous and highly civilized society. The wealth of
mines, industries and commerce and the labor of slaves, alien craftsmen,
and serfs were all vital parts of the Greek economy. To the Greek
aristocracy, these subservient classes were necessary in order to have leisure
time to devote to government, war, athletics, literature, and philosophy.[107]

As years went by, the slave system which began in the seventh century
proved to be "...one of the most fatal causes of disease and decay to the
states of Greece," according to Bury.[108]

Opportunity to Compete

Historians generally agree that during the period that Homer wrote about, participation in athletic games was restricted to members of the aristocracy —kings and chieftans and the warriors that surrounded them.[109] [110]. During the next few centuries the opportunity to compete broadened only slightly. Concerning this aspect of the athletic games, Robinson stated that:

> From the eighth century B.C., through most of the sixth it was still, for the most part, the young man of means and social distinction who could afford to spend his time training for the national festivals. Besides, in those days when skill in athletics was in such high social repute, there was no easier stepping-stone to an advantageous marriage or to a prominent place in affairs of state for an ambitious man than a victory in the games before the eyes of distinguished spectators gathered from all over Greece. The list of persons recorded as victors at the festival of Olympia, in the two centuries after official lists began to be kept, reads like a page from the Social Register. It is to be expected that wealthy aristocrats and tyrants would be entering four-horse chariots in contests but in these centuries future statesmen, generals, sons-in-law of wealthy tyrants and the like were also fighting hard pancratium matches to a far from gentle type of boxing and wrestling and were sprinting in the foot races at Olympia during the stifling heat in August. Such was the social and political prestige of that festival in the early seventh century B.C. that the powerful and rich king of Argos, Pheidon, wantonly usurped control of it for a season.[111]

During the latter part of the sixth century, the participation in athletics by the Greeks increased considerably. One factor that contributed to this change was the growth in the number of festivals throughout Greece in the fifth century B.C.[112] In addition, age categories for competition were introduced in many festivals throughout the Greek world, which undoubtedly served as a stimulus and incentive for younger athletes. At Olympia a category of competition for young men or boys was added in 632 B.C.[113] The age range for the new competitive category at Olympia was apparently "over seventeen and less than twenty years of age."[114] At the Nemean, Isthmiam and Panathenaic Games there were three age classifications for competition and at "purely local competitions there were far more elaborate [age] classifications."[115] The resulting innumerable competitive opportunities for boys of all ages served as an aid to the schools because it kept alive interest in the training previously described.[116]

In spite of numerous opportunities to compete in athletics, participation was essentially limited to a small minority because slaves were not usually permitted to participate in athletic events[117] and the poor people were, for all practical purposes, unable to engage in competitive athletics. Forbes stated that if a Greek "belonged to the middle or upper classes [he] had leisure enough so that he might spend hours daily conversing in the market place or exercising in the gymnasium."[118] This is most likely true, but the middle and upper class citizens were a small minority of the total poulation. The lower class of citizens made up the largest segment of the citizenry. Assuming that the populations of Attica can be viewed as indicative of Greece in general, then a liberal estimate of the percentage of the population that would be in the citizen class after 431 B.C. would be 40 per cent and, at the most, 50 per cent. Research shows that the total population of Attica in 431 B.C. was between 310,000 and 425,000. Of this total it was estimated that 75,000 to 150,000 were slaves, 95,000 to 99,000 were resident aliens and 140,000 to 176,000 resident citizens. Approximately one-fourth of the citizens and resident aliens were adult males.[119]

An estimate of the percentage of the population eligible to participate in athletic contests can be derived by using the midpoint or average of each estimate referred to above. Therefore, if the total population of Attica was 367,500, including 112,500 slaves, 255,000 resident aliens and 158,000 citizens, the citizens, including men, women, and children, make up less than fifty percent of the total population. If it is assumed that three-fourths of the 158,000 citizens were women and children, only 39,500 adult male citizens are left. These 39,500 adult male citizens,* who cover a broad age span, represent slightly less than eleven per cent of the population. The number of the males from this group who could participate in athletic contests was often further reduced because not all citizens had the time and money to engage in athletic training and competition. Thus the opportunities for competition and training in athletics were open to a relatively small percentage of the population in Greece in 431 B.C., a date just a few years later than the peak of the athletic ideal in Athens.**

This is a dimension of Greek athletics that has significant implications for contemporary amateurism as a category of sports competition. A society which makes athletic competition impossible or nearly impossible for fifty percent, and possibly ninety percent, of the population leaves a great deal to be desired as an ideal if one believes that all persons should have an equal opportunity to participate. To what extent the above percentages can be used for other areas of Greece is open to question, but it seems

*This figure corresponds with the estimates given by Zimmern. A maximum of adult male population of Attica of 44,000 and a minimum of 35,000.[120]

**Schobel claims that after 146 B.C. members of non-Greek tribes and states could compete in the Olympic Games.[121]

reasonable to assume that a smaller percentage of the population had the opportunity to compete in other cities. It must also be remembered that Greece was not a static society for a thousand years; therefore, these percentages can only serve as reference points for determining population and athletic percentages during other eras. An additional point that needs to be considered is the fact that the male resident aliens did assume a military defense obligation in Athens similar to that of male citizens.[122] Therefore, they had to train themselves for warfare; but as aliens, they were not eligible to participate in athletic contests at Olympia.

The chariot race, an event of special interest in terms of opportunities to compete was held at Olympia and at some other festivals. This was an event which certainly presented a limited opportunity for competition. While the chariot race is not usually considered an athletic event, as an Olympic event it has some similarity to the equestrian events in the modern Olympics. The chariot race had limited appeal from a participant aspect which was undoubtedly due to the fact that it required considerable wealth to purchase horses and chariots and to train the horses for the races.[123] Thus, by the very nature of this event, there was an added restriction of great wealth. The fact that the wealthy had an advantage in the ancient chariot races and have an apparent advantage in the modern Olympic equestrian events is a contradiction to the stated objectives of the International Olympic Committee from 1949[124] to 1974[125] [126] which were to promote "fair and equal competition." Perhaps the reason this phrase was eliminated from the modern Olympic rules was the inevitably unequal opportunity that existed under recent eligibility rules in some events for persons with little wealth.

The Giving of Awards

At athletic festivals and events during the period prior to 776 B.C., valuable awards were given the winners as a common practice. In fact, I was unable to find any evidence of restrictions on the value of the prizes for winning athletic contests. For example, at the funeral games in honor of Patroclus many valuable awards were given. In these games the rewards given by Achilles for a chariot race were:

> ...a woman to lead away, one skilled in goodly handiwork, and an eared tripod* of two and twenty measures for him that should be first; and for the second he appointed a mare of six years, unbroken, with a mule foal in her womb; and for the third he set forth a cauldron** untouched of fire, a fair cauldron that held four measures, and for a fourth he appointed two talents of gold; and for the fifth a two-handled urn, yet untouched by fire.[127]

For the boxing match Achilles gave a six-year-old unbroken mule for the

---

*A vessel or kettle with three legs.   **A large kettle or boiler.

winner and a two-handled cup for the loser.[128]

In the third contest, a wrestling match, the winner of that match was to receive "...a great tripod to stand upon the fire, that the Achaians prized amongst them the world of twelve oxen; and for him that should be worsted he (Achilles) set in the midst a woman of manifold skill in handiwork, and they prized her at a worth of four oxen."[129] However, before the match was finished Achilles stopped it and said, "Victory is with you both; take then equal prizes and go your ways..."[130]

The prizes for the foot race were a valuable silver mixing bowl that held six measures for the first place, "an ox great and rich with fat" for second place, and half talent of gold for third place.[131]

For the winner of a duel between two armed warriors, Achilles gave a silver-studded sword with its scabbard and baldric.[132] Another consisted of throwing "a mass of rough cast iron." The person who threw it the farthest was given the medal mass to use for "five revolving years."[133]

In the archery contest, the archer who hit the pigeon received ten double-headed axes, and the archer who hit the cord with which the pigeon was tied received ten single-edged axes.[134]

The last event of the games was the javelin throw. First prize for this winner was a cauldron. A spear went to the man who finished second.[135]

It is not certain whether the awards for the Patroclus funeral games are real or fictional, but it is reasonable to assume that athletic contests with awards similar to those described did take place during the era prior to the Olympic games. Hesiod, who lived in the ninth century B.C., tells in The Theogony and The Shield of Heracles of the valuable prizes awarded to victors of athletic contests.[136] Herodotus[137] and Pausanias[138] tell of tripods being given to the winners. Even at the Olympic Games, according to Phlegon, it was not until the seventh Olympiad in 752 B.C. that the olive wreath was introduced as the victor's award in place of prizes of value.[139] Gardiner feels that Phlegon was probably mistaken in his view that prizes of value were given at Olympia before the seventh Olympiad when the olive wreath was introduced.[140] However, Robinson supports the view that awards of cash value were the common practice prior to the seventh Olympiad.[141]

The practice of giving valuable awards at these early games was followed because, according to Hyde, "their value...was regarded not so much in light of rewards to the victor as proof of the generous spirit of the holder of the games."[142] This opinion seems reasonable in view of the fact that the participants in and hosts of these early games were from the wealthy aristocratic levels of society. The implication is that the contestants did not participate for rewards but for the joy derived from the activity and the challenge of the contest. Nevertheless, it does appear reasonable to assume that the valuable prizes did provide some motivation for the competitors even if the prizes were of little value in comparison with the total financial worth of the givers and receivers.

Hyde also implies that when awards are given because of the generous spirit of the giver, such a practice has no relationship with professionalism. If this is true, then gifts to athletes from generous alumni and sports philanthropists, such as Robert Mitchell who financed Billie King's training for three months in Australia, when she was a young amateur, would fall in a similar category.[143] This emphasis indicates that it is the spirit involved in one's motives for competition and that rewards are really a secondary matter.

Awarding winners crowns made from plants was followed in the sixth century at the other Panhellenic festivals. At the Pythian Games which were reorganized in 582 B.C. a crown of bay leaves was awarded the victors in place of the valuable prizes previously given.[144] At the Isthmian Games, a wreath of pine leaves was awarded the winner. A crown of parsley was given the winner of the Nemean Games.[145] However, at the local festivals it was common for valuable awards to be given. Sometimes the most valuable product of the country was given as the prize.[146]

Although no awards of material worth were given at the Olympic Games after the sixth Olympiad, it should be clearly understood that victors did receive very valuable rewards from other sources for winning. Receiving valuable awards was certainly not in conflict with the Greek athletic ideals at this time. The absence of any negative attitude toward financial awards for athletics during the first half of the sixth century is shown by the fact that Solon passed a law about 594 B.C. which awarded one hundred drachmas to victors at the Isthmian Games and five hundred drachmas to the winners at Olympia.[147] The high value of these awards is evident by the fact that a drachma could purchase a bushel of grain.[148] A person who had an increase of five hundred bushels of grain during the year was placed in the top financial category in Solon's division of citizens.[149] It was Solon's hope that these lucrative awards would motivate the Athenians to win more victories at the Isthmian and Olympic Games where people "from every section of the Greek trade world were regularly in the audience."[150] Solon anticipated that the prestige which would come to Athens as a result of these victories would contribute to the commercial prosperity of the city.[151] The results of Solon's rewards apparently had significant effects. Robinson states that:

> One of the immediate results of Solon's law must have been that competition in the national festivals became less exclusively the privilege of the wealthy few. With such inducement a person could afford to leave a gainful occupation long enough for the journey to Olympia and the month of training there. The Isthmus, being nearer, entailed less expense. The investment by the city of

47

such sums, possibly provided by the state-owned silver mines at Laurium, must have paid dividends far exceeding Solon's expectations, for Athens from that time began her rise to first place in Greece on all matters athletic.[152]

Gardiner wrote concerning the trend toward giving lucrative awards:

At Athens, too, and elsewhere, the victor had the right of the front seat at all public festivals, and sometimes of free meals at the Prythaneion. In later times he was exempt from taxation. At Sparta, which at this time seems to have stood aloof in the athletic movement, he had the privilege of fighting next to the king. In later times these honours grew more and more extravagant, especially in the rich cities of the West. As an instance of such extravagance it is recorded that Exaenetus of Agrigentum, who won the foot-race at Olympia in 412 B.C., was drawn into the city in a four-horse chariot, attended by three hundred of the chief citizens in pair-horse chariots. In the fifth century which was characterized by a revival of the worhip of the dead, we find a few cases of athletes worshipped as heroes.[153]

Over the centuries the rewards to athletes continued to grow. In a letter written in 41 B.C., Mark Antony grants athletes exemption from military service, a guarantee of personal safety and other benefits.* Other athletes received pensions for life and exemption form taxes in the third century A.D. Gardiner's information "from some papyri of Hermopolis belonging to the reign of Gallienus (253-260 A.D.)"[154] says:

A victor in any of the Sacred Games had a right secured by the law of the Empire to receive a pension, obsonia, from his city. He had only to present to the Council a demand, made out in triplicate, and the Council had no option but to grant it. The amount of the

---

*Mark Antony's letter was translated by R. S. Robinson from text given by R. G. Kenyon. "A Rescript of Marcus Antonius" The Classical Review 7 (December,1893), pp. 467-78. The letter reads as follows:

The petition previously presented to me in Ephesus by my friend and gymnastics trainer, Marcus Antonius Artemidorus, acting in conjunction with Charopinus of Ephesus, empnymous priest of the world-wide guild of Hieronikai-Stephanitae (i.e. winners in the sacred games and wearers of the wreath) that I write you immediately in regard to the other benefits and honors about which they asked me, to wit, exemptions from military service, public duties, billeting of troops, a truce during the festival (i.e. Ephesian), guarantee of personal safety, privilege of purple—(this petition) I do cheerfully grant because of my friendship with Artemidorus and because I wish to oblige their priest with a view to the glorification and magnification of the guild.

And now when Artemidorus petitioned me again to ask that they might erect a bronze tablet and inscribe upon it the aforesaid privileges, I consented to the setting up of the tablet as requested, choosing to support Artemidorus in every way. You now have a confirmation in writing of these grants.[155]

pension was from 180 to 200 drachmas a month. Most of the athletes mentioned were local athletes and their victories were won at local games, for example, at Sidon, Gaza, Bostra, which can only have been places of secondary importance. Moreover, an athlete could enjoy two or more pensions together. One of them received for two victories in the course of four years, 2 talents and 3,900 drachmas. Of the value of these pensions we can judge from the fact that workmen engaged in building a public stoa, presumably therefore skilled men, received only 4 drachmas a day, and the average wage for a day's labour must have been about 1 drachma. When an ordinary athlete could earn such a pension, what must have been the pension of an Asclepiades or Damostratus?[156]

Even though the professional athlete tended to dominate the athletic scene more and more, it is reasonable to assume that several participants not in the category currently called "professional" athletes competed in the games. Robinson stated that in the period from 146 B.C. to 118 A.D. "contrary to what has often been asserted, amateurs probably did not entirely disappear from the scene;."[157]

The practice of giving valuable prizes to the winners at the games undoubtedly served as an incentive to train and compete in athletics. This was especially true for poor citizens. While men of wealth and social distinction dominated the national festivals through most of the sixth century B.C., "the increase in rich prizes was soon to put the poor man on a level with the rich."[158] Awards were probably an incentive to the Greeks to participate in athletics also while under the rule of the Roman Empire when they were "shut out from many other possibilities of earning a livelihood."[159]

Closely related to the incentive resulting from awards given to athletes and the rise in popularity of festivals was the fact that statesmen began to recognize that local festivals gave an opportunity to display their cities and the products of their cities. The rewards given by Solon to victors at the Isthmian and Olympic Games indicate this attitude, which is also evident in information concerning the Athenian Festival. For example, at the Athenian Festival the prizes for boys' and youths' events in the fourth century B.C. varied between six and thirty amphorae of oil, which records say was well worth having.[160]

The desire of rulers to have outstanding athletes represent their cities at various games also created a situation in which those members of the lower classes who possessed unusual athletic attributes, such as speed, strength and size, which could be readily recognized, were given special opportunities to receive an education and to train in order to bring fame to a city and its rulers. Perhaps this is part of the explanation why men such as the poor fisherman who carried fish from Argos to Tegea were able to compete at Olympia. [161]

Bribery and Awards

The extravagant awards to victors, the prestige of winning, and the rivalry between states, appear to have resulted in athletes being bribed to lose contests. Some such incidents include the following: in the ninety-eighth Olympiad in 388 B.C. Eupous of Thesaly bribed his opponents in boxing. This was apparently the first violation of the rules at Olympia. [162] In the 112th Olympiad in 332 B.C., Callippus of Athens bribed his opponents in the Pentathlon.[163] At the 178th Olympiad in 68 B.C., a Rhodian bribed his opponents in wrestling.[164] At the 192th Olympiad in 12 B.C., Damonicus bribed the father of Sosander in order that his son could win the wrestling match.[165] At the 226th Games in 124 A.D. two boxers, Didas and Sarapammon, agreed to fix their boxing match.[166] If violations of this type were possible at Olympia, with its deep religious association, it seems reasonable to assume that similar violations took place at other festivals.[167]

As the penalty for these incidents at Olympia fines were imposed, and the statues called Zanes were erected with inscriptions including the details of the violations, the names of the offenders, and a warning to others. One inscription was "intended to make plain that an Olympic victory is to be won, not by money, but by swiftness of foot and strength of body."[168] An inscription on another statue declares "that the image stands to the glory of the deity, through the piety of Eleans, and to be a terror to law-breaking athletes."[169] The willingness of the authorities at the ancient Olmpics to impose severe fines promptly appears to have been a significant factor in keeping the Games relatively free from corruption.[170]

Although there were a few instances of bribery at Olympia, it seems reasonable to assume that athletics in ancient Greece was generally free from such problems for hundreds of years. The few recorded instances of bribery prior to the fall of Greece to the Romans in 146 B.C. is a remarkable record. It isn't until about 225 A.D. that we hear Philostratus claim that bribery was common in athletics everywhere, except at Olympia.[171] Certainly, the increasing value of awards since 146 B.C. must have contributed to the increased instances of bribery and corruption during Philostratus' time. However, it must be remembered that athletics were lucratively rewarded even during the fifth and sixth centuries B.C. The total decay in Greek society must be considered when trying to explain the cause of increased bribery in Greek athletics after 146 B.C. Excessive rewards were only part, and perhaps a small part, of the problem.

Specialization in Athletics

The practice of specializing in athletic events began during the fifth century B.C. At that time athletes found that in order to win "it was necessary to concentrate on some particular event and that different events required different development and different training.[172] Boxing, wrestling, and the pancration, the most popular of Greek sports, led the way to specialization.[173] In part, this happened because about 480 B.C.[174] Dromeus conceived the "idea of the flesh diet"[175] to reinforce the special development of athletes. This diet, when combined with a certain exercise program would add weight and strength to one's body. The addition of weight and strength was an obvious advantage in boxing, wrestling, and the pancration, because weight classifications did not exist in Greek Athletics.[176] This trend toward bulky bodies soon began to be condemned by military leaders. For example, the General Epaminodas (420-362 B.C.) complained that heavy-weight wrestlers did not make good soldiers.[177,178] The implication is that athletic training of earlier years did not stress the gaining of excess weight and as a result was better for military purposes. An example of a philosopher who clearly indicated his rejection of the specialized over-developed athlete is Aristotle (384-322 B.C.) who stated that "the athlete's habit of body is not serviceable for bodily fitness as required by a citizen, nor for health and parentage."[179]

With the development of specialization, professional trainers appeared "whose business was to train the competitors for the great games.[180] Gardiner states that the first trainers "were boxers and wrestlers."[181] As a result of the necessity to specialize and to train extensively in order to win at the major festivals, athletics became an extremely time consuming activity for some. One example of a person who apparently spent much time training was Thesgones of Thasos, who won some 1,400 prizes.[182]

Time Spent in Training and Competition

The differences in emphases and rules involving time spent in training and competition for athletes in ancient Greece and contemporary amateur athletes are significant. The Greeks were concerned with establishing minimum standards for training whereas the modern International Olympic Committee, during most of the twentieth century, has been concerned with restrictions on the time spent in training and in competition. For example, at the ancient Olympics as far back as the eighth century B.C., the participants had to swear that they had "strictly obeyed the rules for training...for ten months prior to the games,"[183] and had trained for thirty days at Olympia prior to the beginning of the games.[184] In addition to the time spent at Olympia, it seems reasonable to assume that it took some athletes fifteen to twenty days to travel to the ancient Olympic Games.[185]

51

For the athletes living at Olympia this meant at least thirty-three days away from their regular work for the Olympic Games. Until 468 B.C., the games were only one day.[186] After that time the games were extended to three days. Thus, the combination of competition and festivities lasted for five days. For some, the time spent at Olympia and traveling to and from the games could involve sixty days or more. Futhermore, it is reasonable to assume that the participants in the Olympic Games spent time competing in other games and festivals, too. If one adds to the thirty days, the five days for the games, plus the time spent traveling to and from the games, he realizes that this was not a normal leisure experience. Not everyone in Greece could be absent from his job for at least thirty-three days, but there were no rules then to pervent employers and governments from enabling athletes to participate and from rewarding them for success.

In contrast to the rules for ancient Greek athletes, the rules of the International Olympic Committee from 1962 to 1974[187] clearly stated that to be eligible for the Olympic Games an athlete must have a basic vocation.[188] In addition, from 1938 to 1962[189] an athlete was not supposed to interrupt his employment or studies by attending a training camp for more than two weeks.[190] In 1962 the period allowed for training camps was extended to three weeks[192] and in 1967 the period was extended to four weeks.[192] The eligibility rules from 1962 to 1974 also specifically stated that "those who have neglected their usual vocation or employment for competitive sports at home or abroad" were not eligible for the Olympic Games.[193] The International Olympic Committee also has in principle been opposed to payments for broken time most of the time.[194] These rules create some real difficulty for the athletes of average or less than average wealth or the athlete who works on an hourly basis in contrast to the independently wealthy athlete and the athlete who earns a salary. In October 1974 all of the above restrictions were eliminated from the eligibility rules for the modern Olympic Games.

Rules for Certain Event

Another factor which contributed to the decline in athletic participation was the unsatisfactory rules of some events.[196] Since no size or weight classification existed, the big man had the advantage in boxing, wrestling, the pancration, discus, and perhaps the javelin. The big man also had the advantage in the pentathlon,[197] which consisted of running, jumping, throwing the discus, throwing the javelin and wrestling. The fact that in two of the recorded accounts of pentathlon contests, the winner won the discus, javelin, and wrestling events does lend some support to this view.[198]

The absence of weight categories for boxing, wrestling, and the pancration was unfortunate. In these events it was especially obvious that the big man had an advantage; it would have been fool-hardy for a small man to engage in these contests. Thus, it was only natural that athletes would, by special diets and exercise programs, try to add bulk to their bodies. The practice of adding weight to the body contributed to specializing in events and was the beginning of the trend away from the athletic ideal of the fifth century B.C. As a result of the gluttonous habits of athletes and the bulky bodies that developed, people in ancient Greece began to associate athletes with these characteristics. In the nineteenth and twentieth centuries some people have associated these characteristics with professionalism.

In addition to the absence of weight classifications, the brutality allowed by the rules of boxing, wrestling, and the pancration did not encourage participation by the masses. In boxing a match was not ended until "one of the competitors was knocked out or held up his hand in acknowledgment of defeat."[199] In addition, during the Roman period the boxers wore the "murderous caetus."[200] The caetus consisted of leather thongs wrapped around the boxer's hands and forearms as a type of glove.

In the pancration the object was to get one's opponent to admit defeat. The brutality brought about by this rule is made evident by Epictetus, who wrote in the first century A.D. "Then, when the contest comes, you get hacked, sometimes dislocate your hand, twist your ankle, swallow plenty of sand, get a flogging, and with all this you are sometimes defeated."[202] Pausanias also tells of a pancratiast named Sicy who "used to grip his antagonist by the fingers and bend them, and would not let go until he saw his opponent had given in."[203] and of a wrestler named Leontiseus who "did not know how to throw his opponents, but won by bending their fingers."[204] The brutality of boxing, wrestling, and the pancration certainly must have caused some people to lose their motivation for participating in athletics.

As a result of the failure of the ancient Greeks to eliminate brutality from certain sports, people in Greece began to associate brutality with athletics in the same way they associated gluttonous, bulky athletes with the evils of athletics. In comtemporary society this same association has been made with professionalism and certain evils in sports by many people, especially strong advocates of amateurism. However, it is important to recognize that professionalism or money is not the sole cause of these practices. The rules of the events are the cause of some problems.

SUMMARY

From this survey of athletics in ancient Greece several implications for contemporary amateurism have either been alluded to or specifically mentioned. Perhaps the major implication of the study of athletics at that time is the realization that athletics in ancient Greece is not a perfect model for contemporary amateurism, nor is it an adequate model for a system or framework of athletic competition for the general public. For example, what has been thought of as the Greek athletic ideal by the nineteenth and twentieth century advocates of amateurism was an ideal applicable to only a small minority of the population. This was especially true prior to the awarding of lucrative awards to the victors.

Another significant aspect of athletics in ancient Greece relates to the factors that contributed to the popularity of athletics. These factors were the religious beliefs of the people, the necessity for constant military preparedness, a general love of competition, the educational system with its emphasis on physical activities, opportunities to compete, rewards for winning, and a high value placed on a beautiful, strong, healthy body.

The ancient Greeks had no known restrictions on granting awards to athletes. At some festivals only wreaths were given, but winners were generously rewarded in their own cities. This emphasis is certainly in contrast to the rules of the twentieth century amateurism. The same contrast is evident when comparing time required or allowed for practicing and competing. The Greeks were concerned with minimum standards rather than maxiumum standards. In essence, the Greeks were not concerned with legalistic definitions of how to assure the proper emphasis in athletics. Their whole orientation to athletics was much more positive than that of contemporary advocates of amateurism, who, at times, appear to be preoccupied with legalistic restrictions as a means of achieving the important values to be derived from athletics. In fact, the Greeks did not make a distinction between professional and amateur athletes as defined by modern sports organizations. The Greek system of competition was open to all citizens. From the time of Homer, the athletics in ancient Greece were what is currently defined as "professional."

It is true that the combination of awards and numerous opportunities to compete did help create a class of professional athletes who were able to earn a living from awards. Also the development of an organized class of professional athletes in Greece apparently did discourage the masses from participating in athletics. It is also possible that the valuable awards given to athletes during the last few centuries of the ancient Olympics did reach a point where they created a distorted sense of values. Thus, what the nineteenth and twentieth century men have called the Greek ideal of fifth and sixth centuries B.C. disappeared with the growth of professionalism. This ideal thought athletics a thing of beauty which possessd a utilitarian value in terms of health and personal and state defense. However, the granting of awards and the numerous opportunities to compete should not be given as the primary causes of the destruction of this ideal.

The issue of professionalism in athletics was a secondary symptom and not the primary cause of the decline of athletic festivals and athletic participation within Greece. Changes in religious beliefs and military needs and emphases, class distictions, population trends, economic factors, wars, and the rules of some sports were the chief factors that created a situation in which fewer people participated and more watched than during the fifth century B.C. Because these factors were interrelated and tended to have a cyclic effect, social, political, and religious changes were much more instrumental than professionalism in bringing about the general decline in athletic values.[205]

FOOTNOTES

1   *The Olympic Games* (Lausanne, Switzerland: International Olympic Committee, 1967), p. 43.

2   *Handbook: 1969-1972,* ed. Harold W. Henning (George St. 247, Sydney, N.N.W.; Australia: International Swimming Federation [1969]), p. 29.

3   R. A. Wright, *Greek Athletics* (London: Jonathan Cape, Ltd., 1925), p. 14.

4   Rachel Sargent Robinson, *Sources for the History of Greek Athletics with Introductions, Ancient Text in English Translation, and Explanatory Notes* (Cincinnati, Ohio 45206: By the Author, 1960 Madison Road, lithoprint and copyright, 1955), p.33

5   Ibid., p. 1.

6   H. I. Marrou, *A History of Education in Antiquity,* trans. by George Lamb (New York: The New American Library, 1964), pp. 22-23.

7   Homer, *The Iliad,* Vol. II, trans. by A. T. Murray, 2 Vols., The Loeb Classical Library (Cambridge: Harvard University Press, 1925), xxiii.

8   Homer, *The Odyssey,*Vol. I, trans. by A. T. Murray, 2 Vols., The Loeb Classical Library (Cambridge: Harvard University Press, 1919), viii. 97-384.

9   Homer, *The Odyssey,* Vol. II, xviii. 1-112.

10   Homer, *The Iliad,* Vol. II, xxiii. 630-644.

11   Homer, *The Iliad,* Vol. I, xi. 697-704.

12   Pausanias, *Description of Greece,* Vol. II, trans. by W. H. S. Jones and H. A. Ormerod, 5 Vols., The Loeb Classical Library (Cambridge: Harvard University Press, 1926), v. 17. 5-11.

13   *Herodotus,* Vol. I, trans. by A. D. Godley, 4 Vols., The Loeb Classical Library (Cambridge: Harvard University Press, 1926), i. 144.

14   E. Norman Gardiner, *Athletics of the Ancient World* (Oxford: The Clarendon Press, 1930), p. 27.

15   Ferenc Mezö, *The Modern Olympic Games* (Budapest: Pannonia Press, 1956), p. 13.

16   E. Norman Gardiner, *Athletics of the Ancient World* (Oxford: The Clarendon Press 1967), pp. 36-37.

17   *Greek Elegy and Iambus with the Anacreontea,* Vol. I, trans. by J. M. Edmonds, 2 Vols., The Loeb Classical Library (Cambridge: Harvard University Press, 1931), pp. 192-195.

18   Gardiner, *Athletics in the Ancient World,* p. 42.

19   J. B. Bury, *A History of Greece* (3rd ed.; London: Macmillan and Company, Ltd., 1959), p. 295.

20   Norman E. Gardiner, *Greek Athletic Sports and Festivals* (London: Macmillan Company, 1910), p. 107.

21   Ibid., p. 86.

22   Heinz Schöbel, *The Ancient Olympic Games,* trans. by Joan Becker (Princeton, New Jersey: D. Van Nostrand Company, Inc., 1966), pp. 29-37.

23   See Robinson's analysis of this denunciation, op. cit., p.116).

24   See Robinson, *op. cit.,* Chapter V, pp.123-137; C, "The Philosophers Examine Greek Athletics," Socrates, pp. 123-124; 2. Plato, pp.125-134; 3. Aristotle, pp. 135-137.

25   See detailed discussion in Robinson, *op. cit.,* p. 119.

26   N. L. W. Laistner, *A Survey of Ancient History to the Death of Constantine* (New York: D. C. Heath and Company, 1929), p. 428.

27   Schobel, *The Ancient Olympic Games,* p. 35.

28   Norman E. Gardiner, *Olympia* (Oxford: The Clarendon Press, 1925).

29   Ibid., p. 158.

30   Robinson, *Sources for the History of Greek Athletics,* pp. 158-159.

31   *Velleius Paterculus and Res Gestae Divi Augusti,* trans. by Frederick W. Shipley (New York: G. P. Putnam's Sons, 1924), Res Gestae Divi Augusti, iv. 22.

32   Gardiner, *Athletics of the Ancient World,* pp. 119, 123-24.

33   Tertullian, *Disciplinary, Moral and Ascetical Works,* Vol. XL, ed. by Roy Joseph Deferrari and trans. by Rudolph Arbesmann, Emily Joseph Daley and Edwin A. Quain, 51 Vols. (New York: Fathers of the Church, Inc., 1959), p. 33.

34   Thomas Woody, "Professionalism and the Decay of Greek Athletics," *School and Society,* 47 (April 23, 1938), p. 525.

35   Gardiner, *Athletics of the Ancient World,* p. 107.

36   Robinson, *Sources for the History of Greek Athletics*, p. 208.

37   Ibid.

38   Ibid., p. 208.Translation used with paid permission of author.

39   Ibid.

40   Irene C. Ringwood, "Agonistic Features of Local Greek Festivals Chiefly from Inscriptional Evidence," Ph.D. Dissertation: Columbia University (published by Irene C. Ringwood, Poughkeepsie, N. Y., 1927).

41   John Apostal Lucas, "Baron Pierre de Coubertin and the Formative Years of the Modern International Olympic Movement 1883-1896" (unpublished D.Ed. dissertation, University of Maryland, 1962), pp. 131-32.

42   Ibid., p. 135.

43   William Cranston Lawton, "The Greek Attitude Toward Athletics and Pindar," *The Sewanee Review* 11 (January 1903), p. 36.

44   Pindar, *The Odes of Pindar*, rev. ed., trans. by Sir John Sandys, The Loeb Classical Library (Cambridge: Harvard University Press, 1937), pp. 113-15, *Olympian Odes*, x. 25-55.

45   Lawton, "The Greek attitude Toward Athletics and Pindar," p. 36.

46   Lucas, "Baron Pierre de Coubertin and the Formative Years of the Modern International Movement 1883-1896," p. 130.

47   Clarence Forbes, *Greek Physical Education* (New York: The Century Company, 1929), p. 57.

48   Ibid., pp. 12-14.

49   Norman E. Gardiner, *Greek Athletic Sports and Festivals* (London: Macmillan Company, 1910), pp. 84-106.

50   Ibid., p. 88

51   Ibid., pp. 110-114.

52   Op. cit., Pindar.

53   Gardiner, *Greek Athletic Sports and Festivals*, p. 11.

54   Gardiner, *Olympia*, p. 112.

55   Ibid.

56   Ibid.

57 Marrou, *A History of Education in Antiquity*, p. 67.

58 Jacob Burckhardt, *History of Greek Culture*, trans. by Palmer Hilty (New York: Frederick Ungar Publsihing Company, 1963), p. 47.

59 Schöbel, *The Ancient Olympic Games*, pp. 23-24.

60 Hugh Harlan, *History of Olympic Games Ancient and Modern*, publication of the Bureau of Athletic Research (Los Angeles: Art Jones Printing Company, 1932), p. 14.

61 Robinson, *Sources for the History of Greek Athletics*, p. 62.

62 *Lucian*, Vol. IV, trans. by A. M. Harmon, 8 Vols., The Loeb Classical Library (Cambridge: Harvard University Press, 1925), *Anachersis or Athletics*, 24-25.

63 Edward M. Plummer, "Athletic Games Among the Homeric Heroes," *American Physical Education Review* 2 (December 1897), pp. 200-201.

64 Plato, *Laws*, Vol. II, trans. by R. G. Bury, 2 Vols., The Loeb Classical Library (Cambridge: Harvard University Press, 1926), vii. 796a.

65 Will Durant, *The Life of Greece* (New York: Simon and Schuster, 1939), p. 468.

66 Ibid.

67 Forbes, *Greek Physical Education*, pp. 109, 157, 177, 259-62.

68 Durant, *The Life of Greece*, p. 468.

69 Ibid.

70 Bury, *A History of Greece*, pp. 407-08.

71 Schöbel, *The Ancient Olympic Games*, pp. 34-35.

72 "Eligibility Rules of the International Olympic Committee," *Bulletin*, Lusanne, Switzerland: International Olympic Committee, No. 80 (November 1962), p. 44.

73 *The Olympic Games*, 1967, p. 21.

74 Schobel, *The Ancient Olympic Games*, pp 34-35.

75 Gardiner, *Athletics of the Ancient World*, p. 33.

76 Durant, *The Life of Greece*, p. 467.

77 Plato, *Laws*, Vol. ii, xii. 948^{c-d}.

78 Kenneth Scott Latourette, *A History of Christianity* (New York: Harpers and Brothers, 1953), pp. 23-27.

79 Tertullian, *Spectacles in Disciplinary, Moral and Ascetical Works*, p. 63.

80 Ibid., p. 77.

81 Ibid., pp. 52-56.

82 Ibid., pp. 98-103.

83 Latourette, *A History of Christianity*, p. 222.

84 Ibid., pp. 26-27.

85 Forbes, *Greek Physical Education*, p. 261.

86 Latourette, *A History of Christianity*, pp. 128-29.

87 Wright, *Greek Athletics*, p. 14.

88 Clarence A. Forbes, "Crime and Punishment in Greek Athletics," *The Classical Journal,* 47 (February 1952), p. 202.

89 Gardiner, *Athletics of the Ancient World*, p. 66.

90 Lawton, "The Greek Attitude Toward Athletics and Pindar," p. 38.

91 Gardiner, *Athletics of the Ancient World*, p. 58.

92 Gardiner, *Greek Athletic Sports and Festivals*, p. 88.

93 Ibid.

94 Gardiner, *Athletics of the Ancient World*, p. 118.

95 Marrou, *A History of Education in Antiquity*, pp. 167-69.

96 Forbes, *Greek Physical Education*, pp. 5-6.

97 Gardiner, *Athletics of the Ancient World*, p. 90.

98 Forbes, *Greek Physical Education*, pp. 109, 119.

99 Lucian, *Anacharis, or Athletics*, 20.

100 *Xenophon: Memorabilia and Oeconomicus*, trans. by E. C. Marchant, The Loeb Classical Library (Cambridge: Harvard University Press, 1923), pp. viii-ix.

101 Xenophon. *Memorabilia*, iii. 12. 1-8.

102 Gardiner, *Athletics of the Ancient World*, p. 90.

103 Marrou, *A History of Education in Antiquity*, p. 65.

104 Bury, *A History of Greece*, p. 131.

105 Ibid., pp. 131-32.

106 Burckhardt, *History of Greek Culture*, pp. 45-53.

107 Durant, *The Life of Greece*, pp. 270-80.

108 Bury, *A History of Greece*, p. 118.

109 Marrou, *A History of Education in Antiquity*, p. 23.

110 Gardiner, *Athletics of the Ancient World*, p. 27.

111 Robinson, *Sources for the History of Greek Athletics*, pp. 57-58.

112 Gardiner, *Athletics in the Ancient World*, p. 37.

113 Mezo, *The Modern Olympic Games*, p. 13.

114 Gardiner, *Athletics in the Ancient World*, p. 41.

115 Ibid.

116 Ibid., p. 92.

117 Ibid., p. 50.

118 Forbes, *Greek Physical Education*, pp. 3-4.

119 Alfred Zimmern, *The Greek Commonwealth*, 5th ed. (New York: The Modern Library, 1931), pp. 174-79, 412, 429.

120 Ibid., p. 174.

121 Schobel, *The Ancient Olympic Games*, p. 34.

122 Ibid., pp. 429-431.

123 *Isocrates*, Vol. III, rev. ed., trans. by Larue Van Hook, 3 Vols., The Loeb Classical Library (Cambridge: Harvard University Press, 1954), Socrates, *The Team of Horses*, 33, 34.

124 *Olympic Rules* (Lausanne, Switzerland: International Olympic Committee, 1949), p. 5.

125 *The Olympic Games*, 1962, p. 11.

126 *Olympic Rules*, 1975, p. 5.

127 Homer, *The Iliad*, Vol. II., xxiii. 262-271.

128 Ibid., xxiii. 655-57.

129 Ibid., xxiii. 703-07.

130 Ibid., xxiii. 738-39.

131 Ibid., xxiii. 742-52.

132 Ibid., xxiii. 823-824.

133 Ibid., xxiii. 831-836.

134 Ibid., xxiii. 855-883.

135 Ibid., xxiii. 884-894.

136 Hesiod, *The Theogony* 432-438 and *The Shield of Heracles* 306-314.

137 *Herodotus*, Vol. I, i. 144.

138 Pausanias, *Descriptions of Greece*, Vol. II, v. 17.11.

139 Robinson, *Sources for the History of Greek Athletics*, pp. 42, 239.

140 Gardiner, *Athletics in the Ancient World*, p. 35.

141 Robinson, *Sources for the History of Greek Athletics* p. 239.

142 Walter Woodburn Hyde, *Olympic Victor Monuments and Greek Athletic Art* (Washington: The Carnegie Institution of Washington, 1921), pp. 18-19.

143 Kim Chapin, " Center Courts Is Her Domain," *Sports Illustrated* 28 (June 24, 1968), p. 47.

144 Gardiner, *Athletics of the Ancient World*, p. 36.

145 Ibid., pp. 36-37.

146 Ringwood, "Agonistic Features of Local Greek Festivals Chiefly from Inscriptional Evidence," p. 7.

147 *Plutarch's Lives*, Vol. I, trans. by Bernadotte Perrin, II Vols., The Loeb Classical Library (Cambridge: Harvard University Press, 1914), p. 467, *Solon* 23.3.

148 Ibid.

149 Ibid., *Solon* 18.1.

150 Robinson, *Sources for the History of Greek Athletics*, p. 59.

151 Ibid.

152 Ibid., p. 60.

153 Gardiner, *Athletics of the Ancient World*, p. 99.

154 Ibid., p. 113.

155 Robinson, *Sources for the History of Greek Athletics*, pp. 161-62.

156 Gardiner, *Athletics of the Ancient World*, p. 113.

157 Robinson, *Sources for the History of Greek Athletics*, p. 157.

158 Gardiner, *Greek Athletic Sports and Festivals*, pp. 81-82.

159 Robinson, *Sources for the History of Greek Athletics*, p. 176.

160 H. A. Harris, *Greek Athletes and Athletics* (London: Anchor Press, Ltd., 1964), p. 36.

161 Gardiner, *Athletics of the Ancient World*, p. 42.

162 Pausanias, *Description of Greece*, Vol. II, v. 21.3.

163 Ibid., v. 21.5.

164 Ibid., v. 21.8-9.

165 Ibid., v. 21.15.

166 Ibid.

167 Gardiner, *Athletics of the Ancient World*, pp. 103-104.

168 Pausanias, *Descriptions of Greece*, Vol. II, v. 21.4.

169 Ibid.

170 Gardiner, *Athletics of the Ancient World*, pp. 103-104.

171 Robinson, *Sources for the History of Greek Athletics*, pp. 228-29.

172 Ibid., p. 141.

173 Ibid., p. 126.

174 Robinson, *Sources for the History of Greek Athletics*, p. 118.

175 Pausanias, *Description of Greece*, Vol. III, trans. by W. H. S. Jones, 5 Vols., The Loeb Classical Library (Cambridge: Harvard University Press, 1933), vi. 7.10.

176 Gardiner, *Athletics of the Ancient World*, p. 101.

177 Robinson, *Sources for the History of Greek Athletics*, p. 151.

178 Forbes, *Greek Physical Education*, p. 91.

179 Aristotle, *Politics*, rev. ed., trans. by H. Rackham, The Loeb Classical Library (Cambridge: Harvard University Press, 1944), vii. 14.8.

180 Gardiner, *Greek Athletic Sports and Festivals*, p. 122.

181 Ibid.

182 Pausanias, *Description of Greece*, Vol. II, vi. 11.6.

183 Gardiner, *Olympia*, p. 301.

184 Philostratus, *The Life of Apollonius of Tyana*, Vol. II, trans. by F. C. Conybeare, 2 Vols., The Loeb Classical Library (Cambridge: Harvard University Press, 1912), 5.43.

185 Mezo, *The Modern Olympic Games*, p. 12.

186 Ibid., p. 13.

187 *The Olympic Games* (Lausanne, Switzerland: International Olympic Committee, 1962), p. 19.

188 *The Olympic Games*, 1967, p. 21.

189 *Olympische Gesetz*, ed. by Carl Deim (Berlin: Schriftenreih Des Internationales Olympisches Instituts), Vol. I, 1938, p. 87.

190 *The Olympic Games: Fundamental Principles, Rules and Regulations* (Lausanne, Switzerland: International Olympic Committee, 1958), p. 95.

191 "Eligibility Rules of the International Olympic Committee," *Bulletin* (Lausanne, Switzerland: International Olympic Committee, No. 80, November 1962), p. 45.

192 *The Olympic Games*, 1967, p. 44.

193 *The Olympic Games*, 1962, p. 96.

194 *The Olympic Games*, 1967, p. 45.

195 "New Rules," *Olympic Review*, No. 85-86 (November-December 1974), pp. 585-86.

196 Gardiner, *Athletics of the Ancient World*, p. 204.

197 Ibid., p. 178.

198 Harris, *Greek Athletes and Athletics*, p. 79.

199 Ibid., p. 98.

200 Gardiner, *Athletics of the Ancient World*, p. 49.

201 Harris, *Greek Athletes and Athletics*, p. 107.

202 *The Discourses of Epictetus*, trans. by P. E. Mathison (New York: The Heritage Press 1968), 3.15. 308 pp.

203 Pausanias, *Description of Greece*, Vol. III, vi. 4.1.

204 Ibid., vi. 4.3.

205 Ludwig Dees, *Olympia* (New York: Frederick A. Praeger, 1968), pp. 155-60.

CHAPTER IV

The Development of Sports
in the 19th and 20th Centuries

INTRODUCTION

This chapter will review aspects of the evolution of sports and sports organizations and those societal changes during the nineteenth and twentieth centuries that have special significance to the development of amateurism. The first part of this chapter briefly covers the history of sports between the sixth and the nineteenth centuries. The main part of this chapter deals with the development of sports following 1880. The third part of the chapter is a brief description of sports following 1800.

Sports Between 600 and 1900

Although this chapter is primarily about the evolution of sports during the Nineteenth and Twentieth Centuries, it seems appropriate to comment briefly on the period between the end of ancient athletic games and the emergence of sports in the Nineteenth Century. The insignificance of sports during this period from the sixth through the nineteenth centuries gives added emphasis to the importance of developments in sports and amateurism during the Nineteenth Century. Although people did engage in sports and other recreational activities prior to the Nineteenth Century, such activity was not in the manner of either the ancient Olympics or modern organized sports which are associated with the issue of amateurism. [1] [2]

During medieval times, scholasticism, monasticism, and asceticism were dominant influences that generally condemned and emphasis on the body.

During this period, the monks were "reacting against a decadent age, in which men papmered their bodies and indulged in sensuous and cruel pastimes."[3] However, as in most if not all societies, the soldiers and warriors, who in that era were the knights and nobility, did stress physical skills and attributes that were of military value.[4]

In England during the sixteenth, seventeenth, and eighteenth centuries, sports and pastimes such as running, wrestling, dancing, archery, hawking, bowling, swimming riding horses, pageants, football, club-ball, cock fighting, baiting of animals, playing of chess, card playing, dice games, were common. As these activities began to flourish, so did gambling. However, because of excesses involving gambling and time wasted, many of these activities fell into disreput and laws were passed forbidding the playing of certain games.[5]

During this time, which encompasses the later period of the Renaissance, the Protestant Reformation, and the emerging nationalism of Europe and America, some games that were to evolve into major international sports during the Nineteenth and Twentieth Centuries had their beginning. Only two athletic bodies of any later significance developed during this period. One was the Marylebone Cricket Club which was established in 1787 and was the governing body for cricket.[6] The other was the Jockey Club which was started about 1751 and became the supreme authority and governing body for horse racing in England.[7] Other clubs interested in sports like cricket, yachting and hunting in England, which in some cases date back to the Seventeenth Century, also existed during this era. These clubs were exclusive, upper-class social clubs rather than governing bodies whose interest was in controlling and promoting sports. A partial exception was an archery group called the Society Royal Toxophilete which was formed "about 1790 for the purpose of advancing archery as a sport."[8] Perhaps the nearest any group came to the development of athletic games or festivals of highly organized nature during the Sixteenth, Seventeenth, and Eighteenth Centuries were the promoters or sponsors of Cotwold and Cornish Games, which "consisted of wrestling, cudget-playing,* leaping, pitching the bar,** tossing the pick, throwing the sledge..(and) other feats of strength and activity..."[9]

In America the period from the founding of Jamestown in 1607 until the end of the seventeenth century was basically a period of work and little play for the majority of the settlers. Two factors account for this. Work was vital to survival in the early settlements and sports and amusements that were non-productive were considered sinful by the puritans.[10]*** This same

*A cudget is a short heavy club.

**Similar to throwing a javelin.

***An example of this Puritan attitude toward sports is evident from the following proclamation against horse racing by the Boston Council in 1677:

general attitude toward work and play dominated thinking in much of America during the nineteenth century and even into the twentieth century.

Nevertheless, as the population of America grew and as villages and towns developed, sporting events began to take place. Horse racing, bowling on the green, pitching ye barr, Stool ball (a primitive form of cricket), Kelves,* and cock fighting were sports and amusements which existed in America during the seventeenth century.[12] By the end of the eighteenth century, boxing cricket, shuttlecock, fencing, football, fox-hunting, horse-shoe pitching, lacrosse, lawn bowling, trap ball (a forerunner of baseball), and skittle were part of the American scene.[13]

But as in England, no organized sports-governing bodies or groups had emerged to develop rules and regulations for any sport. However, sports were evolving with unofficial local rules and interpretations, and at times individuals apparently provided some leadership in helping to organize different sports. For example, in 1665 Governor Nicolls of New York organized horse racing by establishing the Long Island race course and instituting rules for horse racing.[14]

The almost complete absence of sports clubs during the eighteenth century in America indicates how unorganized all types of sports were at that time.[15] The first sport club to be established in North America was the Schuylkill Fishing Company which was organized in 1722.[16] There is also a record of a Jockey Club in Charlestown and a Quoits Club in Savannah in existence about the middle of the eighteenth century.[17] From this brief survey of sports to about 1800, it is apparent that organized sports and sports clubs like those that exist today were rare. Because of their absence, it is obvious that the issue of amateurism in sports did no exist prior to 1800.

THE DEVELOPMENT OF SPORTS BETWEEN 1800 AND 1880

This section traces the development of several major sports between about 1800 and 1880 and the subsequent rise of amateurism in sports. In

---

The council being informed, that among other Evils that are prevailing among us, in this day of Calamity, there is practised by some the variety of horse racing, for mony, or monys worth, thereby occasioning much mispence of precious time, and the drawing of many persons from duty of their particular callings, with the hazards of their Limbs and Lives.

It is hereby Ordered that henceforth it shall not be Lawful for any Person to do or practice in that kind, within four miles of any Town, or in any Highway or Common Rode, on penalty of forfeiting twenty Shillings apiece, nor shall any Game or run in that kind for mony, or monys worth upon penalty of forfeiting Treble the value thereof, one half to the partys forming, and the other half to the Treasury, nor shall any accompany or abbett any in that practice on the like penalty, and this to continue til the General Court take further Order.[11]

*A game involving hitting a ball with a stick. It may have been a form of fieldhockey or golf.

some cases the history of a sport prior to 1800 is mentioned, but most of the sports referred to did not develop before 1830 or 1840. The particular sports included in this section were selected because 1) they effectively illustrate the developmental pattern of sports in the nineteenth century, 2) they were associated with the development of amateurism, and 3) they included most of the competitive sports in which the aristocrats and the masses of this period engaged.

During the nineteenth century most organized sports participants were from the aristocratic and upper class segments of society. These included the titled, the wealthy, members of recongized professions, officers in the military services, and students and graduates of public schools and universities.[18] [19] The fact that these early clubs often excluded labourers, artisans, and mechanics from their membership is important in understanding the develpment of social distinction in sports which became associated with the term "amateurism."

It is interesting to note that in the United States there were only 4,306,446 whites and 1,002,037 Negroes in 1800.[20] With so few non-native people in the United States and with all the problems associated with starting a new country, it is understandable that organized sports had not come into existence by then.

The First Sports Clubs in America

Excluding the fishing, hunting, quoits, and jockey clubs, mentioned earlier, the first sports club in America was the Boston Cricket Club which was active in 1809.[21] [22] The next oldest club was the United Bowmen Club of Philadelphia which was organized in 1828 and disbanded in 1859. An Olympic Club was operating in Philadelphia in 1833, but it is not certain when it was founded.[23] Other sports and athletic clubs may have existed before 1830 in America, but if they did, they were apparently of little lasting significance. Thus, the first three decades of the nineteenth century were relatively insignificant in the history of sports and amateurism.

Rowing

In England rowing goes back several centuries.[24] It involves the commercial use of boats and barges on inland waterways. With the expansion of this type of commerce, "the Thames River in England became one of the most congested waterways during the reign of Henry VII (1509-1547)."[25] As rowing by paid oarsmen expanded, a natural accompaniment was boasting concerning "...the ability of certain men, and the result was boat racing, usually for side bets."[26]

By the early part of the nineteenth century private rowing clubs had come into existence, and school and universities were taking up rowing. For example, the Leander (rowing) Club was founded about 1818 or 1819, and there is some evidence that other rowing clubs existed before that time in England. Eton is recorded as having a boat in 1811, and "College boat racing was in existence at Oxford in 1815."[27]

The first intercollegiate rowing race took place between Oxford and Cambridge in 1829, ten years before Oxford University had formed a boat club.[28] In 1839 the Henley Regatta, the most famous regatta in the world was first rowed.[29] For the first race the organizing committee ruled that "every boat shall be steered by an amateur member of the Club or Clubs entering for the cup." and "no fouling be permitted."[30] This was one of the first specific rules concerning amateurism.

Up until 1882 the Henley Stewards were the major governing voice in rowing. Some believed "that the Henley Stewards would come to hold in rowing the position which is held in cricket by the M.C.C. (Marylebone Cricket Club), and in golf by the Royal and Ancient Club."[*31] In 1878 the Metropolitan Rowing Association was formed in order to have a method of selecting a crew to form the best English team to compete against foreign competition.[22] During 1879 this newly formed association issued the first definitions of an amatuer oarsman in England, and soon afterward the Henley Stewards issued their classic definition of an amateur.

In 1882 the name of the Metropolitan Rowing Association was changed to the Amateur Rowing Association, and it became the official governing body for rowing in England. "Its primary object was stated to be the maintenance of the standard of amateur oarsmanship ·as recognized by the rowing clubs..."[33] With these developments, rowing entered a new era in England.

By 1800 boating was becoming quite popular in America. Evidence indicates that in Boston, New York, and Philadelphia races were conducted "...between four-oared barges owned by gentlemen who employed professional crews."[34] Although there is some disagreement about when the first regattas were held in America, there is evidence that regattas and rowing clubs began to develop during the 1830's. Apparently the first recorded boat race in America took place in 1811, and the first rowing club was organized in 1834.[35**]

According to *The Spirit of the Times* "...the first amateur boating organization known to America Waters, was the Castle Garden Amateur Rowing Association, numbering twelve to thirteen district clubs which was founded

*The Marylebone Cricket Club is recognized as the governing body for cricket throughout the world and the Royal and Ancient Club holds an exalted position in golf.

**Whitney in the Encyclopedia of Sports states that "...the first boat race of which there is any record..." was held on May 24, 1842, by members of the Detroit Boat Club,[37] but Menke states that "the first actual regatta in the United States is believed to be the one held on the Hudson River...in 1948."[38]

in 1837."[36] This association lasted many years, and its annual regattas attracted hundreds of spectators. No definition for an amateur appears to have been used in governing these regattas. At a regatta on the Hudson River in 1848, Menke said that "all oarsmen were eligible. There was no distinction between amateurs and professionals, but the professionals dominated the scene, since they made sculling a profession."[37] In 1852 the first intercollegiate rowing race in the United States took place. This race between crews from Harvard and Yale is considered the first intercollegiate contest of any kind in the United States.[40]

During the 1850's, 1860's and 1870's numerous rowing clubs emerged in America.[41] In both England and America rowing became one of the most popular sports during the second half of the nineteenth century. As the popularity of rowing grew, the number of clubs and associations grew. In Philadelphia, one of the areas where rowing was most popular, the Schuylkill Navy was formed in 1857. It was an association of twelve large boating clubs. Nine years later the Hudson River Amateur Rowing Association was formed by nine clubs[42] and by 1868 it was reported to have become the strongest association in America.[43] The next year the first international rowing race took place betweeen Oxford and Harvard.[44]

Numerous problems were created with the rapid rise in popularity of rowing. There was no uniform understanding and definition of amateurism, and there were no uniform racing rules. These problems showed the need for a national governing organization for rowing. Consequently in 1872 delegates from several boat clubs met and "adopted a definition of an amateur and a code of racing laws and elected a judiciary committee...who were instructed to give a National Regatta in 1873."[45] In 1873 a second convention was held, and the National Association of Amateur Oarsmen was formed. This new organization attempted to bring some order to rowing in the United States.[46]

Track and Field (Athletics)

What is known as track and field in America and athletics in England evolved from pedestrianism in the nineteenth century.[47] [48] In England pedestrianism or professinal racing dates back to the latter part of the eighteenth century. Pedestriansim involved running or walking any distance from fifty yards[49] to as far as from New York to San Francisco.[50] The races were usually arranged by challenges which were issued by one of the competitors, sometimes through columns in newspapers like *The Spirit of the Times*.*

*The following is an example of a challenge:

Poughkeepsie, February 26, 1863. Seeing Mickey is not satisfied with his defeat by me some two years ago, I will now make him a match to run him 5 miles, and jump 500 hurdles 3 feet high. The one that runs it the quickest, and knocks down thee least to win; and I will pick up 100 stones

Pedestrianism was especially popular from the 1840's through the 1880's, but it died out with the development of bicycle racing and amateur track and field meets.

Because there were no official rules or governing bodies for pedestrianism before 1860, numerous problems involving cheating, gambling, throwing of races, and all sorts of corrupt practices became associated with the races in England and the United States.[53] As a result of the many evils associated with pedestriansim, the sport fell into disrepute and people in the upper classes began to look with disfavor on participants in the pedestrian races. In fact, it was almost social ostracism for upper class people to be involved in athletics that existed prior to 1860.[54] One of the best descriptions of professional running in the nineteenth century is by William Curtis.

> During the early years of American amateur athletic sport, all the methods of management were naturally copied from the professionals. Running was limited almost entirely to matches, as there were no open competitions in which athletes could enter, and the distances were in nine cases out of ten one of the two extremes — one hundred yards or ten miles. As there were but two starters in these match races, the methods of getting away were more primitive than at present and had been cunningly devised by veteran professionals to give the expert an advantage over the novice.
>
> Several styles were in common use, the oldest being what was called the "break start." The judge stood in the starting line, then men went back fifteen or twenty paces, stood side by side, joined fingers lightly and trotted up to the judge. As they passed on either side of him, his body broke the touch of their fingers and they dashed away at full speed. If the judge thought the start fair he said nothing, but if he thought either man had an unfair advantage they were recalled.
>
> This method was subsequently doctored into the "lead pencil" start. Instead of touching fingers, each man held one end of a lead pencil or short stick and started much as in the original style, dashing away just as the lead pencil or stick touched the judge's body, and being subject to recall if the start was manifestly unfair.
>
> As the men's hands were so close together and their bodies must necessarily have been almost if not quite abreast as the passed the judge, it would seem to those who never experimented with

one yard apart, with him, the one that does it in the shortest time to win; each race to be for $25 a side, and the Editor of the *Spirit* to be stakeholder. As soon as Mickey puts up a deposit as a forfeit, I will send the same amount of money, and name the place to run.   Jas. B. Kensley.[51]

this start that neither man could gain an appreciable advantage, but the cunning of professional runners had devised methods of outwitting inexperienced opponents. A few steps from the judge the expert would slacken his trot and the other would do almost invariably the same. Just as he reached the judge the expert would suddenly quicken. As it required some fraction of a second for the other to follow this example. the men would pass the judge almost exactly abreast, the expert more than likely a few inches in the rear, but he would be running, while the other was only trotting. The advantages thus gained would amount to two or three yards in the first twenty-five yards of the race.

A more complicated style was the "mutual consent" start. A line was drawn across the track, fifteen or twenty feet behind the starting scratch. The men were placed between these lines and told to start by mutual consent, and whenever both men touched the ground in front of the starting scratch at the same time with their persons it was considered a start.

A race of this kind between two experts was amusing. The men stood between two lines facing each other, pranced up to the starting mark sideways, and the one who was ahead would put his foot down over the mark, hoping the other would follow. If he did, it would be a start, with the first man a foot or two in front; but if the second man did not like the start, he held back, did not put his foot over the mark, and the first man was ordered back for a fresh trial.

Starts of this style frequently lasted over an hour, especially if one of the runners was extremely anxious for a race, and eventually this system was modified by inserting in the articles of agreement a clause substantially as follows: "Start by mutual consent; if not inside an hour (or some other specified time), then start by pistol." Resort to the pistol was necessary in so many cases that it gradually supplanted the mutual consent system, and became the customary way of starting sprints.

The expert found it easier to outwit the novice in the mutual consent start than in the older 'break' start. The ordinary method, which was almost invariably successful, was as follows: after two or three purposefully ineffectual starts, in which the expert would get over the mark so far in front of the novice that there would be no chance for the rear man following, the expert would hang back as they neared the mark a few inches, even a foot, in front, and he usually thought this a fine opportunity to step over. But just after the expert slowed he started again at quickened speed, and followed the novice over, with the result that although a few inches behind as both got over the mark, he was fairly in his stride and moving at three-quarter speed while the novice was still partially turned sideways and not yet fairly running. Of course, the novice lost.

These professional wolves usually travelled and prowled in pairs, one going first to a town, securing some employment, exhibiting his proficiency as a runner to a select few, and finally making a match with and beating the local champion. Then the winner would explain that he knew a man in a neighboring town who thought he could run, and whose friends would back him heavily, but who was really several yards slower than championship speed and could be beaten easily. Negotiations would be opened with the stranger and a match arranged. All the men who won the first race wished to double their gains, while those who lost were anxious for their chance to get even, so, the betting was heavy. The stranger won of course; the town was pretty thoroughly cleaned of spare money, and the partners changed their names and moved to fresh harvest fields.

If, after beating the local champions in races on even terms and under ordinary conditions, any money still remained in sight, the professional tried to secure it by offering contests on novel terms, and with such conditions that it seemed to the uninitiated, foolhardy and sure to lose. One of these was called the "lying down" start. The novice stood in his usual position, while the professional would lie flat on his back, with his head at the scratch and his feet pointing away from the finish, and the race started by a pistol shot. To men unacquainted with this trick, it seemed as if the novice must win, and the elderly know-it-alls, standing about, shifted their quids and wisely drawled out: "Why, Jimmy will be down at the other end fo the field before the other fellow gets started."

But it did not work that way. When the pistol sounded, the professional turned on his face, rose to his hands and feet, and found himself in an attitude now universally adopted by present sprinters (the crouch start), and which is much better than the old-fashioned erect position. This primary movement cost the professional about half a second, or five yards, and as this was about half the handicap, he could beat the novice in 100 yards. He usually caught his man near the seventy fifth yard mark.

Another favorite game, especially in smaller towns, was the "fence rail" race. The novice stood on the mark as usual while the *professional went back twenty or twenty-five yards, and carried on his left shoulder a fence rail borrowed from the nearest rail fence. The rail was nicely balanced on his shoulder and was held in place by the runner's left hand, while his right arm was left free. The race was usually fifty yards, rarely more than sixty yards, unless the novice was notably slow. The conditions were that the professional should move up as he pleased and take a flying start, while the novice stood on the mark and did not move until the professional reached the mark and the judge said "Go," or fired his pistol.*

This match, as in the "lying down" start looked to the uninitiated as a sure thing for the novice, but he really had no chance, as with two men of equal speed, the rail bearer would frequently beat the other. When the professional reached the mark he was running at full speed, while the time needed for the judge to see him at the mark and give his signal, and for the novice to hear the signal and get in motion used up the larger part of a second, and the result was that the professional had a seven or eight yard start, which was quite enough to make a fifty or sixty yard race sure, as the rail would not delay him more than six or seven yards in the distance.[55]

According to Webster, 1817 marked an important milestone in athletic history, because that was the year that the Necton Guild was founded. This guild was the first English athletic club, and it conducted athletic meets between 1819 and 1826. Webster also says that amateur matches were held prior to 1825 at either Uxbridge, Newmarket Road, or Lord's Cricket Grounds.[56] This information is slightly at variance with that given by Menke who claims that the first amateur athletic races in England were held about 1825 on the Newmarket Road and at Lord's Cricket Ground in London.[57] If these races were amateur, it is probably safe to assume they were some sort of "closed" competition for club members, or upper class people of the era, and excluded lower-class pedestrians. The early limited meaning of the term "open" competition is made clear by Wilkinson in his book published in 1868. While describing how to handle entries in a meet, Wilkinson states, "In case of open contests great care must be taken that none but those of 'gentlemen' amateurs be accepted."[58]

In 1834 some informal track rules and minimum performance standards were specified for some meets in England. Various English schools and universities had begun to conduct different types of races as early as 1925,[59] but the first recorded school race or meet was in 1837.[60]

About the same time, The Scotland Highland Games had developed a great popularity. Originally, these games were amateur in spirit, but professional aspects developed over the years. Nevertheless, in many parts of Scotland the games continued throughtout the nineteenth century.[61]

In 1850 the Much Wenlock Olympian Society, founded by Dr. William P. Brookes, conducted the first Olympian Games which consisted of a cricket match, quoits, football, and running. Over the years the games grew and were popular enough to attract Pierre de Coubertin as a visitor in 1890.[62]

In the United States, track and field activities were also beginning to develop during the nineteenth century. According to James E. Sullivan*, who was president of the United States AAU from 1906-1908, the first amateur track and field meet in the United States was held in Hoboken, New Jersey, on September 4, 1838.[63] However, I have some doubts about the actual existence of an amateur track and field meet in 1838, since I was not able to find any reference other than Sullivan's to it.

During the 1850's the Scottish Caledonian Societies were coming into prominence. The first Caledonian Festival, which became an annual event was sponsored by the Caledonian Society of Boston in 1853. This was the first known organized athletic event in the United States, if one discounts Sullivan's reference to the 1838 meet. In 1857 and 1858 the New York and Philadelphia Caledonian Societies began their annual contest. From there the contests spread to other cities. A typical Caledonian festival included fifteen to twenty-five events. Some of the common events were throwing or putting light and heavy stones and hammers, long jumping, high jumping, hurdle races, sack races, three-legged races, and dancing. The usual prizes were three to five dollars in cash for first place, a dollar fifty to three dollars for second place, and two dollars or less for third place. Prizes up to fifteen dollars were fairly common, and the New York Caledonian Society once offered fifty dollars for first place in a race and "a Canadian society reported a cash prize of $150.00 for first place in addition to a $100.00 medal in 1876."[65] Participation in contests was usually limited to members of the societies, but thousands of non-Scotsmen came as spectators to some of the festivals. Over the years the Caledonian clubs established a wholesome example for the developing sports in America and even though the Caledonian Games awarded cash prizes, they not only forbade gambling, but were able to maintain an environment free of gambling.[66]

In 1870 the Caledonian clubs formed the American Caledonian Association, and in 1875 the organization changed to the Scottish-American Club because of the developing issue of amateurism.[67] This change was necessary because the participants in the Caledonian festivals accepted cash prizes. As a result of this, the athletes were technically professional according to the

---

*Sullivan was also secretary of the United States AAU from 1899 to 1905 and again from 1909 to 1914.[64]

developing definitions of an amateur in the 1860's and 1870's. The early definition of an amateur said that a $100.00 medal was legal as a prize but a three dollar cash prize was illegal.

If the Caledonian clubs are excluded as genuine athletic clubs, then the first athletic club in North America was the Montreal (Canada) Pedestrian Club which held its first annual race in 1865. About this time the H.M.A. Association of Paterson, New Jersey, an amateur athletic club, was organized. Sullivan says it conducted the first properly organized amateur athletic meeting in the United States. The meeting took place in the spring of 1866 on the race track of the Passaic County Agricultural Society.[69]*

The New York Athletic Club, founded in 1866, is frequently considered the first athletic club in America because of its prominent role in the development of athletic clubs in America. If the term athletic club is interpreted to mean a club especially interested in track and field activities, the New York Athletic Club may qualify as the first such club in the United States. This club was organized and patterned after the first English amateur athletic club, the Mincing Lane, which was founded in 1863 and changed its name to the London Athletic Club in 1866.[71] One of the significant services that the New York Athletic Club performed in its early years was the revising, improving, and codifying of "...the rules governing competition with such intelligent skill that its laws of athletics and rules for the government of athletic meetings were subsequently adopted by the National Association of Amateur Athletes of America without alteration or amendment."[72] The important influence on athletics in the United States by the New York Athletic Club during its early history is further evident from the following observation by Korsgaard.

> Since its inception the New York Athletic Club has exercised a role of leadership unmatched by any other club. The form of organization, constitution, and bylaws, rules, or laws for the conduct of athletics and other games, served as models for many of the hundreds of athletic clubs which were to follow in its wake in the last three decades of the nineteenth century.[73]

In England amateur athletic sports were becoming quite popular about 1862. This is evident from an article reprinted in *The Spirit of the Times* from

---

*This is apparently the first of the semi-annual pedestrian contests referred to in the following portion of an article in The Spirit of the Times:
THE AMATEUR FOOT—RACE AT PATERSON — The fifth semi-annual pedestrian contest of thee H.M.A. Association of Paterson, came off on the race-course on Wednesday last. This Association is composed of the young men of the most select families in Paterson, and has for its object the cultivation of athletic sports and the consequent promotion of physical development. The attendance was very large and fashionable, including great numbers from New York, Newark, Paterson, and other places.[70]

the *London Field* about the first track meet held by the New York Athletic Club in 1868. In this article the following statement is made: "... we may safely say that the times and distance accomplished are quite as good as those of our gentlemen six years ago, when amateur sports first became widely developed in Great Britain."[74]

In this same year, 1868, Wilkenson stated that athletic meetings had become general throughout the Kingdom and scarcely a cricket or football club existed which did not hold an annual athletic meeting.[75]

The first intercollegiate track and field contest took place between Oxford and Cambridge in 1864.[76] In America the first official intercollegiate track and field meet, which was between athletes from Harvard, Yale, Princeton, and Columbia, did not take place until 1874.[77] This first meet and a larger one the next year provided the stimulus for organizing The Intercollegiate Association of Amateur Athletes of America (ICAAAA) in 1875 for the purpose of promoting and controlling intercollegiate track and field meets.[78]

The Amateur Athletic Club was founded in England in 1866. This was a union of clubs for the primary purpose of inaugurating and managing an annual amateur championship.[79] During the same year the Amateur Athletic Club and the London Athletic Club conducted the first track and field meet for the championship of England.[80] [81] In 1866 the Amateur Athletic Club also issued the following definition of amateur. This was apparently the first such definition in the world:

> Any gentleman who has never competed in an open competition, or for any prize money, or for admission money, or with professionals for a prize, public money, or admission money, and who has never in any period of his life taught or assisted in the pursuit of athletic exercises as a means of livelihood; nor as a mechanic, artisan or labourer.[82]

In the next few years athletics began to develop rapidly in the United States and England. In the United States, the New York Athletic Club held its first amateur track meet in October 12, 1868. The events were open to any amateur "...young men in the neighborhood of New York city who had ever developed ability in any branch of athletic sports."[83]

As a result of developements in track and field the New York Athletic Club sponsored the first annual American amateur athletic meeting in 1874 with "the advice and consent of every amateur athletic club in this country."[84] In 1879 the National Association of Amateur Athletes was formed, and the New York Athletic Club transferred to this new organization the responsibility for sponsoring the annual championship meet.[85]

About a year later the Amateur Athletic Association was founded in

England to replace the Amateur Athletic Club in controlling and promoting track and field activities.[86] Thus, with the formation of the Amateur Athletic Association in England and the National Association of Amateur Athletes of America, a new era began in track and field.

Cricket

Cricket, a game that was very popular among the English people and has been taken by the English wherever they have gone, has some interesting connections with the development of amateurism. Like many other sports, cricket has its origins shrouded in antiquity. One of the earlist references to an actual contest was in 1705.[87] An important date in the history of Cricket is 1787. This is when the Marylebone Cricket Club was founded. This Club, which became the most important cricket club in the world, evolved from the White Conduit Club which was founded in 1782.* The first recorded match at the Marylebone Cricket Club was in 1788.[89] In the same year a meeting took place at the club "...at which time all the previous rules were revised and the basis of the game was definitely established."[90] In the eastern American colonies cricket was well-known in 1747, and Boston had an active cricket club in 1809. By the middle of the nineteenth century cricket seemed destined to become as popular with the Americans as it was with the English. But the faster game of baseball, which was just becoming popular, captured the interest of the Americans, and cricket was soon on the decline.[91]

While amateurism as a category of sport evolved during the early part of the nineteenth century, the regulations in cricket contained some major differences in comparison to the traditions in athletics (track and field) and rowing. For example, the Marylebone Cricket Club hired four practice bowlers (pitchers) in 1826 and a fifth practice bowler in 1836. By 1896 the Club had a professional staff of fifty-two players.[92] This shows that professional assistance or instruction was not viewed negatively by cricket players as it was by people associated with rowing. Also, in cricket no problem existed concerning amateurs competing against professionals as was the case in athletics. This is evident by one of the most popular matches in England, the Gentlemen (amateurs) vs. the Players (professionals), which has been a fixture since 1806.

In discussing the development of cricket and the acceptance of the professional player, Ford stated that:

> The original popularity of the game was no doubt due to the
> amateurs who devoted themselves to its practice and extension;

*The White Conduit Club was an offshoot of a West End convivial club called the Je-ne-sais-quoi.[88]

but it was only natural in the process of events that another class should spring up consisting of men who have great ability for the same game but neither the spare time, nor the spare money necessary for its cultivation; and, as the keenness between counties and clubs increased, the paid services of this class were enlisted, till professional cricketers became the backbone of the game; and it is not too much to say that thousands of men are now (1911) earning a livelihood by means of cricket.[93]

Baseball

The American game of baseball evolved from cricket, the English game of rounders, and the New England game of town ball. The Olympic Club in Philadelphia had a Town Ball Club as early as 1833, but the first baseball club organized was the Knickerbocker Club of New York in 1845.[94] Originally, this club was restrictive about membership, and the members attempted to keep baseball a sport exclusively for gentlemen.[95] The first recorded game of baseball was played in 1846 between the Knickerbocker Club and a group called the New York Club.[96]

By 1855 interest in baseball had grown and it was becoming a game popular with workmen as well as gentlemen. With the development of teams by laborers, the exclusive clubs, such as the Knickerbockers Club, began to accept workmen as players. For example, in 1856 Henry [Harry] Wright, a professional bowler and employee in a jewelry factory, was allowed to join the Knickerbocker Club.[97]

In 1857 the first baseball association was established when twenty-five clubs from around New York formed the National Association of Base-Ball Players to clarify the rules of the game.[98] Two years later in 1859 the first intercollegiate baseball game was played between Williams and Amherst. While the National Association of Base-Ball Players is usually considered to have been an amateur organization, no clear definition of an amateur player existed during the early years of the association. By 1866, 200 clubs belonged to the association.

About the same time it became clear that success in baseball required making a business of playing ball. "But players could not afford to do that without some remuneration and as a result, most of the so-called amateur teams soon had among their members men who received compensation in one way or another for their services."[99] An attempt was made in 1868 to correct this situation by recognizing professionals in baseball. Consistent with this concern, Section Nine, Rule Five of the baseball rules was amended in 1869 to read as follows: "All players who play base-ball for money, or who shall at any time receive compensation for their services as players shall be considered as professional players, and all other players shall be regarded as amateurs."[100] However, it appears that this rule was either overlooked or proved to be meaningless.

During the same year, the Cincinnati "Red Stockings" announced their plans to become the first regular professional baseball team.[101] By 1871 the professional and quasi-professional elements in the game developed to the point where a new organization entitled the National Association of Professional Base-Ball Players was formed and the National Association of Base-Ball Players was discontinued.[102] In 1876 the National League came into existence, and the National Association of Professional Base-Ball Players was disbanded.

Yachting

Yachting, a sport currently on the Olympic Games schedule, was one of the most expensive sports in which to participate during the nineteenth century. For this reason, the sport was usually limited to people with considerable wealth. The history of yachting in England goes back to at least 1661, In 1720 the Water Cock Club, which was perhaps the first yacht club, was established; and in 1775 the Royal Thames Club, the second oldest, was established.[103]

Yachting began in America in 1884 when the New York Yacht Club was organized. The following year the Club had its first race. During the next two decades numerous yacht clubs were formed in England and America. In 1851 the "America's Cup" race which has become an important race between the United States and England, was first scheduled.[104] However, until 1875 when the Yacht Racing Association was formed in England, the rules and regulations for racing were in "...a somewhat chaotic condition...."[105]

During the early part of the nineteenth century, membership in yacht clubs was exclusive. This exclusiveness was evident from records of the meeting of the Lough Erne Yacht Club in 1815. At this meeting it was agreed "...that the qualifications for membership of the club should be the ownership of a vessel not under ten tons that all members should ballot for the election of any new member, and that two black balls should exclude."[106] In 1820 this club was granted permission to change its name to the "Royal Yacht Club." The word royal would seem to imply that it was an upper class club."

In yachting during the nineteenth century, the awarding of prize money was not a problem. This is evidenced by the fact that the New Thames Yacht Club between 1867 and 1908 distributed more than 20,000 pounds in prize money.[107] It was not until 1946 that the first written definition of an amateur was agreed upon by the International Yacht Racing Union. The writing of this definition of an amateur was brought about by the necessity of having a definition for the XIV Olympiad in 1948. Bland made the following comment about the development of a definition of amateur for yachting:

> It may be of interest to record that previously neither the Yacht Racing Association, the governing body in this country (United Kingdom), nor the International Yacht Racing Union, has ever framed, or thought it desirable to attempt to frame, any definition of an amateur.[109]

Football, Soccer, and Rugby

Association football or soccer as it is known to Americans is one of the oldest sports in the world, but "...there was no generally recognized code of rules, or governing body, until 1863. In that year...largely owing to the influence of Cambridge and the public school men the Football Association was formed."[110] The first international game was played in 1870 between England and Scotland.[111]

Rugby, another English sport, began to evolve from English football back in 1823 when William Ellis, a student at Rugby, accidentally or spontaneoulsy decided to run with the ball in a football (soccer) game. However, the game of rugby did not develop immediately. The first known rugby game was not played until 1841, and the first rugby governing body, the English Rugby Union, was not formed until 1871, the same year that the first international rugby match between England and Scotland took place.[113] The major problem of amateurism in rugby developed "some considerable time prior to 1895.[114] The basic issue involved was the secretive payments being made to the players on some clubs.

American football evolved from the combination of soccer and rugby.[115] A type of football was played at Yale in 1806, but the first intercollegiate football game, which was really a variation of soccer, was not played until 1869.[116] The first rules for football were written down in 1871. In 1876 representatives of American colleges organized an intercollegiate football association and adopted the Rugby Union Rules with a few slight modifications to govern their games.[117] Thus, American style football developed primarily after 1876.

As interest in American football developed, problems of proselyting, subsidizing, brutality, and commercialism became associated with the sport.[118] As in other sports, many of the problems were partially due to the absence of a governing body which could provide leadership and control. Primarily in response to the problems of professionalsim, eligibility of athletes, and brutality in football, the Intercollegiate Conference of Faculty Representatives (Big Ten)[119] was formed in 1895, and the Intercollegiate Athletic Association of the United States was formed in 1905. In 1910 the title of the Intercollegiate Athletic Association of the United States was changed to the National Collegiate Athletic Association.[120]

Some Other Sports

In order to more completely present the historical setting in which amateurism emerged, a few facts about cycling, golf, tennis, riflery, and swimming are included in the next few paragraphs. These sports were involved in varying degrees in the evolution of amateurism, and they help exemplify the development of sports in the nineteenth century.

Bicycle racing which is included in the Olympic program developed after 1870.[121] The Bicycle Union, the first governing body for cycling in England, was formed in 1878. This was the first sports governing body in England to eliminate the "mechanic" or "worker" clause from its definition of amateur.[122]

Although golf had been played in Scotland since the fifteenth century, it was not until 1860 that the first tournament took place.[123] In 1886 the amateur championship of England and Scotland was begun, and in 1895 the first amateur championship in the United States was conducted.[124] [125]

Riflery, because of its close association with the military services, is a sport that is significant in relation to the purposes of amateurism and the objectives of the modern Olympic Games. As early as 1846, there was a prominent rifle club called the Philadelphia Schuetzen Verein, and by 1871 when the National Riflery Association was founded, "...there were a score of amateur clubs interested in long-and-short-range shooting."[126] The first international riflery match for Americans took place in 1874 between the American Rifle Club of New York and a team from Ireland that had just defeated the teams from England and Wales.[127]

A type of tennis was played as early as 1810 in England, but no championship matches took place until 1862.[128] In 1873 lawn tennis was invented in England, and in 1874 it was introduced to Americans.[129] In 1881 the United States Lawn Tennis Association was formed. In England the first amateur tennis championship open to all amateurs was held in 1887.[130] During the early part of the twentieth century, tennis was part of the Olympic Games.

As early as 1837 competitive swimming meets were conducted in London under the auspices of the National Swimming Society of England. The date 1837 coincided with the first year of the reign of Queen Victoria which is of interest because the development of swimming in England coincided with the Victorian campaign for urban hygienics. This campaign led to the construction of numerous public baths where people could swim both as a pastime and in competition.[131] In 1862 an organization called the Associated Swimming Club directed a competitive swimming meet in England. This group was replaced seven years later by the first governing body for swimming, the Amateur Swimming Association of England.[132] [133]

The Influence of Thomas Arnold

Thomas Arnold was a major influence in the development of sports in the nineteenth century. He was headmaster of the Rugby School from 1828-1842. There he created an atmosphere conducive to athletics and reforms that was accepted and expanded upon by all the English schools in the forties and fifties. Thomas Hughes' best seller, *Tom Brown's School Days,*[134] was perhaps the primary instrument in spreading Arnold's views of sports in education. The acceptance and encouragement of athletics in the schools that resulted from the reforms at Rugby coincided with the rapid development of the sports reviewed earlier in this chapter. Arnold's philosophy of sport and education as understood by Pierre de Coubertin was also very instrumental in de Coubertin's thinking and motivation while he founded the modern Olympic Games.[135]

Attempted Olympic Festivals

During the nineteenth century at least three attempts were made to establish and conduct "Olympic Games." The first attempt was the founding in Scotland of the Much Wenlock Olympian Society which conducted its first annual Olympian festival in 1850.[136] These festivals appear to have been fairly local in nature, but they did continue for several decades.

More ambitious attempts at re-establishing and conducting the Olympic Games were the Games staged in Greece in 1859, 1870, and 1888. Unfortunately, these games were not completely successful due to financial, political, and organizational problems. However, they are part of the historical sports picture in the nineteenth century. They also serve as a small connection between the ancient and modern Olympic Games.[137] [138]

Some Technological and Social Changes

Numerous technological developments contributed to the Industrial Revolution which took place during the second half of the nineteenth century. Five major technological developments which show the tremendous progress of the era were 1) the vulcanization of rubber in 1830, 2) the expansion of railroads,* 3) the sinking of the first oil well in 1859, 4) the development of new printing processes, and 5) the invention of the incandescent light bulb in 1879. These and many other technological developments had a big impact on the social and economic life of the citizenry of Americans and affected their athletic interests. With the expansion of railroads, athletic teams and spectators could travel with increased speed and ease to numerous far away places. With the development of printing, the daily

*The first railroad in the United States was built in 1830.

83

reporting of scores became a reality by 1870. By late 1880's photographs of athletic events began to appear in the papers.[139] Following the invention of the light bulb in 1879, gymnasiums began to appear, and the interests in indoor sports increased.

As a result of the Industrial Revolution, big cities were developed and there were changes in living patterns.* With the rise of cities an environment was created in which people were more apt to turn to games and sports for physical exercise and enjoyment than they were in a rural or frontier setting.

One fact of life in the cities for the laboring man during the nineteenth century that limited his involvement in sports was the length of the work week. As late as the 1860's some laborers had to work fourteen hours a day, six or seven days a week, and as late as 1900 the average work week for most laborers was still six ten-hour days. Government workers were more fortunate than most workers, though, for they were granted an eight-hour day in 1869.[141] Since the long work day left the laborer little leisure time, sports were dominated and controlled by the upper classes during this period.

THE DEVELOPMENT OF SPORTS FROM 1880

Cultural Changes

From about 1880 athletics and sports literally entered a "boom" period in the United Kingdom, the United States, and Europe.[142] This tremendous interest coincided with the continuing technological developments, the trend toward the shorter work week, the growing awareness of the need for exercise and play, the growing acceptance of sports by religious groups, the continued trend toward urban living, and many other factors. Specific technological developments that influenced society and sport during the latter part of the nineteenth and twentieth centuries and exemplify the technological advances in the current century are the development of the pneumatic tire, the streetcar, the automobile, the airplane, the radio, television, and improvements in the telephone. All these developments have influenced cultures around the world and sports within these cultures.

During the last twenty years of the nineteenth century, most, if not all, of the sports developed were at first participated in primarily by the upper classes who engaged in sporting activities during their leisure. This class had the time and money to organize the first organizations, clubs, and associations which controlled and promoted various sports. Their position in these clubs and associations enabled them to exert control over participation in

*In 1800 about six per cent of the population of the United States lived in cities of 2,500 population or larger. By 1830 the percentage of people in urban areas had increased to about ten per cent and by 1850 to about twenty-eight per cent.[140]

sports. This created some of the issues surrounding amateurism today. As members of the laboring class in England and America gained a shorter working week, they too had time to engage in sports. At the same time promoters, manufacturers, and businessmen viewed the emerging laboring and middle classes as a new source of profit and started to cater to them. The growing participation in sports by the masses is certainly a significant aspect of sports since 1880.*

During this time, the leaders of the Third Republic of France were trying to rebuild France after the defeat of the Republic in the Franco-Prussian War in 1871. Emphasis was placed on physical education to promote military and nationalistic objectives. The first track meet was held in France in 1883, and the first national athletic meet was held in 1889. In 1887 the *Union Des Societies Francois de Sport Athletiques* was founded, and in 1891 de Coubertin became General Secretary of this Union.[144]

The Emergence of National and International Organizations

Numerous national and international sports organizations developed after 1880. This development illustrates the growing interest in sports. Some of these organizations were: The Amateur Athletic Association in England in 1880,[145] the United States Lawn Tennis Association in 1881;[146] the Amateur Rowing Association of England in 1882;[147] the Amateur Athletic Union of the United States in 1888;[148] the Amateur Golf Association of the United States in 1894;[149] the International Olympic Committee in 1894; the Intercollegiate Athletic Association of the United States in 1905;[150] and the National Federation of State High School Athletic Associations in 1920.[151]

Other developments of this era that illustrate the sports trend were the invention of basketball in 1891,[152] the invention of volleyball in 1895,[153] and the growth of interschool athletics in secondary schools and colleges.

Although there were organizations developing to control and promote sports in this era, there was a complete absence of international sports organizations prior to 1892. The absence of international federation made it difficult for athletes to compete internationally because of differences in (1) the rules and (2) understanding who and what was amateur. When writing about his reason for founding the Olympics, de Coubertin included these two factors in an article in 1898.

> *Modern athletics need to be unified and purified. Those who have followed the renaissance of physical sports in this century (19th) know that discord reigns supreme from one end of them to*

---

*For the interested reader, the article entitled "1879 the Beginning of the an Era in American Sports" by Lewis is an excellence reference that deals with this period of change in greater depth.[143]

another. Every country has its own rules: it is not possible even to come to an agreement as to who is an amateur and who is not.[154]

The founding of the modern Olympic Games provided a great impetus to national organizations to organize on an international basis. However, it was not until 1920 that the International Olympic Committee delegated to various international sports federations the responsibility for conducting competition in their respective sports at the Olympics Games. The first international federations organized were the International Skating Union[155] and the International Rowing Federation in 1892.[156] The next federations to develop were the International Football Federation in 1904,[157] the International Yacht Racing Federation in 1906,[158] the International Athletic Federation in 1913,[159] and the International Fencing Federation in 1913.[160] In recent years, international federations have been established in almost every sport. The founding of the International Softball Federation in 1952 was one of the most recent federations formed.

The tremendous growth during recent years in the popularity of the Olympic Games, and sports in general, for both the spectator and the participant is obvious to any newspaper reader or television viewer. With this increased interest in sports and popularity of national and international championships, the concern about issues involving amateurism is more acute than ever before.

SUMMARY

The developments in sports during the nineteenth century were in stark contrast to the absence of athletic festivals in the period since the ancient athletic games. Even in the nineteenth century no significant development took place during the first three decades. In the 1830's, 1840's, and 1850's sports clubs and organizations began to emerge, but not until 1860 did sports and athletics develop to a point where organizations and written rules and regulations were considered necessary by most participants. After the American Civil War (1861-1865), interest in sports renewed in the United States, and the need to regulate sports became more evident. This trend resulted in the formation of numerous sports-governing bodies during the 1860's, 1870's, and the 1880's in England and the United States. During this time the London Athletic Club, founded in 1863, and the New York Athletic Club, founded in 1866, played a large role in the development of other clubs, rules for many sports, and sports associations.

Prior to 1892 there was little international competition. But in 1894, international competition in sports received a big boost with the formation of the International Olympic Committee. At first this Committee was very weak, but over the years, the International Olympic Committee and the Olympic

Games have developed into one of the most, if not the most, influential and powerful organizations and festivals in the world.

International sports competition has become common in recent years. Technogical advances in transportation and communication have encouraged this trend. In addition, the trend to urbanization, the shorter work week, and changes in religious attitudes have all contributed to the development of sports in the nineteenth and twentieth centuries. With the development of sports, amateurism emerged as a category of competition. The evolution of amateurism during the nineteenth and twentieth centuries will be discussed in the next two chapters

FOOTNOTES

1   Joseph Strutt, *The Sports and Pastimes of the People of England*, with additions and index by William Hone (London: William Tegg and Company, 1875), pp. xvii-lxvii.

2   B. Deabold Van Dalen, Elmer D. Mitchell and Bruce L. Bennett, *A World History of Physical Education* (Englewood Cliffs, New Jersey: Prentice-Hall, Inc., 1953), pp. 95-172.

3   Ibid., p. 102.

4   Ibid., pp. 109-116.

5   Strutt, *The Sports and Pastimes of the People of England*, pp. xxvi-lxv.

6   Pelham Warner, *Lord's 1787-1945* (London: George G. Harrap and Co., Ltd.,1947), p. 17.

7   Alfred E. T. Watson, "Racing," *The Encyclopedia of Sports and Games*, III (London: William Heinemann, 1911), p. 399.

8   Frank G. Menke, *The Encyclopedia of Sports* (New York: A. S. Barnes and Company 1953), p. 21.

9   Strutt, *The Sports and Pastimes of People in England*, pp. xxxvi-xxxvii.

10   Foster Rhea Dulles, *America Learns to Play*, 2nd ed. (New York: D. Appleton-Century Company, 1940), pp. 3-21.

11   John and Otto Bettman Durant, *Pictorial History of American Sports* (Cranbury, New Jersey: A. S. Barnes and Company, Inc., 1965), p. 6.

12   Ibid., pp. 5-9.

13   William C. Ewing, *The Sports of Colonial Williamsburg* (Richmond, Virginia: The Dietz Press, 1937), pp. 21-28.

14   Durant, *Pictorial History of American Sports*, p. 9.

15   Ewing, *The Sports of Colonial Williamsburg*, pp. 1-2.

16   Durant, *Pictorial History of American Sports*, p. 10.

17   Dulles, *America Learns to Play*, p. 64.

18   Guy M. Lewis, "1879: The Beginning of an Era in American Sports," *Proceedings 72nd Annual Meeting National College Physical Education Assocation for Men* (1968), p. 137.

19   H. Hewitt Griffin, *Athletics* (London: George Bell and Sons, 1891), pp. 5-20.

20   Edward B. Reuter, *Population Problems* (New York: J. B. Lippincott Co., 1937), p. 61.

21   Dulles, *America Learns to Play*, p. 64.

22   Harry Clay Palmer, *et. al., Athletic Sports in America, England and Australia* (Chicago: Hubbard Brothers Publishers, 1889), p. 682.

23   Menke, *The Encyclopedia of Sports*, p. 82.

24   Strutt, *The Sports and Pastimes of the People of England*, pp. 88-90.

25   Menke, *The Encyclopedia of Sports*, p. 736.

26   Ibid., p. 737.

27   R. C. Lehman, *The Complete Oarsman* (Philadelphia: George W. Jacobs and Company, 1908), p. 9.

28   Ibid., p. 4.

29   D. H. McLean, "Rowing," *The Encyclopaedia of Sports and Pastimes*, IV (London: Heineman, 1911), p. 53.

30   Lehman, *The Complete Oarsman*, p. 14.

31   Ibid., p. 250.

32   Ibid., p. 251.

33   Ibid.

34   John Allen Krout, *Annals of American Sport*, Vol. 15 of Pagaent of America (New Haven, Connecticut: Yale Universtiy Press, 1929), p. 77.

35   Menke, *The Encyclopedia of Sports*, p. 737.

36   *Spirit of the Times*, December 2, 1871, p. 251.

37 Caspar Whitney, "Rowing in the United States," *The Encyclopaedia of Sports and Games*, IV (London: William Heineman, 1911), p. 76.

38 Menke, *The Encyclopedia of Sports*, p. 737.

39 Ibid.

40 Ibid.

41 Frederick William Janssen, *A History of American Amateur Athletics and Aquatics* (New York: Outing Company, Limited, 1887), pp. 153-57, 166-67.

42 Whitney, "Rowing in the United States," p. 78.

43 *Wilkes' Spirit of the Times*, April 25, 1868, p. 147.

44 Whitney, "Rowing in the United States," p. 78.

45 Janssen, *A History of American Amateur Athletics and Aquatics*, p. 153.

46 Ibid.

47 Shearman Montague, "Athletics or Athletic Sports," *The Encyclopaedia of Sports and Games*, I (London: William Heineman, 1911), p. 95.

4 Griffin, *Athletics*, p. 2.

49 Robert Korsgaard, "A History of the Amateur Athletic Union of the United States" (Unpublished report of a Type C [D.Ed.] project; Teachers College, Columbia University, 1952), p. 9.

50 Menke, *The Encyclopedia of Sport*, p. 888.

51 *Wilkes' Spirit of the Times*, March 7, 1863, p. 11.

52 Krout, *Annals of American Sport*, pp. 186-200.

53 *Porter's Spirit of the Times*, September 5, 1857, p. 5.

54 Griffin, *Athletics*, p. 7.

55 Archie Hahn, (ed.) *How to Sprint*, Spalding Athletic Library, "No. 500B" (New York: American Sports Publishing Company, 1929), pp. 189, 191, 193, 195, 197.

56 F. A. M. Webster, *Athletics of Today* (London: Frederick Warne and Co., Ltd., 1929), pp. 4-6.

57 Menke, *The Encyclopedia of Sport*, pp. 888-89.

58 H. F. Wilkinson, *Modern Athletics* (London: Frederick Warne and Co., 1868), p.16.

59   Webster, *Athletics of Today*, pp. 6-7.

60   Menke, *The Encyclopedia of Sport*, p. 889.

61   Griffin, *Athletics*, p. 5.

62   John Apostal Lucas, "Baron Pierre De Coubertin and the Formative Years of the Modern International Olympic Movement 1883-1896," (Unpublsihed D.Ed. dissertation, University of Maryland, 1962), pp. 46, 69.

63   James E. Sullivan, "The Growth of American Athletics," *Official Athletic Rules of the Amateur Athletic Union of the United States*, A Group XII, No. 311 (New York: Spaldings' Athletic Library, August 1908), pp. 60-64.

64   Korsgaard, "A History of the Amateur Athletic Union of the United States," pp. 372-80.

65   Korsgaard, "A History of the Amateur Athletic Union of the United States," p. 25.

66   Ibid., pp. 22-26.

67   Lewis, "1879: The Beginning of an Era in American Sports," p. 142.

68   Korsgaard, "A History of the Amateur Athletic Union of the United States," p. 31.

69   Sullivan, "The Growth of American Athletics," pp. 60-64.

70   *Wilkes' Spirit of the Times*, June 20, 1868, p. 317.

71   Janssen, *A History of American Amateur Athletics and Aquatics*, p. 124.

72   Ibid., p. 128.

73   Korsgaard, "A History of the Amateur Athletic Union of the United States," p. 32.

74   *Spirit of the Times*, January 2, 1869, p. 315.

75   H. F. Wilkinson, *Modern Athletics*, p. 14.

76   Menke, *The Encyclopedia of Sports*, p. 889.

77   Arnold William Flath, *A History of Relations Between the National Collegiate Athletic Association and the Amateur Athletic Union of the United States, (1905-1963)* (Champaign, Illinois: Stipes Publishing Company, 1964), p. 12.

78   Krout, *Annals of American Sport*, p. 188.

79   Griffin, *Athletics*, p. 13.

80   Ibid., p. 14.

81   Menke, *The Encyclopedia of Sports*, p. 889.

82   Griffin, *Athletics*, pp. 13-14.

83   Janssen, *A History of American Amateur Athletics and Aquatics*, p. 126.

84   Ibid., p. 128.

85   Ibid.

86   Griffin, *Athletics*, p. 18.

87   W. J. Ford, "Cricket," *The Encyclopaedia of Sports and Games*, I, (London: William Heineman, 1911), p. 483.

88   Warner, *Lord's 1787-1945*, p. 17.

89   F. G. J. Ford, "Lords and the M. C. C. ," *The Encyclopaedia of Sports and Games*, I (London: William Heineman, 1911), p. 483.

90   Menke, *The Encyclopedia of Sports*, p. 301.

91   Menke,*The Encyclopedia of Sports*, p. 302.

92   Ford, "Lords and the M. C. C.," p. 484.

93   Ford, "Lords and the M. C. C.," p. 440.

94   Menke, *The Encyclopedia of Sports*, p. 69.

95   Dulles, *A History of Recreation*, p. 187.

96   Durant,*Pictorial History of American Sports*, pp. 39-40.

97   Dulles, *A History of Recreation* pp. 187-88.

98   Palmer, *Athletic Sports in America, England and Australia*, p. 26.

99   Ibid., pp. 26-27.

100   *Spirit of the Times*, December 19, 1869, p. 277.

101   Krout, *Annals of American Sport*, p. 122.

102   Dulles, *A History of Recreation*, p. 188-90.

103   Dunraven and Francis B. Cooke, "Yachting," *The Encyclopaedia of Sports and Games* IV (London: William Heineman, 1911), pp. 354-58.

104   "American Cup," *The Encyclopaedia of Sports and Games*, IV (London: William Heineman, 1911), p. 439.

105   Dunraven, "Yachting," p. 362.

106 Ibid., pp. 358-59.

107 Ibid., p. 358.

108 Ernest A. Bland, ed., *Olympic Story* (London: Rockliff, 1948), p. 129.

109 Ibid.

110 C. B. Fry, "Association Football," *The Encyclopaedia of Sports and Games*, II (London: William Heineman, 1911), p. 259.

111 "International Football," *The Encyclopaedia of Sports and Pastimes*, II (London: William Heineman, 1911), p. 272.

112 Menke, *The Encyclopedia of Sports*, p. 753.

113 "International Football," p. 272.

114 Ibid., p. 256.

115 Menke, *The Encyclopedia of Sports*, p. 353.

116 Durant, *Pictorial History of American Sports*, p. 17.

117 Howard J. Savage, *et. al., American College Athletics*, Bulletin No. 23 (New York: The Carnegie Foundation for the Advancement of Teaching, 1929), p. 20.

118 Harold Frindell, "The Origin and Development of the National Collegiate Athletic Association - A Force for Good in Intercollegiate Athletics" (Unpublished M.A. thesis, New York University, 1938), p. 5.

119 Carl D. Voltmer, *A Brief History of the Intercollegiate Conference of Faculty Representative* (New York: Western Intercollegiate Conference, 1935), p. 1-6.

120 Frindell, "The Origin and Development of the National Collegiate Athletic Association - A Force for Good in Intercollegiate Athletics," pp. 1-32.

121 G. Lacey Hillier, "Cycle Racing," *The Encyclopaedia of Sports and Games*, II (London: William Heineman, 1911), pp. 57-63, 66.

122 Griffin, *Athletics*, p. 17.

123 Menke, *The Encyclopedia of Sports*, p. 424.

124 "Golf," *The Encyclopedia of Sports and Games*, II (London: William Heineman, 1911), p. 343.

125 Menke, *The Encyclopedia of Sports*, p. 426.

126 Krout, *Annals of American Sport*, p. 169.

127 Ibid., p. 170.

128 G. E. A. Ross and E. B. Noel, "Tennis," *The Encyclopaedia of Sports and Games*, IV (London: William Heineman, 1911), p. 269.

129 Menke, *The Encyclopedia of Sports*, p. 871.

130 Ross, "Tennis," p. 270.

131 Peter G. McIntosh, "The British Attitude to Sport," *Sport and Society*, ed. by Alex Natan (London: Bowes and Bowes, 1958), p. 15.

132 Menke, *The Encyclopedia of Sports*, pp. 827-28.

133 Archibald Sinclair, "Swimming," *The Encyclopaedia of Sports and Games*, IV (London: William Heineman, 1911), p. 229.

134 Thomas Hughes, *Tom Brown's School Days*, edited with introduction and notes by Charles Swain Thomas (New York: The Macmillan Company, 1908).

135 Lucas, "Baron Pierre De Coubertin and the Formative Years of the Modern International Olympic Movement 1883-1896," pp. 44-78.

136 Ibid., pp. 42-47.

137 Victor Banciulesco, "A Forerunner of the Revival of the Olympic Games," *Bulletin*, Comite International Olympique, 83 (August 1963), pp. 55-56.

138 Jean Ketseas, "A Restatement," *Bulletin*, Comite International Olympique, 83 (August 1963), pp. 56-57.

139 John Richard Betts, *America's Sporting Heritage: 1850-1950* (Addison-Wesley Publishing Company, 1974), pp. 62-67, 79.

140 Bureau of the Census, *Historical Statistics of the United States, Colonial Times to 1957* (Washington, D. C.: United States Government Printing Office, 1960), p. 14.

141 Harry J. Carmen and Harold C. Syrett, *A History of the American People Since 1865*, Vol. II of *A History of the American People* (New York: Alfred A. Knopf, 1956) p. 158.

142 Dulles, *America Learns to Play*, p. 10.

143 Lewis, "1879: The Beginning of an Era in American Sports," pp. 136-145.

144 Lucas, " Baron Pierre De Coubertin and the Formative Years of the Modern International Olympic Movement 1883-1896," pp. 74-80.

145 Edward Joseph Grant, "Athletics," *Encyclopaedia Britannica*, 1967, II, p. 682.

146 Harry Alexander Scott, *Competitive Sports in Schools and Colleges* (New York: Harpers, 1951), p. 21.

147 Lehman, *The Complete Oarsman*, p. 345.

148 Korsgaard, "A History of the Amateur Athletic Union of the United States," p. 64.

149 Scott, *Competitive Sports in Schools and College*, p. 22.

150 Frindell, "The Origin and Development of the National Collegiate Athletic Association - A Force for Good in Intercollegiate Athletics," p. 32.

151 *Official Handbook 1970-71* (Chicago: National Federation of State High School Athletic Associations, 1970), p. 21.

152 Krout, *Annals of American Sport*, p. 266.

153 Ibid., p. 219.

154 Pierre De Coubertin, "The Redemption of Athletics," *Mind and Body*, 5 (October, 1898), p. 167.

155 J. H. Johnson, "Skating," *The Encyclopaedia of Sports and Games*, IV (London: William Heineman, 1911), p. 166.

156 Bland, *Olympic Story*, p. 62.

157 *Statuten Reglement Kongressreglement Der F. I. F. A.* (Hitziseg 11, Zurick: Federation Internationale De Football Association, 1963), p. 1.

158 Dunraven, "Yachting," p. 365.

159 Grant, "Athletics," p. 682.

160 *Statuts et Renseignements Generaux* (53 Rue Vivienne, Paris: Federation Internationale D'Escrime, 1966), p. 1.

CHAPTER V

The Early Development
of Amateurism

INTRODUCTION

This chapter explores the development of amateurism as a category of sport. The primary emphasis is on amateurism in the nineteenth century, although a few pages near the end of this chapter cover events during the early part of the twentieth century. Amateurism, as it relates to the modern Olympic Movement, is discussed in the following chapter.

Since the early development of amateurism in sports is primarily an English and American phenomenon, the events included in this chapter are essentially limited to developments in these countries. Furthermore, since the development of amateurism concerned mainly baseball, cricket, football (soccer), rugby, rowing and athletics (field and track), it is these sports that are the focus of this chapter.[1]

The first part of the chapter discusses the early use of the word "amateur" and the beginning of the controversy surrounding amateurism. The second part of the chapter reports on early efforts to define amateurism, the emergence of associations of athletic clubs, and attempts to define amateurism after 1872. The latter part of the chapter reviews the distinction between amateurism and athletic eligibility in educational institutions and attempts to define amateurism in the United States in the early part of the twentieth century.

EARLY USE OF THE WORD "AMATEUR"

Amateur is a French word derived from the Latin word *Amatorem* which means "one who loves or is fond of; who has a taste for anything."[2] In France during the reign of Louis XIV (1643-1715) the word amateur came into use and meant "...a connoisseur of the fine arts."[3] In Great Britain, the word was first used in 1784 with a similar meaning. Some sources say that the first use of the word "amateur" in sports referred to ringside spectators at a prize fight as "gentlemen amateurs" in 1801.[4] Menke disagrees with this date. He states that the word amator (amateur) was *probably* first used in regard to sports in England in 1788"...to separate 'Gentleman Jack' Jackson, aristocrat, collegian and boxer, from the heavy-weight bare-knuckles fighters of his time who fought for side bets or small purses put up by somebody in funds..."[5]

Menke's assumption that Jackson was referred to as an amateur prior to 1800 is highly dubious, but he was a gentleman sportsman of his time. Prior to 1800 the word "professional" had emerged to identify athletes who competed for money and/or who were looked down upon socially, but the word "amateur" was not yet used to identify a category of athletes.

In 1803 the word was used primarily to "...denote a person understanding and loving or practicing the polite art of painting, sculpture, or architecture, without any regard to pecuniary advantage."[6] During the early 1800's the word amateur generally meant "one who cultivates anything as a pastime, as distinguished from one who prosecutes it professionally; hence sometimes used disparingly; as a dabbler, or superficial student or worker."[7] During the early part of the nineteenth century the term "amateur" also was used to connote one who had no professional training and was a dilettante.

The shift in meaning of "amateur" is explained in the *Encyclopaedia Britannica*:

> The original meaning of the word, indicating one who participates in any art, craft, game, sport or other activity solely for pleasure and enjoyment, has been largely supplanted by an acquired secondary meaning indicating a person of inferior or superifcial skill, ability or proficiency, as compared with others who specialize in and are expert in the field.[8]

The difference between an amateur and a professional athlete during the first half of the nineteenth century was primarily a social rather than a financial or skill distinction. For example, there was nothing wrong with amateurs accepting money from bets on their own races during this period. In fact, some amateurs seem to have prided themselves on the fact that they could afford to lose a bet. The social distinction of amateurism was exemplified by the fact that mechanics, artisans, and laborers were not considered amateurs.[9]

During the early part of the nineteenth century the aristocratic or upper class segment of society was the first to participate in sports such as horse-racing, fencing, cricket, royal tennis, and yachting. In England, which was probably more class conscious than the United States, the upper class included the titled, the wealthy, officers in military and civil services, members of the clerical, medical, legal professions, and students and professors at universities and public schools.[10] [11] These were the early gentlemen amateurs who could engage in sports in an amateurish manner and gamble in their leisure.

The class below the upper class, the middle class, was the group primarily responsible for enlarging and organizing the modern sports movement in England. However, because these middle class people had upper class aspirations, they conducted their affairs with an upper class code of behavior. This resulted in the continued exclusion of laborers, artisans, and mechanics from their sports clubs.[12]

In the United States, where there were no titled classes, the early sports clubs were organized by the upper and the middle classes. The fact that these early American clubs also excluded laborers, mechanics, and artisans from their membership is important in understanding the developement of amateurism.

The importance of class distinction to sportsmen of that day can be seen from reports of an incident that took place in Williamsburg, Virginia in 1730. " 'James Bullock, a Taylor' (sic), was brought before the York County Court for taking part in a horse race. There was no objection whatever to the sport but the Court declared that it was 'contrary to Law for a Labourer to make a race, being a sport for only Gentlemen;' so 'Taylor' was fined 'one hundred pounds of tobacco and caske.' "[13] This class consciousness continued into the nineteenth century and was a significant factor in the development of the exclusive category of sports called amateur competition.

The annual cricket match in England between the Gentlemen and the Players which began in 1806 also points up the social distinction of that day. In this contest the Gentlemen were considered the amateurs and the Players the professionals until 1962.[14] This early event emphasizes the fact that many considered it acceptable for an amateur to play against a professional in cricket, assuming that the social distinction was kept. However, many English gentleman of the nineteenth century thought it "not proper" or fair to compete with or against violators of the amateur tradition.[15]

Another aspect of amateurism that developed simultaneously with the concept of social distinction was the view that people who engaged in manual labor for their livelihood and had an advantage in certain athletic events because of the strength and skill developed on the job. Griffin made the following statement about this aspect of amateurism in athletics during the nineteenth century:

> *At first it was difficult to define an amateur, and the rough and ready demarcatal division was the body versus the brains, wages versus salary; it is being considered that a man who earns wages by the physical labor of his body was by reason of his employment, better fitted for athletics than one who secured his salary by his mental powers.*[16]

As a result, the laboring class was viewed as professional in most, if not all sports, by gentlemen amateurs.[17] This view seems most apparent in the development of rowing and track and field. This job distinction in amateurism was intimately related to the social distinction discussed earlier.

The social, physical strength and skill aspects of the growing division between amateurs and professionals in sports were, in part, explained by the fact that "the traditions of English amateur sports are predominantly of the universities and the greater [more important] English public schools."[18]

The truth of this statement is obvious when one recalls the role played by the English public schools and universities in the development of sports such as rowing, football, rugby, and track and field. Outside of these schools and universities, amateur competition in track and field athletics was almost unknown until about 1860.[19]

The nineteenth century students of the public schools and universities in England tended to be the children of the English gentlemen or people aspiring to become gentlemen, and these students were only one step away from being gentlemen themselves. They certainly were not preparing to be mechanics, artisans, and laborers. Also, the educational value given to sports by such men as Thomas Arnold, headmaster at Rugby, and Pierre de Coubertin helped people associate sports closely with schools. Thus, the early development of amateurism stems from what may be called two "closed groups," the gentlemen class of society and the school system.

THE BEGINNING OF THE CONTROVERSY

The first controversy over professionalism took place in 1823 at an intercollegiate rowing race at Oxford. In that year the Christ Church team refused to row "because Stephen Davis, the boatbuilder, rowed for Brasenose and Issac King (a waterman*), in the Jesus boat."[20] As a result, the Christ Church men ran along the bank shouting "no hired waterman" at the Brasenose rowers. After that year" '...watermen ceased to row in the races.' "[21] However, professional watermen were acceptable as coxswains by non-

---

*A waterman was any person who works in or near water.

school teams. During the same period betting on athletic events did not eliminate anyone from the amateur classification. An example of this was the Leander Club vs. Oxford Club rowing race in 1831 in which two hundred pounds were bet on the outcome of the race with the Leander Club using a professional coxswain.[22]

At that time it was the custom in rowing "...to allow fouling; that is, to let one boat impede the other when it chose to and was able to do so. This, of course, made the office of coxswain one of far greater importance than it is now..."[23] Recognizing the importance of the coxswain, Cambridge University agreed to use professionals* as coxswains in races with the Leander Boat Club in 1837 and 1838, but the Cambridge crew had "...made it an express stipulation that no fouling was to be lawful."[24] Nevertheless, the match resulted in a number of fouls and encouraged the university men to stay clear of professionals. Some university gentlemen at this time felt that "fouling" in rowing should be abolished; and since watermen could not be trusted with fair play, they must be eliminated from positions as umpires, members of the crews, and coaches in the university races.[25]

Consistent with this view was the rule of the organizing committee of the first Henley Royal Regatta in 1839. This rule says "that every boat shall be steered by an amateur member of the Club or Clubs entering..." and no fouling was to be permitted.[26]

In 1841 the Oxford University Boat Club ruled that no crew would be allowed to start the races who had employed a waterman in the capacity of trainer or coach within three weeks of the first race. This rule was suspended between 1871 and 1873 because of the difficulty in finding amateur coaches. Nevertheless, Oxford crews were trained by professionals in 1839, 1840, 1841, 1846, and 1857.[27] From this information it is clear that a division between or among gentlemen and amateurs and watermen was beginning to develop during the early decades of the eighteenth century, but not until 1879 was the first official definition of amateur established for rowing in England.

Until about 1855, the term "amateur," when used in reference to a category of sports competitors, was still in the embyonic stage as an issue.[28] Consequently, little use of the word appears in literature prior to 1855. Most of the organized sports at this time were developed in schools or by upperclass segments of society. As a result, the competition within the various clubs and schools tended to be exclusive because of the characteristics of the students in public schools and members of the upper levels of society. This exclusiveness made it unnecessary for many organizations to specify in their

*Professionals here refers to people who made their living rowing boats on rivers or building boats.

titles that they were amateur. The National Association of Base-Ball Players in the United States, which was formed in 1857 as an amateur organization, is an example of an organization that apparently did no find it necessary to use the word amateur in its title or define an amateur in its rules. During this period, there was no agreement or understanding as to who was or was not an amateur.

THE BEGINNING OF EFFORTS TO DEFINE AMATEUR

The Castle Garden Amateur Rowing Association, founded in 1837, was perhaps the first organization to use the word amateur in its title, but no one knows exactly what the association meant by the term "amateur."[29] Similarly several other organizations that were founded in the late 1830's, the 1840's, and the 1850's used the word "amateur" in their titles. If there ever was an official definition of the term by these organizations, no record is available.

Not until the American Civil War (1861-1865) did serious concern develop over the need to define amateurism in sports. The first official definition of an amateur published by any organization in the world was a definition issued by the Amateur Athletic Club of England in 1866. According to its definition, and amateur was:

> Any gentlemen who has never competed in an open competition, or for public money, or for admission money, or with professionals for a prize, public money, or admission money, and who has never at any period of his life taught or assisted in the pursuit of athletic exercises as a means of livelihood; nor is a mechanic, artisan, or labourer.[30] [31]

The same year, Edwin D. Brickwood, writing under the pen name of Argonaut, presented his own definition of an amateur. This definition expresses Brickwood's understanding of who was an amateur in 1866, and it was the first published definition of an amateur. He says:

> "Amateurs must be officers of Her Majesty's Army, Navy, or Civil Service, members of the Clerical, Medical, or Legal professions, of the Universities of Oxford, Cambridge, Dublin, London, Durham, Edinburgh, Galscow, St. Andres's, or Aberdeen, and the Queen's Colleges in Ireland, or Eton, Radley, Westminster, and other public schools, or of any estblished club not composed of tradesmen or working mechanics, which would be allowed by the stewards of the Henley-on-Thames Regatta to compete for their Grand Challenge Cup, Stewards' Cup, Silver Goblets, or Diamond Sculls."[32]

The two definitions quoted have basically the same meaning, but Argonaut provides some additonal insight into the class of people who made up the category of gentlemen amateurs in 1866.

In the same year, the New York Athletic Club, which was to play a major role in the development of amateur sports in America, was founded. However, the idea of amateurism was somewhat confusing in America during this period. A letter written on August 21, 1867, by William Curtis, who was an outstanding athlete and one of the founders of the New York Athletic Club and the Amateur Athletic Union, provides valuable insight into the confusion surrounding amateurism in America at this time. In this letter Curtis protested against the reported time for a racing crew by the Hudson River Amateur Rowing Association. Portions of the letter read as follows:

The Hudson River Amateur Association carefully excludes from its contests all professional oarsmen, a prominent member tells me, not because they are afraid the professionals would carry off all the prizes, but to protect themselves against the tricks and devices and manoeuvres (sic) and frauds which are said to prevail among their professional brethern. Every member of the club knows that this time is false — too absurd to do much harm, but still utterly false. If they caused it to be published, no professional oarsmen can hope to rival them either in effrontery or mendacity. If they did not, then by neglecting to contradict it they brand themselves as partners in the most unblushing hoax ever thrust upon oarsmen. If these men were some nameless crew from the far West, the matter would be beneath notice; but the H.R.A.R. Association will attain a much lower rank than its founders anticipate if its members are allowed to falsify the record so grossly and go "unwhipt of justice."

If this club is right and I am wrong, I will give them a chance to defend their reputation, and at the same time punish me pecuniarily for my interference. I will bet $1000 to $500 that this crew cannot pull their boat over a three-mile course of the H.R.A.R. Association in 18m. 35s. any day they may name within thirty days of the publication of this challenge. If they take refuge behind "the pulling for money laws" of the H.R.A.R. Association, I will procure a set of colors-value not less than $500 as an outside bet with any individual member of the club, which will not infringe the rules. Finally, I am told by a member they will enter the three-mile six-oared gig race of the H.R.A.R. Association, September 12, 1867. If they do not wish to pull before this time, I will bet $1000 to $500 that the same boat and crew do not make 18m. 35s. on

*that day, another $1000 to $500 that they do not win the race, and
a third $1000 to $500 that the winning boat does not make 18m.
35. I enclose $250, which you can apply as forfeit on my part for
any one of these races they may choose.* [33]

In Curtis's letter, a prevailing negative, untrusting attitude of the upper
classes toward professional athletes can be detected. He also indirectly calls
attention to the fear among club members that professionals may win the
races and prizes. This fear was apparently associated with the social separation of the classes of people during that period. To be defeated by a common laborer would be unpleasant and embarrassing for a gentleman. The
letter also makes it quite clear that gambling among athletes was common.
Willingness to gamble was certainly no problem for Curtis, who became a
leader in amateur athletics during the next two decades. One role of leadership assumed by Curtis in 1868 was the promotion of the first amateur track
and field meet sponsored by the New York Athletic Club. There is no information to show how the club distinguished between professionals and amateurs for that meet. [34]

In the United States the first organization to define more specifically who
was not an amateur was the Hudson Amateur Rowing Association. In April
1868 several constitutional amendments were presented to the membership
among which were the following:

> *8. In all races rowed between clubs composing this association
> the crews must be* bona fide *members of the respective clubs at
> the time of the acceptance of the challenge.*
> *9. Any member of this association who shall hereafter row for
> money shall forever be debarred from participating in the regattas
> thereof.* [35]

There is no record of whether the amendments were approved by the
membership. If they were approved, they were ignored because on July 18,
1868, *The Spirit of the Times* contained the following report on a boat race
between two members of clubs belonging to the Hudson Rowing Association:

> BOAT RACE FOR AMATEURS FOR $500—*A boat race between
> Mr. Alden S. Swain, of the Atlanta Boat Club, and Mr. James G.
> White of the Gulick Boat Club took place on the 11th inst., from
> off the Elysian Fields for $500.* [36]

This advertisement is an example of the confusion surrounding amateurism during the 1860's in England and the United States. The winning of
money was obviously not the sole criterion for a person being classified as a
professional nor was there universal agreement that the accepting of money
for winning made one a professional. In fact, in England the sponsors of

meets were encouraged by early sports leaders to give prizes "...of as valuable and varied a nature as funds will allow."[37] This practice in amateur sports developed to the point where the winning and selling of prizes made it difficult to distinguish between amateurs and professionals. Thus, "pot hunting" had become commonplace in England by 1880.[38]

By about 1869 an amateur in athletics was generally thought to be someone who 1) had not competed in athletics for money, 2) had not taught athletic skills as a means of a livelihood, 3) had not competed in an open race.[40] However, not everyone agreed with this definition.

In addition, a distinction between the terms "amateur" and "gentlemen amateur" emerged.[41] The term "gentlemen amateur" referred to a distinction based on social class or position; whereas the term "amateur" referred to a category of athletes that met the criteria listed above. Consequently, by 1870 three categories of athletes existed: the professional, the amateur, and the gentleman amateur.

A series of events documented in the minutes of the minutes of the London Athletic Club, the leading athletic club in England, effectively illustrates the class distinction in sports during the early 1870's. One of these occured at a special general meeting of the club on October 19, 1870 when a member moved "That any Member of the London Athletic Club (willfully) entering for or competing in any sports confined wholly or partly to tradesmen or to members of tradesmen's cricket or rowing clubs shall be at once ejected from the Club."* The motion failed. A few days later on November 2, the committee of the of the Club dealt with the same unresolved issue by unanimously passing the following resolution which the club secretary was to send by circular to members of the club: "The Committee thinking the position of the Club may be affected if Members compete at athletic meetings held by firms of tradesmen express an earnest desire that Members will not enter at such meetings."* It should be noted that the position stated in the resolution is not as harsh or demanding as the motion proposed earlier.

Another excellent example of the problem associated with tradesmen competing against gentlemen amateurs took place at a race sponsored by the London Athletic Club in 1872. In this race the eligibility of W. J. Morgan, an employee of a large dry-goods and furnishing store (Shoolbred's Establishment) was challenged "...on grounds that he [the employee] was not a 'gentleman amateur,' and also that on a recent occasion he had made use of abusive, indecent language when competing in a similar race."[42] No evidence was found for the latter accusation and the committee voted to allow

*From the original minutes of the London Athletic Club currently held by the club archivist, Michael D. Pope.

the employee, a tradesman, to enter the walking race.* This incident created considerable turmoil within the London Athletic Club and as a result a special general meeting was held on December 2 and the following compromise resolutions were adopted:

1. Any Amateur wishing to compete in any open race held by this club, he not being a Member of the Clubs mentioned in the next Regulation must be introduced by two Members of the Club, and if any such entry be objected to by any Member of this Club the acceptance or rejection thereof shall be determined by ballot of the committee at a meeting to be held previous to the date fixed for the race at which one black ball in five shall exclude. Entries for open races to close a fortnight before the date of running.

2. Members of the following Clubs are considered eligible to compete in the open races of the Club without introduction specified in the preceeding Regulation, but subject nevertheless to the power reserved to the Committee in the Regulation No. 3. The Universities, Public Schools, Officers of the Army and Navy, A.A.C., Civil Service A.C., United Hospitals A.C., South Norwood A.C., Crystal Palace A.C., Thames H. and H.[43]**

These resolutions permitted a minority to control the outside entries in athletic events sponsored by the London Athletic Club, and, as a result, perpetuated the gentleman amateur distinction. In spite of this exclusiveness toward athletic events sponsored by the London Athletic club, members of the club would compete in athletic meetings sponsored by other clubs in which "horrid tradesmen"[44] were allowed to compete. This exclusive position by the London Athletic Club was not well received outside the club as is evident from reading the following quotation from *The Spirit of the Times:*

> *It is indeed surprising to find a club whose members so well versed in the history of athletics so far behind the age, for with hardly an exception the English sporting press ridicules the idea of this exclusiveness, and tells them that they are foolish to attempt keeping such an obsolete distinction.*[45]

Because of the dissatisfaction expressed by clubs excluded from these 1872 resolutions, members of the London Athletic Club passed a new resolution on January 29, 1873 that allowed members of all athletic, rowing, and

---

*From the original minutes of the London Athletic Club, dated December 2, 1872.

**From the original minutes of the London Athletic Club, dated November 20, 1872.

cricket clubs to compete in events sponsored by the club. This resolution was a big step leading toward the elimination of the "gentleman amateur" distinction.[46] During the years that followed the London Athletic Club continued to help remove the barriers that separated sportsmen.

As one can see from this evidence, great confusion surrounded the theory and practice of amateurism during the 1860's and the early 1870's. This confusion is effectively summarized by Korsgaard in the following paragraph.

> The evils associated with sports were not, however, banished simultaneously with the advent of athletic clubs. Many athletes continued to compete for hundreds of dollars 'a side.' An athletic club member might run in his club's closed games one week and run in a matched race or row in a sculling race for $500 a side the next week. The following week it would not be unlikely that he would run for a medal in some open games conducted by an athletic club. Betting had nothing to do with one's amateur status, even after a concept of amateurism had been promulgated by the New York Athletic Club in 1872. Despite the fact that this club awarded only medals, the contestants and their backers continued to bet on the outcome of an event so that in many instances the stakes were actually considerable higher than the medal offered. Eventually it was suggested that the net result was the same and that it made no difference whether the person ran for a cash prize or the stakes of a bet.[47]

Without a universal definition of amateur, the clubs used several different methods to limit entries to amateurs. The following statement is a good example of this effort to control and enforce amateurism. It is from the Schuylkill Navy National Amateur Regatta in 1872.

> The regatta is to be strictly what its name imports, 'amateur;' and the better to assure this and to prevent the possible creeping in of professionals unawares, the names of the different crews, entered from various quaters are to be promptly published, thus giving opportunity for all concerned for the presenting and consideration of objections.[48]

According to this announcement, entries were to be limited to those who could compete under their real name. Since competing under a false name was a common practice, the promise to publish the names of all crews for possible objections probably eliminated some professionals.[49] However, this type of announcement seems to have left room for several interpretations about who was eligible to compete. From the announcement it is not clear whether tradesmen or athletes, such as members of the Harvard crew who had competed against professionals, were eligible. Nor is it known if an athlete who had won money wagering on his own races was eligible. These are examples of the types of questions that clubs apparently tried to interpret and enforce.

As sports increased in popularity during the 1860's and the 1870's, the ambiguousness of what was meant by the term amateur and the inconsistency in interpreting eligibility, became increasingly troublesome. As a result, it became evident that a specific definition of an amateur that everyone agreed on was needed.

While the advocates of amateurism at this time were concerned with earning money from sports, prize medals with values as high as $100 were offered in an attempt to attract participants.[50] This seems to be in contradiction to the amateur spirit that was supposedly being promoted during this era. Certainly it is a contradiction to what has been called the amateur spirit during the nineteenth and twentieth centuries.

ATTEMPTS TO DEFINE AMATEURISM
AFTER 1872 IN THE UNITED STATES

In August 1872 at the first meeting of the National Association of Amateur Oarsmen of America (officially formed in 1873), a definition of an amateur was formulated and adopted by the delegates present. According to Janssen, this was the first definition of amateurism ever published in the United States by any club, association, or committee.[51]* This statement written in 1888 indicates that there was no national concensus as to who was an amateur prior to 1872. Prior to this date:

> Different customs prevailed in various localities; men who were amateurs on one river were professionals on another; protests were judged by no law but the pleasure of each regatta committee, and this chaos hindered the progress of amateur rowing and made a National Regatta an impossiblity.[52]

The definition of an amateur formulated in 1872 and formally adopted in 1873 by the National Association of Amateur Oarsmen in America is as follows:

> One who does not enter into open competition; or for either a stake, public or admission money, or entrance fee; or compete with or against a professional for any prize, who has never taught, pursued, or assisted in the pursuit of athletic exercises as a means

*This statement is true if it is assumed that the brief attempts to define amateurism or limit participants by organizations such as the Hudson Amateur Rowing Association and the National Association of Baseball Players are excluded or were never published. I have not been able to find any earlier complete definition of an amateur.

of livelihood; whose membership of any rowing or other athletic club was not brought about, or does not continue, because of any mutual agreement or understanding, expressed or implied, whereby his becoming or continuing a member of such a club would be of any pecuniary benefit to him whatever, direct or indirect, and who has never been employed in any occupation involving any use of oar or paddle;...and who shall otherwise conform to the rules and regulation of the National Association of Amateur Oarsmen.[53]

Since track and field athletics in the United States did not arrive at an official definition of amateurism as early as the rowing clubs, there remained considerable confusion in their meets about who was an amateur. The following except from the announcement by the New York Athletic Club for its fall games in 1872 shows its method of explaining who was eligible:

At the fall games,...the following will be open to amateurs of the United States, under the club definition...for presentation of gold medals; value $100 each. Entries close October 5, and should be made to the secretary...who will furnish all particulars concerning the definition of an amateur, rules, etc.[54]

The definition of an amateur in these meets is unknown. Another attempt to establish control over the entrants in an amateur contest is the following announcement by the New Jersey Association for its spring games in 1874:

The following programme..(is) open to amateurs, subject to the following conditions: Contestants must be members of a college or of a recognized amateur athletic club, and forward a certificate to that effect. Gentlemen not members of any club will be required to furnish a letter of introduction from a recognized athletic club, guaranteeing his being an amateur. These conditions are in full accord with the suggestions made by us last fall, when the difficulty ocurred at the New York Athletic Club games and can be readily complied with by any bona fide *amateur of good standing. It will also be an assurance to those who do enter that their opponents are veritable amateurs and that the quasi-professional element will be rigidly excluded (sic).*[55]

In 1876 at the seventh annual games of the New York Athletic Club, the following stipulation on competitors was issued:

No competitor will be allowed to enter under a false name, and the right to refuse or strike out any entry is reserved. In order to assure bona fide entries, an entrance fee of $2 will be charged for each game which will be returned to all those who finish in their

*respective games. An amateur is any person who has never com-
peted in an open competition for public or admission money, nor
has at any period of his life taught or assisted in the pursuit of athletic exercises as a means of livelihood.*[56]

The first attempt to organize American athletic clubs into an association
took place in 1873 with the formation of the National Amateur Gymnastic
and Athletic Tournament Association. Since the Association never received
much support, it discontinued operations in 1874.[57] In the same year an attempt was made to form an organization called the North American Amateur Association, but it never officially came into being.[58]

In 1875 the Intercollegiate Association of Amateur Athletes of America
was founded to "foster and maintain competition among its members in
track and field athletics on a high plane of true amateurism, sportsmanship,
and friendly relationships.' "[59] Despite the growing concern over professionalism in athletics, the first constitution of the Intercollegiate Association
of Amateur Athletes of America "...contained no statement concerning eligibility. The amateur status evidently was taken for granted."[60]

A third attempt to organize athletic clubs took place in 1878 when the
American Association of Amateur Athletes was founded.[61] This organization
ceased to exist the same year. In 1879 the Columbia College Boat Club tried
to form another organization called the National Athletic Association.[62] This
organization also did not succeed. This was partially due to the fact it was
composed of non-athletic clubs. However, it did publish one of the first detailed definitions of amateur. It said:

*An amateur athlete is one who practices athletics for his own
physical improvement or pleasure, and not as a business or for
gain.*

*A person who violates any one of the following rules will not be
considered an amateur, in the sense of this definition:*

*Rule 1. No amateur can compete in an open competition or for
a stake, or for public money or for gate money.*

*Rule 2. No amateur can compete with a professional; but an
amateur shall be held blameless for competing with a professional
whose entry has been accepted, in a game or contest open to amateurs only, and given by a recognized amateur athletic club —
provided that, if aware of the status of the professional, he enters
his protest before starting.*

*Rule 3. No amateur can teach or pursue or engage in athletic ex-
ercises as a means of livelihood.*

*In addition to the above the following will be enforced on or
after March 25, 1879:*

Rule 4. No amateur can compete in public games not under the direction of or given by a recognized amateur athletic club.

Rule 5. No amateur can compete in public games, the profits or any part of the profits from which are to be devoted to any other object than charity or the future encouragement of athletic exercises among amateurs.

Rule 6.No amateur can, as a condition of his competing, demand the appointment or withdrawal of any specified individual as an officer at any amateur athletic meeting nor can he ask or demand , as a condition of his competing, the refusal of the entry of any amateur; nor can he claim any privileges not accorded other contestants.

Rule 7. No amateur can offer his entry for any games under an assumed name, or from a club of which he is not a member.

Rule 8. No amateur, when entered for a handicap race, can refuse to give his public record when asked for it by the club under whose direction the race is given.

Rule 9. No amateur can have his expenses or any part of the same, in connection with any contest defrayed except by the athletic club of which he is a member. But this rule shall not operate where any recognized athletic club defrays the expenses of all contestants alike.

Rule 10. No amateur can accept compensation of any kind, directly or indirectly, as a condition of, or because, of this connection with any athletic club or games, or for the use of his name in such connection.

Rule 11. No amateur can enter for any games in which the prizes are articles of merchandize or trade.

Rule 12. No athlete can sell or hypothecate his prizes nor dispose of them for any equivalent.

Rule 13. No amateur can bet on any contest for which he has entered, nor receive, directly or indirectly, the profits or any share of them, of a bet on any such contest.

Rule 14. Any person guilty of conduct which may tend to bring amateur athletic sports into disrepute shall not be deemed an amateur.[63]

In the same year, 1879, the National Association of Amateur Athletes of America, which was the forerunner of the Amateur Athletic Union in the United States, was formed by most of the leading athletic clubs. The first definition of amateurism adopted by the Association was:

An amateur is any person who has never competed in an open contest, or for a stake; or for gate money, or under a false name; or

*with a professional for a prize, or where gate money is charged;
nor has ever at any peiod of his life taught or pursued athletic exercises as a means of livelihood.*[64]

In essence, this definition is the same as that given in 1872 by the National
Association of Amateur Oarsmen of the United States. In reflecting on this
definition, Savage and others made the following observation:

*...one fact concerning this definition is noteworthy — its negative
phasing. A subsequent amateur definition by the same body, effective in 1885, continued the negative attitude and particularized
in much detail the circumstances in which an amateur becomes a
professional. Thus amateurism of the day was defined as the
absence of professionalism. This negative attitude permeates all
attempts to define the amateur status during the next thirty
years.*[65]

ATTEMPTS TO DEFINE AMATEUR AFTER 1872 IN ENGLAND

Prior to 1878 a definition of an amateur in rowing in England was not considered necessary because the terms "gentleman" and "amateur" were considered to be basically synonymous. The social or class restrictions of clubs
tended to automatically control who entered races. The question of earning
money from prizes or bets did not enter into the issue of being a gentleman
or an amateur either, except that it was understood that a gentleman did not
make his living from prizes or bets. However, it was acceptable to bet considerable sums of money on matches. In fact, as late as 1861, the amateur
championship of the Thames was a sweepstakes with each competitor risk-
ing five pounds and the winner taking the pool.[66]

By 1878 conditions were beginning to change as confusing, contradictory
rulings were appearing in different regattas. This caused a group of representatives from different prominent rowing clubs to meet and publish the
following definition of an amateur:

*An amateur oarsman or sculler must be an officer of Her Majesty's
Army or Navy or Civil Service, a member of the Liberal professions, or of the Universities, or Public Schools, or of any established boating or rowing club not containing mechanics or professionals; and must not have competed in any competition for either
a stake, or money, or entrance fee, or with or against a professional
for any prize; nor have ever taught, pursued or assisted in the pursuit of athletic exercise or any kind as means of a livelihood, nor
have ever been employed in or about boats, or in manual labor;
nor be a mechanic, artisan or labourer.*[67]

However, this definition was not totally satisfactory to the clubs involved. Therefore, in 1879, the Henley Stewards issued the following definition of an amatuer. This definition was in effect until 1937.[68]

No person shall be considered as an amateur oarsman or sculler—

1. Who has ever competed in any open competition for a stake, money or entrance fee.

2. Who has ever competed with or against a professional for any prize.

3. Who has ever taught, pursued, or assisted in the practice of athletic exercises or any kind as a means of gaining a livelihood.

4. Who has been employed in or about boats for money or wages.

5. Who is or has been by trade or employment for wages, or mechanic, artisan, or labourer.[69]*

These definitions of an amateur by the two rowing groups clearly convey the social distinction of amateurism in practice during this era.

In 1879 the Metropolitan Rowing Club was formed as a governing body for rowing in London, and it adopted the definition of an amateur drawn by the Henley Stewards in 1879. In 1882 the Metropolitan Rowing Club changed its name to the Amateur Rowing Association. This new organization soon became the governing body for rowing throughout the United Kingdom.

With the growing popularity of rowing, an increasing number of working class people started to partiacipate in the sport. Since they were unable to get the Amateur Rowing Association to eliminate the restrictions against people who had been or were "by trade or employment for wages, a mechanic, artisan, or labourer," they founded a new organization in 1890 without this restriction. The new organization was called the National Amateur Rowing Association.[71]

The year 1879 was an important one for amateurism. It was in this year that the Bicycle Union was formed. It was the first amateur sports organization in England to omit the "merchandise clause" from its definition of an amateur.[72] Another problem which developed was a controversy in cricket over certain amateur players. In effort to settle the issue, the Marylebone Cricket Club passed the following resolution in 1879.

That no gentleman ought to make a profit by his services in the cricket field, and that for the future no cricketer who takes more than his expenses in any match shall be qualified to play for the

---

*From the first point of the above definition it should be noted that it was illegal to compete in any open competition for money, but it was legal in races confined to members. This interpretation was accepted until 1894.[70]

Gentlemen against the Players at Lord's but that if any Gentleman feels difficulty in joining in the match without pecuniary assistance, he shall not be debarred from playing as a Gentleman by having his actual expenses defrayed.[73]

In spite of this rule, the great cricketer, Dr. W. G. Grace, having just completed his medical training in 1879 was presented with a purse of 1458 pounds and a marble clock, "...that was intended to purchase a medical practice."[74] In 1895 a committee of the Marylebone Cricket Club and the journal *Sportsman* collected 2,377 pounds and two shillings and the *Daily Telegraph* collected 5,281 pounds and nine shillings for Dr. Grace.

Even though Dr. Grace had received these gifts and others "...he always maintained in the eyes of controlling committees an amateur status."[75] Such were the various ways amateurism was interpreted by leading sports organizations and individuals in the latter part of the nineteenth century. It was not until 1962 or early 1963 that the Marylebone Cricket Club eliminated the category of an amateur in first class cricket, and thus solved the controversy and the hypocrisy which existed.[76]

In 1894 the Amateur Rowing Association revised its amateur code to read as follows:

The Association shall consist of Clubs which adopt the following definition of an amateur, viz.

No person shall be considered an Amateur Oarsman, Sculler, or Coxswain

1. Who has ever rowed or steered in any race for a stake, money, or entrance fee:

2. Who has ever knowingly rowed or steered with or against a professional for a prize;

3. Who has ever taught, pursued, or assisted in the practice of athletic exercises of any kind for a profit.

4. Who has ever been employed in or about boats, or in manual labour, for money or wages.

5. Who is or has been by trade or employment for wages a mechanic, artisan, labourer, or engaged in any menial duty.

6. Who is disqualified as an amateur in any other branch of sport.

And in the next clause of the Constitution it is laid down that—

An amateur may not receive any contribution towards his expenses in competing in a Race or a Regatta except from the Club which he represents, or a bona fide Member of such Club; but the Committee shall have power to make special rules for any International Regatta or Competition.[77]

112

This definition was more stringent than the earlier definition because the words "...or engaged in any menial duty" were added to the "Mechanics Clause." It also omitted the word "open" from line one of the rules. This meant that amateurs could not compete for money or stakes in closed club competition as well as open competition after 1894.

In the 1897 edition of his book, *Rowing*, Lehman added the following explanatory note to the 1894 Amateur Rowing association rules to help clarify their meaning.

PROFESSIONAL

Up to 1894 A.R.A. gave a very wide interpretation to the term "professional," which was held to include "any person not qualified as an amateur under A.R.A. Rules." Mechanics, artisans, labourers, men engaged in menial duty, or employed in manual labour for money or wages, were, therefore, not merely disqualified as amateurs, but were considered to be professionals, and competition against them for a prize involved disqualification to the amateur so competing. In 1894, however, the whole code of the A.R.A. was submitted to the revision of a sub-committee and their report, subsequently adopted by the full committee, laid it down that from this time on the word "professional" must be interpreted "in its primary and literal sense," i.e. one who makes money by rowing, sculling, or steering with or against a professional for a prize is still disqualified, but the amateur status of one who rows or steers with or against mechanics, artisans, etc. (provided, of course, that the race is not for a stake, money, or entrance fee), is not affected. At the same time it must be remembered (Rule 1 of Rules for Regattas) that at regattas held in accordance with A.R.A. rules no mechanic, artisan, etc. can be admitted to compete, and by Clause XI of the Constitution no member of any club affiliated to the A.R.A. is permitted to compete at a regatta not held in accordance with A.R.A. rules. The result would seem to be, therefore, that whereas an amateur who is not a member of a club affiliated with A.R.A. can compete against mechanics, artisans, etc., at a regatta not held in accordance with A.R.A rules without incurring any penalty, a member of a club affiliated to the A.R.A. can compete against this class only in a private match. Any member of an affiliated club transgressing Clause XI would unquestionably render himself liable to suspension under Clause VIII of the constitution. There are now, therefore, three classes of oarsmen, viz, amateurs, non-amateurs, and professionals.

NON-AMATEURS

The A.R.A. holds that "apprenticeship is no disqualification." Nobody, therefore, is to be disqualified for serving an apprenticeship, even if it involves (as in the case of engineers and nurserymen) manual labor for a money payment. But such manual labour on the part of one who has passed through his ordinary apprenticeship and still continues at the work for a year or two would disqualify.

The committee has held that disqualification attaches, for instance to—

1. A watchmaker's assistant who works, or has worked, at the bench.

2. A baker's assistant who not only helps to make bread, but also delivers it.

3. Engravers and etchers.

4. A man having an interest in a boat-letting business, and taking in or starting boats at a raft.

But not to—

5. A 3rd engineer, sea-going who goes to sea and works for money, where such sea-service is necessary to qualify him for passing his examinations for the position of chief engineer.

6. A draughtsman in an engineering firm, though working for wages.

Decisions 3 and 6 are not easily to be reconciled.[78]

From Lehman's comments, one can see the development of a third class of participants in sports, "the non-amateur." This same definition of the Amateur Rowing Association was used for the rowing races in the 1908 Olympics[79] and was still in force at least until 1925.[80]

In 1880 the practice of making payments to players in the Football Association in England for "broken time" started. Because of the difficulty in controlling this practice, the Association legalized it in 1885 and thus made a distinction between amateurs and professionals by openly recognizing professionals in football.[81]

During the early 1880's, members of the Rugby Football Union, which was formed in 1871, became concerned about possible professionalism in Rugby. Consequently, the Union passed a regulation in 1886 "designed to prevent private gain from games."[82] However, the issue of professionalism continued to exist. This was particularly true in relation to the practice of payment for "broken time."

This issue of "broken time" payments developed into a critical problem in the Rugby Union of England. By 1892 and 1893, Union members were fully aware that "broken time" payments were being made in spite of a strengthening of the Union rules against such payments. Since it was obvious that the rules were being broken, some clubs believed that "...honesty demanded a modification of the regulations governing professionalism."[83] Consequently, a specific proposal to legalize payments for "broken time" was set forth in 1893, but it was voted down by the Union. This rejection resulted in the formation of the Northern Rugby Football Union in 1895 by twenty-two clubs which had withdrawn from the Rugby Union.[84] Originally, the Northern Rugby Football Unions strictly limited its professionalism to six shillings a day for lost time. In 1898 the rules were amended so that remuneration was unlimited, but it "...debarred players from participation in the game unless they also regularly followed some other occupation."[85]

This same issue of "broken time" appeared again in 1924 in England, and has been debated and discussed by the International Olympic Committee at many meetings until 1974.

NEW ATHLETIC ASSOCIATIONS DEFINE AMATEURISM

Track and field athletics had also been going through a period of transition during this era in England and the United States. In England the Amateur Athletic Association was formed in 1880. It issued the following definition of an amateur.

> *No person shall be considered an amateur who has either competed with or against a professional for any prize; who has either taught, pursued, or assisted in the practice of athletic exercise of any kind as a means of obtaining a livelihood.*[86]

This definition was revised and expanded into a new one which apparently was issued in 1885:

> *An amateur is one who has never competed for a money prize or monetary consideration, or for any declared wager or staked bet; who has never engaged in, assisted in, or taught any athletic exercise as a means of pecuniary gain; and one who has never taken part in any competition with anyone who is not an amateur.*
>
> *To this definition the only exceptions are as follows:*
>
> *(a) That Amateur athletes shall not lose their amateur status by competing with or against professionals in the Cricket matches or in ordinary Club Football matches for which no prizes had been given, or in Cup Competitions permitted by the National Football Associations or National Rugby Unions of England, Ireland, Scot-*

land, or Wales, providing that such competitions or matches form no part of, nor have connection with any Athletic Meeting.

(b) That Competitions-at-arms between Volunteers and Regulars shall not be considered as coming within the scope of the A.A.A. Laws.

(c) That Competitors in Officer's Races at Naval and Military Athletic Meetings (such races being for officers only, and for which money prizes are not given) shall be exempt from the laws of the A.A.A. disqualifying runners for competing at mixed meetings.

(d) That the "Championship of Army" Races be exempt from the effect of this Rule.

(e) That a paid handicapper is not ipso facto a professional.

(f) That those Sailors and Soldiers of His Majesty's Forces (including the territorial Army), who do not individually accept money prizes, be exempt from the loss of their amateur status by reason of competing in Navy and Military Competitions confined to Sailors and Soldiers. [87]

In an attempt to eliminate "pot hunting," one of the abuses of the amateur spirit at this time, which resulted from the expensive prizes that were being given at meets the Amateur Athletic Association stated in 1885 that "no prize shall be offered in a handicap of greater value that ten pounds, ten shillings.[88] About the same time, the Amateur Athletic Association made a statement condemning the practice of selling prizes. However, there is no evidence that there was ever a penalty for selling prizes at that time.[89]

In 1885 the National Association of Amateur Athletes of America also revised its definition of an amateur. This definition is in essence the same as the previous definition; but the organization was aware of the need to clarify questions concerning amateurism and developed a detailed statement saying who was and who was not an amateur. This statement which is quoted below was the most comprehensive definition of amateurism up to this time.

An amateur is any person who has never competed in an open competition, or for money, or under a false name; or with a professional for a prize, or where gate money is charged; nor has ever at any time taught, pursued or assisted at athletic exercises for money, or for any valuable consideration. But nothing in this definition shall be construed to prohibit the competition between amateurs for medals, cups or other prizes than money.

And it is hereby expressly declared that this definintion is not retroactive, and that all past acts of amateurs shall be judged in acccordance with the provisions of the old defintions; and that the foregoing definition shall take effect on and after the 1st day of May, 1885.

To prevent any misunderstanding in reading the above, the Association draws attention to the following explanations and adjudications:

An athlete has forfeited his right to compete as an amateur and has thereby become a professional, by —

(a) Ever having competed in an open competition (i.e. competition, the entries to which are open to all, irrespective as to whether the competitors are amateurs or professionals, and whether such competition be for a prize or not) in any athletic exercise over which this Association has declared its jurisdiction.

(b) Ever having competed for money in such athletic exercise.

(c) Ever having competed under a false name in any such athletic exercise.

(d) Ever having knowlingly competed with a professional for a prize, or where gate money is charged in any such athletic exercise.

(e) Ever having taught or pursued as a means of livelihood any such exercise.

(f) Ever having directly or indirectly accepted or received remuneration for engaging in any such athletic exercise.

An athlete shall hereafter forfeit his right to compete as an amateur, and shall thereby become a professional, if at any time after the foregoing defintion shall take effect, he shall —

1. Directly or indirectly receive payments for training or coaching any other person in any athletic exercise over which this Association shall declare its jurisdiction.

2. Directly or indireclty receive payment for services personally rendered in teaching any such athletic exercise.

3. Directly or indirectly receive payment for services rendered as Referee, Judge, Umpire, Scorer Manager, Director, or in any other capacity, at any professional exhibition or contest of any athletic exercises whatsoever.

Note. — Nothing herein shall be construed to prohibit the acceptance by any amateur of his necessary travelling expenses incurred by any Refreree, Judge, Umpire, Scorer or Starter, in going to and from the place of any amateur contest.

4.Directly or indirectly, run, manage, or direct, for prospective profit any professional exhibition or contest.

An amateur shall not hereafter forfeit his right to compete as an amateur, and shall not become a professional, by —

(a) Receiving compensation for services rendered as ticket taker or ticket seller in any contest or exhibition of amateur athletics.

(b) Receiving compensation for services personally rendered as Secretary, Treasurer, Manager, or Superintendent of any amateur athletics.

(c) Receiving compensation as editor, correspondent or reporter of, or contributor to any sporting, athletic, or other paper or periodical.

(d) Running, managing, or directing for prospective profit any sporting, athletic, or other paper or periodical.

(e) Receiving compensation for services personally rendered as official handicapper under the direction and authority of the National Association of Amateur Athletes of America.

(f) Receiving from a club of which he shall be a member the amount of his expenses necessarily incurred in traveling to and from the place of any amateur contest.[90]

Approximately three years later, on January 21, 1888, the Amateur Athletic Union was founded. It issued its own definition of amateur, which, in essence, was the same as that of the National Association of Amateur Athletes of America. The Amateur Athletic Union defined an amateur as:

One who has not entered in an open competition; or for either a stake, public or admission money or entrance fee; or under a fictitious name; or has not competed with or against a professional for any prize or where admissions fee is charged; or who has not instructed, pursued or assisted in the pursuit of athletic exercises as a means of livelihood, or for gain or any emolument; or whose membership of any Athletic Club of any kind was not brought about or does not continue, because of any mutual understanding, express or implied, whereby his becoming or continuing a member of such club would be of any pecuniary benefit to him whatever direct or indirect; and who shall in other and all respects conform to the rules and regulations of this organization.[91]

During the next two years the Amateur Athletic Union and the National Association of Amateur Athletes of America fought a vigorous battle for the control of amateur athletics in America.[92] Both groups started giving out substantial awards to competitors as a means of attracting athletes to their respective meets. A good example of this bidding war was the hundred dollar gold watches given as prizes by the Amateur Athletic Union.[93]

AMATEURISM AND ELIGIBILITY IN EDUCATIONAL INSTITUTIONS

Just as educational institutions played an important role in the development of sports, they also played an influential role in the development of amateurism. For example, in 1882 Princeton decided to amend its eligibility rules to exclude all students whose college expenses were paid because they participated in athletics. A few years later in 1888 the Intercollegiate Association of Amateur Athletes of America revised it rules and included a rather comprehensive and lengthy list of items regarding the eligibility of college athletes. Part of the revised rules stated that athletes could not compete for money prizes or sell trophies for money.[94] This mixing of rules regarding academic eligibility and amateurism by educational institutions has resulted in confusion about the distinction between the two. To clarify this distinction, it seems helpful to think of eligibility rules in colleges and universities as regulations related primarily to academic standing, and rules on amateurism by educational institutions as regulations related to non-academic and monetary affairs. This is an important distinction for proper understanding of the problems of amateurism and the roles of the universities in the evolution of amateurism.

Secondary schools and colleges and universities are "closed systems" with certain specific educational objectives in contrast to athletic clubs which exist without such objectives. As a result, educational institutions must establish rules and standards in athletics in order to prevent abuses that may detract from the institutions' basic objections. Therefore, the eligibility rules or standards for eduational institutions are not necessarily applicable to "open" competition. For example, regulations limiting the number of days a person may spend at a training camp may be very important in an educational setting, but unecessarily restrictive in a non-educational setting.

An example of college eligibility rules in which certain regulations on amateurism are incorporated are the following rules adopted by the Intercollegiate Conference of Faculty Representatives, commonly called the Western Intercollegiate Conference or Big Ten, in 1895 when that Conference was founded.

1. Each college and university which has not already done so shall appoint a committee on college athletics which shall take general supervision of all athletic matters in the respective college or university, and which shall have all the responsibility for enforcing the college or university rules regarding athletics and all intercollegiate sports.

2. No one shall participate in any game in athletic sports unless he be a bona fide *student doing full work in a regular or special course as defined in the curriculum of his college; and no person who has participated in any match game as a member of another college team until he has been a matriculate in said college under the above conditons for a period of six months. This rule shall not*

119

apply to students who, having graduated at one college, shall enter another college for professional or graduate study.

3. No person shall be admitted to any intercollegiate contest who receives any gift, remuneration, or pay for his services on the college team.

4. Any student of any institution who shall be pursuing a regularly prescribed resident graduate course within such institutions, whether for an advanced degree or in one of its professional schools, may be permitted to play for a period of the minimum number of years required for securing the graduate or professional degree for which he is a candidate.

5. No person who has been employed in training a college team for intercollegiate contests shall be allowed to participate in any intercollegiate contest as a member of any team which he has trained, and no professional athlete or person who has ever been a member of a professional team shall play at any intercollegiate contest.

6. No student shall play in any game under an assumed name.

7. No student shall be permitted to participate in any intercollegiate contest who is found by the faculty to be delinquent in his studies.

8. All games shall be played on grounds either owned by or under the immediate control of one or both of the colleges participating in the contest, and all games shall be played under student management and not under the patronage or control of any other corporation, association or private individual.

9. The election of managers and captains of teams in each college shall be subject to approval of the committee on athletics.

10. Before every intercollegiate contest a list of men proposing to play shall be presented to the other or others, certifying that all members are entitled to play under conditions of the rules adopted, such certificate to be signed by the registrar or the secretary of the college or university. It shall be the duty of the captain to enforce this rule.

12. We call upon the expert managers of football teams to so revise rules as to a reduce the liability to a minimum. [95]

The position indicated by these rules is important because since its founding, the Western Intercollegiate Conference has been one of the most influential athletic conferences in the country.

AMATEURISM DURING THE EARLY TWENTIETH CENTURY

In the early part of the twentieth century the problem of defining an amateur intensified for universities and national and international athletic associations. During this period the officials of most, if not all, leading American colleges held an official position regarding eligibility for athletes that was "...ironclad in opposition to professionalism..."[96] To these colleges a professional was any "...student who in any way, either individually or as a member of a team,...accepted remuneration for playing or for training athletes[97]..." and as a result was "...excluded from representing the college."[98] Nevertheless, professionalism and the rule evasions were common on the college campus during the first two decades of the twentieth century. This was partly due to the problem of athletes playing summer baseball for pay.[99] [100] Many universities and athletic conferences definitely prohibited an athlete from accepting money for his athletic skills, but university officials found it difficult to prevent athletes from participating in summer baseball for pay. As late as 1928, at the Twenty-first Annual Meeting of the Association for New England Colleges for Conference on Athletics, "The general opinion seemed to be...that summer baseball could not be controlled, and therefore it was futile to legislate against it."[101]

In order to control intercollegiate athletics, the Intercollegiate Athletic Association* was formed in 1905. At the first meeting the Association set forth the following statement regarding eligibility and amateurism.

Each institution which is a member of this Association agrees to enact and enforce such measures as may be necessary to prevent violations of the principles of amateur sports such as

A. Proselyting

> *1. The offering of inducements to players to enter colleges or universities because of their athletic abilities, and of supporting or maintaining players while students on account of their athletic abilities, either by athletic organizations, individual alumni, or otherwise, directly or indirectly.*
> *2. The singling out of prominent athletic students of preparatory schools and endeavoring to influence them to enter a particular college or university.*

B. The playing of those ineligible as amateurs.
C. The playing of those who are not bona-fide students in good and regular standing.
D. Improper and unsportsmanlike conduct of any sort whatsoever, either on the part of the contestants, the coaches, their assistants, or the student body.[102]

*The name was changed to National Collegiate Athletics Association in 1910.

In 1910 a committee of this same organization, which was to become the major college athletic association in America, set forth a new definition of an amateur in which amateurism was first expressed with some positive emphasis.[103]

> 1. An amateur in athletics is one who enters and takes part in athletic contests purely in obedience to the play impulses or for the satisfaction or purely play motives and for the exercise, training, and social pleasure derived. The natural or primary attitude of mind and motives in play determines amateurism.
>
> 2. A professional in athletics is one who enters or takes part in any athletic contest from any other motive than the satisfaction of pure play impulses or for the exercise, training, and social pleasures derived, or one who desires and secures from his skill or who accepts of spectators, partisan or other interest, any material or economic advantage or reward.[104]

According to Savage, the last stage of defining amateurism negatively appeared in the official handbook of the Intercollegiate Association of Amateur Athletes in America in 1913.

> An amateur is a person who has never competed in any open competition, or for money, or under false name; or where gate money is charged; nor has at any time taught pursued, or assisted at athletic exercise for money, or for any valuable consideration.[105]

During the same year the International Athletic Federation was formed; and it issued one of the first, if not the first, definition of an amateur by an international sports federation. This definition, which was rather lengthy, apparently was "partially American in origin." It contained statements such as 1) an amateur was "one who competes only for the love of the sport," and 2) "competing for money or any other pecuniary reward makes the competitor a professional in all sports."[106] One restriction in the definition that is of special interest to Americans is:

> 5. One who teaches, trains, or coaches for money or other pecuniary consideration is a professional, except, however, that so far as competition in his own country, and there only, is concerned, an employee or representative of the state or school or other educational institution, who teaches, trains, or coaches as an incident to his main vocation or employment, may, or may not, be a professional, as the Association of the country of such a person shall decide.[107]

The definition in 1913 did not "...prohibit competition between amateurs and professionals, although it stipulated that such shall be regulated with

122

stringency."[108] This provision had been removed some time prior to 1936, possibly in 1921.[109]

The chaos and turmoil over eligibility rules and amateurism rapidly became intolerable in America. Consequently, on December 29th and 30th, 1915, the Intercollegiate Association of Amateur Athletes of America called a congress to deal with the matter.[110] By the end of 1916 three major sportsgoverning bodies in the United States, the Intercollegiate Association of Amateur Athletes of America, the National Collegiate Athletic Association, and the Amateur Athletic Union had "...reached substantial agreement in defining an amateur sportsman as 'one who engages in sport solely for the pleasure and physical, mental, or social benefits he derives therefrom and to whom sport is nothing more than an avocation.' "[111]

After 1916, a slow trend developed toward including the positive aspects of amateurism in the definitions of the term. By 1936 at least four of the international sports federations included in their definition the concept that an amateur is one who competes for the love of sport.[112]

SUMMARY

In this chapter the historical development of amateurism, primarily in England and the United States, has been reviewed. The first use of the word "amateur" in reference to sports was in 1801. From then until about 1866, amateurism was in a slow-growing embryonic state. At this point what might legitimately be called the second stage or period of development began. This period lasted until 1872 and coincided with the post-Civil War era in the United States.

A third stage of development began in 1872. It was at this time that organizations in the United States and England made numerous attempts to define amateurism. This was also a time when numerous athletic clubs emerged. Two significant associations were founded during this period. They were the Amateur Athletic Association of England in 1880 and the Amateur Athletic Union of the United States in 1888.

The last part of this chapter dealt with some of the developments at the end of the nineteenth century and the beginning of the twentieth century. This period may appropriately be referred to as the fourth stage of the development of amateurism. The date of 1894, when the first modern Olympic Congress met, and the date 1895, when the Western Intercollegiate Conference (Big Ten) was founded, are appropriate dates with which to begin this period. This was the era when national organizations such as the National Collegiate Athletic Association in the United States was founded and several international sports federations, such as the International Amateur Athletic Federation, came into existence to control and administer international athletics. Amid these national and international developments, the International Olympic Committee became a significant force in national and international athletics. The important role that the Olympic movement and the affiliated international sports federations played in the development of amateurism is the topic of the next chapter.

FOOTNOTES

1   Howard J. Savage, *Games and Sports in British Schools and Universities*, 2nd ed., bulletin no. 18; (New York: The Carnegie Foundation for the Advancement of Teaching, 1928), pp. 193-98.

2   James A. Murray, ed., *A New English Dictionary on Historical Principles*, Vol. IA, ed. by James A. Murray (Oxford: The Claredon Press, 1888), p. 265.

3   Norris Dewar McWhirter and Pincus Sober, "Amateur," *Encyclopaedia Britannica*, 1967 ed., I, p. 707.

4   Ibid.

5   Frank G. Menke, *The Encyclopedia of Sports* (New York: A. S. Barnes and Company, 1953), p. 4.

6   *A New English Dictionary on Historical Principles*, p. 265.

7   Ibid.

8   McWhirter, "Amateurs," p. 707.

9   Ibid.

10   "Gentlemen Amateurs," *The Sporting Mirror*, I (April 1881), p. 80.

11   Edwin Daupier Brickwood, writing under pen name of "Argonaut," *The Arts of Rowing and Training* (London: Horace Cox, 1866), p. 152.

12   Peter C. McIntosh, "The British Attitude to Sport," *Sport and Society*, ed. by Alex Notan, (London: Bowes & Bowes, 1958), pp. 15-18.

13   William C. Ewing, *The Sports of Colonial Williamsburg* (Richmond, Virginia: The Dietz Press, 1937), pp. 1-2.

14   *Wisden Cricketer's Almanack 1963* (13 Bedford Sq., London WC1: Sporting Handbooks, Ltd., 1963), p. 1073.

15   Savage, *Games and Sports in British Schools and Universities*, p. 189.

16   H. Hewitt Griffin, *Athletics* (London: George Bell and Sons, 1891), p. 9.

17   *The Spirit of the Times*, March 1, 1873, p. 35.

18   Savage, *Games and Sports in British Schools and Universities*, p. 10-11.

19   Griffin, *Athletics*, p. 5.

20   Lehman, *The Complete Oarsman* (London: Methuen and Co., 1908), pp. 11-12.

21   Ibid.

22 Ibid., p. 12.

23 Ibid., p. 13.

24 Ibid., pp. 12-13.

25 Ibid., p. 13.

26 Ibid., p. 14.

27 Ibid., p. 16.

28 "Gentlemen Amateurs," *The Sporting Mirror*, I (April 1881), p. 79.

29 *The Spirit of the Times*, December 2, 1871, p. 251.

30 H. Hewitt Griffin, *Athletics*, pp. 13-14.

31 H. F. Wilkinson, *Modern Athletics* (London: Frederick Warne and Co., 1868), p. 16.

32 Edwin Daupier Brickwood, *The Arts of Rowing and Training*, p. 152.

33 Wilkes', *Spirit of the Times*, August 24, 1867, p. 8.

34 Menke, *The Encyclopedia of Sports*, p. 889.

35 Wilkes', *Spirit of the Times*, April 25, 1868, p. 148.

36 *The Spirit of the Times*, July 18, 1868, p. 387.

37 Wilkinson, *Modern Athletics*, p. 22.

38 Tintagel, "Pot Hunting," *The Sporting Mirror*, May 1881, pp. 122-23.

39 *The Spirit of Times*, December 19, 1869, p. 277.

40 *The Spirit of the Times*, October 2, 1869, p. 105.

41 *The Spirit of the Times*, March 1, 1873, p. 35.

42 *The Spirit of the Times*, December 28, 1872, p. 316.

43 Ibid.

44 Ibid.

45 Ibid.

46 *The Spirit of the Times*, March 1, 1873, p. 35.

47   Robert Korsgaard, "A History of the Amateur Athletic Union of the United States" (Unpublished report of a Type C [D.Ed.] project; Teachers College, Columbia University, 1952), p. 35.

48   *The Spirit of the Times*, April 27, 1872, p. 162.

49   Montague Shearman, *Athletics* (London: Longmans, Green, and Co., 1898), pp. 39, 206.

50   Montague, *Athletics*, p. 206.

51   Frederick William Janssen, *A History of American Amateur Athletics and Aquatics* (New York: Outing Company, Limited, 1887), p. 153.

52   Ibid.

53   Ibid., p. 157.

54   *The Spirit of the Times*, December 2, 1871, p. 251.

55   *The Spirit of the Times*, May 2, 1874, p. 273.

56   *The Spirit of the Times*, September 2, 1876, p. 101.

57   Robert Korsgaard, "A History of the Amateur Athletic Union of the United States," p. 39.

58   Ibid., pp. 39-40.

59   Harry Alexander Scott, *Competitive Sports in Schools and Colleges* (New York: Harpers, 1951), p. 19.

60   Howard J. Savage, *et. al. American College Athletics*, Bulletin no. 23 (New York: The Carnegie Foundation for the Advancement of Teaching, 1929), p. 36.

61   Korsgaard, "A History of the Amateur Athletic Union of the United States," p. 40.

62   *The Spirit of the Times*, April 12, 1879, p. 224.

63   *The Spirit of the Times*, March 22, 1879.

64   Savage, *American College Athletics*, p. 37.

65   Ibid.

66   R. D. Burnell, *Henley Regatta A History* (London: Oxford University Press, 1957), p. 3.

67   Lehman, *The Complete Oarsman*, pp. 248-49.

68   Burnell, *Henley Regatta a History*, p. 46.

69 Lehman, *The Complete Oarsman*, pp. 249-50.

70 Ibid., p. 252.

71 Burnell, *Henley Regatta a History*, p. 45.

72 Griffin, *Athletics*, p. 17.

73 Pelham Warner, *Lord's: 1787-1945* (London: George G. Harrap and Co., Ltd., 1946), p. 76.

74 Savage, *Games and Sports in British Schools and Universities*, p. 195.

75 Ibid., p. 196.

76 *Wisden Cricketers' Almanack* (100th ed., London: Sporting Handbooks, Ltd., 1963), pp. 138-40, 1073.

77 Lehman, *The Complete Oarsman*, p. 252.

78 R. C. Lehman, *Rowing*, The Isthmian Library, No. 4 (London: A. D. Innes and Co., 1897), pp. 325-327.

79 Lehman, *The Complete Oarsman*, pp. 335-36.

80 Savage, *Games and Sports in British Schools and Universities*, p. 186.

81 Ibid., p. 194.

82 John H. Smith, "Northern Union Football," *The Encyclopaedia of Sports and Games*, II, (London: William Heineman, 1911), pp. 256-57.

83 Ibid., p. 256.

84 Savage, *Games and Sports in British Schools and Universities*, p. 195.

85 Smith, "Northern Union Football," p. 257.

86 Leslie Higdon, Administrative Officer of the Amateur Athletic Association (London), personal correspondence to the writer on July 14, 1969.

87 "Rules for all Competition Under A.A.A. Law," *The Encyclopaedia of Sports and Games*, I, (London: William Heineman, 1911), p. 115.

88 Ibid., p. 116.

89 Ibid., p. 123.

90 Janssen, *A History of American Amateur Athletics and Aquatics*, pp. 12-13.

91 Ibid., p. 13.

92   Korsgaard, "A History of the Amateur Athletic Union of the United States," pp. 70-93.

93   *The Spirit of the Times*, December 15, 1888, p. 738.

94   Savage, *American College Athletics*, p. 38.

95   Carl D. Voltmer, *A Brief History of the Intercollegiate Conference of Faculty Repre-sentatives* (New York: Western Intercollegiate Conference, 1935), pp. 6-7.

96   Howard J. Savage, *American College Athletics*, p. 43.

97   Ibid.

98   Ibid.

99   Ibid., pp. 41-42.

100 "Summer Baseball vs. Amateurism," *Outing*, 67 (February 1916), pp. 455-61.

101 Savage, *American College Athletics*, p. 42.

102 *Proceedings of the First Annual Meeting* (The Intercollegiate Athletic Association, 1906), p. 33.

103 Savage, *American College Athletics*, p. 42.

104 *Proceedings of the Seventh Annual Convention* (The National Collegiate Athletic Association, 1912), p. 34.

105 Savage, *American College Athletics*, p. 43.

106 Ibid., p. 49.

107 Ibid.

108 Ibid., p. 50.

109 *XIth Olympiad Berlin, 1936 Handbook General Rules and Programmes of the Competitions* (Berlin: Organisationskomitee Fur Die XI Olympiade, 1936), pp. 28-33.

110 Savage, *American College Athletics*, p. 43.

111 Ibid., p. 44.

112 *XIth Olympiad Berlin, 1936 Handbook General Rules and Programmes of the Competition*.

CHAPTER VI

Amateurism and the Modern Olympic Movement

INTRODUCTION

The Olympic Games were revived just prior to the end of the nineteenth century. This began a new movement which was destined to have a monumental effect on amateurism throughout the world. It was not long after 1896 that the idea of an Olympic festival every four years captured the attention of the entire sports world. The magnetism of the Olympic Games soon elevated the status of an Olympic gold medal to a position where it was regarded as one of the highest awards in athletic competition. To compete and win became the almost universal goal of outstanding athletes throughout the world.

As the Olympic Games evolved toward this position of esteem, the role of the International Olympic Committee in the development and control of amateurism during the twentieth was of tremendous importance. Since participating in the Olympic Games became the goal of most world class athletes, the Olympic Movement was in a unique position to influence amateurism as a category of sport on every level throughout the world. This control was established by the development of a working relationship, which still exists, between international sports federations, the national Olympic committees, and the International Olympic Committee. Because of this unique set of circumstances, the development of amateurism as an international phenomenon during the twentieth century can be effectively studied by reviewing the history of the International Olympic Committee and its relationship with the various international sports federations. This chapter is a survey of this history as it relates to amateurism.

AMATEURISM AND THE BEGINNING OF THE MODERN OLYMPIC MOVEMENT

Numerous social and technological changes had taken place in the late nineteenth century. At that time a powerful laboring class was emerging, nationalistic feelings were high, and influential sports associations were developing. In this setting Pierre de Coubertin began to make plans in about 1892 for the founding of the modern Olympic Games. In January of 1894, de Coubertin sent out the second of two circulars to world sports societies in an effort to interest them in his plans for the modern Olympic Games. In this circular de Coubertin expressed his views on amateurism.

> *Above all stands the question of conserving for athletics the noble and chivalric character it had in the past, so that it may hereafter play efficiently the same role in the education of modern peoples which Greek leaders assigned to it. Human imperfection steadily tends to transform the Olympic athlete into the gladiator of the circus. We must choose between two athletic formulae which are contradictory. To defend themselves against the spirit of sordid gain and professionalism which threatens a successful invasion, amateurs in most countries have established a complicated legislation full of incompatible compromises; too often, moreover, it is the letter and not the spirit of the law which controls. There is a need of reform but before inaugurating it, discussion is preemptory. The subjects prepared for the congress relate to the compromises and contradictions of existing amateur regulations. The guarantee of the international understanding which we wish to promote, if not to be realized just yet, at least to be furthered. The reestablishment of the Olympic Games on a basis and under conditions conformable to the needs of modern life would bring together every four years representatives of all nations, and it is permissable to suppose that these peaceful and courteous contests would supply the best of internationalisms.* [1]

To de Coubertin the real issue of the 1894 congress was not amateurism, but the revival of the Olympic Games. Nevertheless, he used the problem of amateurism as bait to attract people to the congress. [2] [3] This fact appears to be indirectly evident in the outline of the program for the congress in 1894 in which the items related to re-establishing of the Olympic Games appear almost as an appendage, rather than the main concern. De Coubertin appears to have had considerable insight into the problems of amateurism during the 1890's as is indicated by the main outline of the program for the congress in 1894 which sums up most of the basic questions and problems related to amateurism during this era. The outline is as follows:

AMATEURISM AND PROFESSIONALISM

1. Definition of an amateur: reasons for the definiton. Possibility and utility of an international definintion.

2. Suspension, disqualification, and rehabilitation. Facts which respectively sustain them and the means of proof.

3. Can we justly maintain a distinction between different sports, in regard to what constitutes an amateur, especially in racing (gentlemen riders) and pigeon shooting? Can a professional in one sport be an amateur in another?

4. The value of medals or other prizes. Must it be limited? What steps are to be taken concerning those who sell prizes won by them?

5. Gate money. Can it be divided between the associations interested or the contestants? Can it be used toward the expenses of the visiting association? Within what limits can the expenses of teams or their members be borne, either by their own or the opposing association?

6. Can the general defintion of an amateur be applied to all sports? Must it comprise special restrictions for cycling, rowing, track athletics, etc.?

7. May an amateur bet? Does betting disqualify? Means to arrest the development of betting.

OLYMPIC GAMES

8. The possibility of re-establishing the Olympic Games. Under what conditions would it be feasible?

9. Conditions to govern participants. List of sports to be represented. Frequency of the re-established Olympic games, etc.

10. The nomination of an international committee for carrying out the plans adopted. [4]

At the athletic congress on June 22, 1894, the following resolutions regarding amateurism were passed.

1. Any infraction of the rules of amateurism disqualifies as an amateur. A disqualified amateur may be reinstated on proof of ignorance of the law, or of good faith.

2. The value of objects of art given as prizes need not be limted. Whosoever obtains money by means of the prizes he has won loses his qualification as an amateur.

131

3. Gate money may be divided between societies, but never between competitors. Teams may have their traveling expenses paid by the societies to which they belong.

4. Betting is incompatible with amateurism. Societies should prevent or restrict betting by every means in their power, and especially by opposing any official organization of betting in the grounds in which competitions are held.

5. The answers to items three and six on the aggenda for the June 22 meeting were no.

6. The committee considers that the tendency off all sports should be toward pure amateurism, and that there is no permanent ground in any sport to legitimize money prizes.

7. As regards horse-racing, pigeon shooting, and yachting, the general defintion of amateur does not for the moment apply.[5]

The resolution passed at the congress which founded the Olympic Games in 1894 was apparently the definition of amateurism used at the Olympics in 1896 and 1900.

AMATEURISM AND THE OLYMPIC MOVEMENT: 1900-1921

The resolution passed in 1894 in no way settled the growing problem of determining who was eligible for the Olympic Games and other international sports contests; therefore, in 1902 the International Olympic Committee sent the following questionnaire in three languages to all sports associations in an effort to collect data upon which to develop a workable definition.[6]

I. What is your definition of an amateur?

II. Will you kindly send us copies of rules and regulations of your union and club?

III. What are the chief questions which you would suggest for discussion at the Brussels' Congress?[7]

According to Pierre de Coubertin, the responses to these questions "...did not produce very many or any luminous replies."[8] [9] For the 1904 Olympic Games in St. Louis the statement on amateurism was revised to read as follows:

No person shall be eligible to compete in any athletic meeting, game, or entertainment given or sanctioned by this Union [Amateur Athletic Union of the United States] who has:

1. Received or competed for compensation or reward in any form, for the display, exercise, or example of his skill in or knowledge of any athletic exercise, or for rendering personal service of any kind to any athletic organisation, or for becoming or continuing a member of any atletic organisation; or

2. Has entered any competition under a name other than his own, or from a club of which he was not at that time a member in good standing; or

3. Has knowingly entered any competition open to any professional or professionals, or has knowingly competed with any professional for any prize or token; or

4. Has issued or allowed to be issued in his behalf any challenge to compete against any professional, or for money; or

5. Has pawned, bartered, or sold any prize won in athletic competition; or

6. Is not a registered athlete.[10]

The following statements on amateurism were agreed upon by the International Olympic Congress in 1905 in Brussels.

1. An amateur is any person who has never taken part in a race or meeting or competition open to all comers, for a prize in money or for gate money, or with professionals, and who has not been during his lifetime a professional or hired teacher of physical exercises.

2. The Congress thinks that a professor or hired teacher of physical exercise should be considered an amateur for the sports that he does not teach, on condition that in the practice of these sports he has never committed an act of professionalism, and under control of the federation to which the association belongs where he wishes to practise them as an amateur.

3. The acceptance of actually incurred travelling expenses is not considered as professionalism.[11]

For the 1908 Olympic Games in London, the major regulations pertaining to the question of amateurism were as follows:

Art. 3: *The Olympic Games are exclusively confined to amateurs.*
Art. 4: *The definition of an amateur qualified to compete in any sport will be found under the detailed regulations under the heading of that sport.*
Art. 7: *The amateur status of every competitor must be guaranteed by the association which, in his own country, governs the sport in which he desires to enter as a competitor, or, where no such governing committee or association exists, by a special committee of experts appointed by the Olympic Committee of that country.*
Art. 8: *All entries will be made through the governing associations, or where associations do not exist by amateur clubs, through the Olympic Committee of each country, who will be responsible to the British Olympic Association for the competence of such ama-*

teur clubs to guarantee that the competitors entered by them are amateurs within the conditions laid down in the British Olympic Association's regulations for the several sports, as set forth in the programme of the Olympiad.[12]

In essence, the amateur definitions which existed in Great Britain for sports were the definitions used for the 1908 Games.*

One consequence of this procedure for determining the amateur rules used in the 1908 Olympics was that the host country tended to hold its own athletes rigidly to its own defintions, but had "...to accept entries from other countries upon the basis of the amateur definitions in force in those countries, and in the particular sport in each country..."[14] This situation prompted the demands for unifications of the amateur rules following the games.[15]

The amateur codes as used for continental and transatlantic competition around 1908 "...stipulated that one ceased to be an amateur:

1. by accepting a cash prize;
2. by competing against a professional;
3. by receiving a salary as a teacher or instructor of physical exercise;
4. by taking part in competition open to all comers."[16]

In these interpretations which came from England, item four clearly conveys the custom of keeping competition closed to athletes who do not belong to the right group or social level of society.[17]

Following the London Games, the *Sporting Life*, an English journal, became interested in the subject of amateurism and set out to gather information on the issue from representatives of sport throughout the world. After a few months, the journal turned over to the International Olympic Committee a huge file of over 150 items. De Coubertin's attitude about the data collected by the *Sporting News* was not exactly enthusiastic. He claimed that after "looking carefully through it [the file] with the hope of finding new elements, I [he] had to acknowledge that here too was only the same old thing."[18] From the material collected by the *Sporting News*, Count de Bertier de Sauvigny prepared and submitted an exhaustive report to the International Olympic Committee in 1909. The report concluded that the International Olympic Committee should ask the various sports federations, associations, and societies associated with the IOC their views on the question of amateurism.[20] This was done by means of the following questionnaire in 1909:

1. *Do you agree that one should not be able to be a professional in one sport and an amateur in another?*

*For a compilation of definitions of amateurism used by various sports organizations in England, Scotland, Ireland, Australia and some others in 1908 see Appendix E in The Official Report of the Olympic Games of 1908 by the British Olympic Council[13]

2. Do you agree on the other hand that a teacher may be an amateur in sports he does not teach?

3. Do you agree that an amateur who has become a professional may not regain his amateur status? Do you permit exceptions to this rule? if so, which?

4. Do you permit reimbursement of transport and hotel expenses to an amateur? Up to what limit?

5. Do you agree that one can lose one's amateur status by simple contact with a professional?[21] [22]

De Coubertin claims that he worked with Count de Bertier de Sauvigny in preparing the report for the 1909 IOC meeting in Berlin. In addition, he claims that he proposed solutions to the problems of amateurism that the committee members where apprehensive about approving. According to de Coubertin, this resulted in a modification of the report.[23] In 1913 He explained his views on the situation as follows:

Its conclusions were frank and distinct; how much trouble, dispute, and marking time we would have avoided by adopting them. And in particular we would have considerably weakened, if not nipped in the bud, that baleful phenomenon, the sham amateur, which began to spring up...Any source of continuous direct profit of appreciable value was denounced—considerable indulgence was requested for minor offenses. The principle of requalification was permitted on the condition that there was one sole tribunal to apply it, completely independent and offering every safeguard—a sort of The Hague Court for sport. The oath was laid down—a detailed oath in writing for ordinary competitions, a verbal oath taken on each competitor's national flag for Olympic celebrations. Payment was allowed in circumstances justifying it on condition that it only covered transport and accommodation, not pocket money.

We strictly refuse to allow that an amateur could be deprived of his status simply for having competed with a professional and even less for competing with an athlete suspended by his federation or having taken part in a competition which it did not authorize—an astounding and absurd claim which more than one federation had managed to impose.

A clear distinction was made between the teaching side and the professional side. Conditions were put forward as a foundation for a legislation based on all these ideas, which were revolutionary yet wise and in line with the democratic and cosmopolitan future which was coming into being and to the impending demands of which I liked to draw my IOC colleagues' attention. They were much less reluctant to accept them than one would have thought, and the most aristocratic of the group were not the most reactionary, far from it.

However, several of them were apprehensive, and keeping in contact with opinion in their countries' sports circles, they were afraid of violent clashes. Modifications to several parts of the Report, in the form at least, were requested. The text appearing in the "Olympic Review" of August 1909 is the revised text. I should have liked to find the original text as presented to the IOC in Berlin. However, it is not in its place in the archives and I cannot lay hand to it.

This apprehension which I have mentioned led the Committee to pick out a few questions from the Report in order to submit them to the federations and groups concerned.[24]

De Coubertin's observation of the responses to the questions sent out by the IOC in 1909 were as follows:

The replies were madly contradictory. There did not seem to be any agreement whatever between one sport and another in the same country, or between different countries for the same sport. Statements, no arguments. Inconsistencies, nothing really considered. In making this observation, in retrospect, I appreciated the apprehension of my colleagues who were afraid to "dare." Perhaps they saved us alot of trouble in this way. But from then on amateur problems lost what little interest they still had for me. I stuck to my conviction that [a] teacher and professional should not be put on the same footings, that the oath—not as a show, but detailed and signed—is the only way of being informed of the sporting past of an athlete, as a false oath disqualifies him forever in every field, that class distinction should never play a role in sport, that the time when you could ask an athlete to pay for his travel and accommodation is over, that amateur status has nothing to do with the administrative rules of a particular sports group, etc. and that there are a lot of sham amateurs against whom action should be taken and a lot of sham professionals to whom indulgence should be shown, etc.[25]

Although there were varying opinions expressed regarding the issue of such matters as money for expenses, reinstatment and disqualifications by respondents to questions sent out by the IOC, there was general agreement "...that an amateur is an athlete who follows sports for sport's sake, and not for any pecuniary inducement."[26]

In spite of these efforts to develop a universally acceptable definition of amateurism in time for the 1912 Olymic Games in Stockholm, no solution was agreed upon. Therefore, the Olympic Games in 1912 had the problem of defining an amateur. This was a "delicate" task, because "...the various athletic associations in various countries had long ago adopted such widely varying laws in this respect."[27] Consequently, the regulations regarding amateurism established for the Games were essentially the same as for the 1908 Games in London. According to the report of the Swedish Olympic Committee, international federations existed for only cycling, football, and swimming in 1912.* As a result, the Swedish Olympic Committee was forced to formulate specific definitions of an amateur for most sports in which competition was held.** The general amatuer rule which served as a norm for developing the specific eligibility rules for the various sports was as follows:

The competition shall be confined to amateurs according to the following definition:

> *An amateur is one who has never*
> *1. competed for a money prize or for monetary consideration, or in any way drawn pecuniary gain from the exercise of sport;*
> *2. competed against a professional;*
> *3. taught in any branch of sport for payment;*
> *4. sold, pawned, hired out or exhibited for payment, any prize won in competition.*[31]

The report by the Swedish Olympic Committee of the Olympic Games in 1912 indicates that a definition of amateur was far from being universally understood and agreed upon at that time.[32] However, the Olympic Games in 1912, as well as in other years, were instrumental in bringing about some uniformity in the defining of amateurism as well as some understanding of amateurism.

POST WORLD WAR I ERA: 1921-1926

Largely due to the interruption of the Olympic Movement by World War I, no major decisions regarding amateurism took place between 1912 and 1921. However, in 1921, an important congress involving the International Olympic Committee, the International Sports Federations and the National Olympic Committees took place at Lausanne, Switzerland. At this congress, the representatives officially established the following procedure for deter-

---

*Other information indicates that international federations existed for yachting and skating at this time also.

**For a compilation of the amateur definitions used in the 1912 Olympic Games, consult the Official Report of the Olympic Games in Stockholm 1912[12] or "A study of Amateurism in Sports" by Eugene A. Glader.[30]

mining the amateur status of participants for the Olympic Games:

A. That the contests in the Olympic Games be open only to amateurs as herein defined.
B. That the definition of an amateur for each sport be that of the International Federation governing such sport.
C. That the National Federation, which in any country governs a particular sport must certify on the entry form that each competitor is an amateur according to the rules of the international federation of that sport, and this certificate must be countersigned by the National Olympic Committee of that country, which must also declare its belief that the competitor is an amateur under the definition of the International Federation concerned. (The international rule must be understood to contain a minimum severity rule, but every National Federation is entitled to make that rule more restrictive in its own country.)
D. That in the matter of protests on the grounds of the amateur status of an entrant, the International Federation of the sport in which such entry was made shall decide such protest. [33]

This pronouncement was not a definition of an amateur, but a clear statement indicating that the various international sports federations were to determine who was an amateur and who was eligible to compete in the sports over which they had jurisdiciton at the Olympic Games. From this procedural statement in 1921, the eligibility rules for the Olympic Games gradually became more specific and restrictive until 1971. Since this procedure did not resolve the problem of defining an amateur or of determining who was eligible to compete in the Olympic Games, another congress involving the International Olympic Committee and delegates from the National Olympic Committees and the International Sports Federations was held in 1925 at Prague. By bringing delegates of different International Sports Federations and the National Olympic Committees together with the IOC, many international sports leaders hoped that a uniform definition of an amateur, applicable to all sports, would be decided. However, the congress itself did not have the power to force its decisions on the various sports federations. It could only recommend a definition of an amateur to the various federations. [34] Nevertheless, the impact of the decisions at the Prague Congress on most, if not all, international sports federations appears to have been significant.

The two major issues of amateurism discussed at the Prague Congress were 1) whether there should be a distinction between an instructor or professor and a professional, and 2) whether amateurs should be permitted payment for "broken time." [35] The following statement regarding amateurism and eligibility for all athletes at the Olympic Games was agreed upon at the Technical Congress at Prague.

1. Amateurism.

The amateur status as defined by the respective International Federations shall apply to athletes taking part in the Olympic Games.

At the same time, all athletes taking part in the Games must comply with, as a minimum, the following conditions:

A. Must not be a professional in any branch of Sport,

B. Must not have been re-instated as an Amateur after knowingly becoming a Professional.

C. Must not have received compensation for lost salaries.

The International Associations and the National Olympic Committees are requested to study the suggestions contained in the articles 4 and 7 of the report issued by the Commissionn on Amateurism, at the Congress, viz:

4. Trainers, Advisors, and Instructors, and Coaches who teach competitive games for money directly or indirectly can neither compete in the Olympic Games nor serve as Judges or members of the Juries. Professors or Teachers who do not specifically train or teach competitive Sports and exercises may take part in the Games and serve as Judges and Members of the Juries.

7. Lengthy sporting competitions which take place in a country far away from that of the competitor are to be condemned, and it is recommended as a general rule that no competitor remains from his home more than one fortnight in a year to take part in Sporting competitions. At the same time it is recongized that for important international competitions such as the Olympic Games and National competitions in very large countries, certain exceptions are necessary. These exceptions should be infrequent and rigidly controlled. [36]

In order to personalize and hopefully to guarantee conformity to the amateur rule, the International Olympic Committee also ruled that all participants in the Olympic Games must declare their amateur qualifications by signing the following oath. "I, the undersigned, declare on my honour that I am an amateur according to the Olympic Rules of amateurism."[37] This was the first time such a declaration was necessary in order to participate in the Games.

AMATEURISM AND THE OLYMPIC MOVEMENT: 1926-1940

In spite of all the effort put forth at the Prague Congress in 1925 to develop a uniform definition of an amateur, the issue of payment for "broken-time" emerged again in 1926 and 1927. In 1926 the International Football Association met in Rome and agreed on a formula for compensating employees for lost wages. This formula was then preesented to the International Olympic Committee for approval because it was not in harmony with the rules established at Prague in 1925. On August 8, 1927, the executive committee of the International Olympic Committee met and ruled that the International Football Federation could take part in the 1928 Olympic Games and agreed "that the salary paid by an employer to an athlete who is absent from his work whilst taken (sic) part in competition in which the I.F.A. permits compensation for broken-time...will at the request of the employer be repaid to him by the National Football Association concerned, and the player himself not receiving directly any compensation."[38]

The intent of this agreement was to allow for a temporary acceptance of the decision on "broken-time" arrived at by the International Football Association Congress in Rome in 1926, since it was too late to call the entire International Olympic Committee together before the 1928 Games. The intent of the executive committee was to rule on a dimension of the "broken-time" issue which they felt was not considered at the congress in Prague in 1925.[39]

The purported purpose of this decision regarding compensation for "broken-time" by the International Football Association was to eliminate the anomaly at the time of regarding an employee who received pay from his employer while away from his job as an amateur, while an athlete whose employer would not pay him, but accepted money from a third party, was considered a professional. A related problem in amateurism over the years has been the situation where a salaried worker who continued to be paid while away from his job and competing in athletics was considered an amateur, but an hourly wage earner who continued to receive wages while participating in athletics away from his job was considered a professional.

Although this decision was an interim decision by the executive committee of the International Olympic Committee applicable only to the 1928 Olympic Games, the British Football Association withdrew from the International Football Association and did not participate in the 1928 Olympic Games in protest of this decision.[40] At the regularly scheduled meeting of the International Olympic Committee on August 3, 1928 in Amsterdam after the Games that year, the new rules of the International Football Association were rejected as not being in accordance with the rules for the Olympic Games.[41] This decision reaffirmed that the definition of an amateur agreed upon at Prague in 1925 was still the official standard of eligibility for the

Olympic Games, and no-exceptions were to be allowed.

However, the issue of "broken-time" did not disappear. The next problem relates to the issue of "broken-time" involved a disagreement over what was a holiday or vacation with pay and what was a "broken-time" payment. Consequently, the issue was discussed again at the April, 1929, meeting of the International Olympic Committee. At this time no decision was reached, and it was agreed to place the issue on the agenda for the May 1930 meeting in Berlin.[42] Part of the reason why the issue of "broken-time kept arising was the increasing number of major tournaments or championships and the inevitable need and/or desire of world class athletes to train longer and compete more often in major competition in order to prepare for contests such as the Olympic Games and other world tournaments.

Having athletes participate in several major trounaments was also found to be helpful by national sports federations and the National Olympic Committees as they sought to select their best athletes to represent their respective countries in the Olympic Games. Preliminary athletic meetings were also being found to be a good way for organizations to raise money.

Because the increasing number of major tournaments seems to have been at the core of the issue of "broken-time," Count de Baillet-Latour, President of the International Olympic Committee, cautioned the members of the IOC in 1930 and 1931 about what he considered were "...an excessive number of spectacular sports meetings where competitors are few and the spectators are numerous."[43] Count de Baillet-Latour stated his concern over the issue in his opening address at the Berlin Congress in 1930 with these remarks:

> Unfortunately, whatever may be your verdict on this subject of the definition of the International Football Federation; whatever the methods you may suggest for bringing it into line with the rules governing Olympic qualification; whatever may be the formula, which you may decide on to do away with the existing irregularities and inconvenience — you will only succeed in disguising under another mask the actual abuses, if amateur sport remains as it is at present. The excessive number of international matches makes it quite impossible to exclude broken-time or compensation paid in some indirect and underhand way. To definitely suppress broken-time without trying to find a solution of the question would encourage certain practices, which are indulged in today for propaganda purposes and would not be justified; it is absolutely necessary that sports should be neither political or commercial; that the number of important matches sportfetes should be very considerably reduced so that in order to take part in sport the period of the annual holiday would suffice. The holiday added to the free times which each individual has at his or her disposal Sat-

*urday afternoons and Sundays, would allow the amateur to in-
dulge in sports little more than a third of the year, and this is quite
sufficient.*[44]

The decision of the Berlin Conference was to reaffirm as the official eligibility rules for the 1932 Olympic Games the statement on amateurism
agreed upon in Prague in 1925.[45] Further clarification of the amateur code
was made in October 1930 at the Council of Delegates of the International
Olympic Committee in Paris. The ruling agreed to at this time for the 1932
Olympic Games was:

*An athlete taking part in the Olympic Games must satisfy the fol-
lowing conditions:*

*a. Must not be, or knowlingly have become, a professional in
the sport for which he is entered, or any other sport.*

*b. Must not have received reimbursement or compensation for
loss of salary.*

*A holiday given under the normal conditions of a business or
profession or a holiday accorded under the same conditions on
the occasion of the Olympic Games, and provided that it does not
lead to reinbursement for lost salary, direct or indirect, does not
come within the provisions of Section b.*[46]

One of the results of the many discussions and agreements between 1925
and 1930 by members of the International Olympic Committee and the representatives of the various international sports federations was progress
toward a standardized definition of an amateur among the nations engaging
in international competition. However, just as there appeared to be some
hope that a permanent agreement on a definition of amateurism had been
reached, new problems developed. One such problem involved the so-
called "contamination" principle which implied that an amateur lost his
amateur standing by competing with or against a professional. Count de
Baillet-Latour's suggestion for solving this problem in 1932 was:

*Why not simplify the whole matter by doing away with the
compulsory disqualification of an amateur simply because he
may have competed against a professional regardless of the circumstances? The foregoing problem would be much less complicated if we were to differentiate between organized competition
and social or informal competition. In my opinion, we should disregard the latter entirely in so far that participation in such competition should have no bearing upon the amateur or professional
status of the individuals. We should engage with others in physical activities of a friendly, social, or recreational nature. This even
if the said activities are athletic pastimes, provided of course that*

such participation is not part of an organized program in the nature of a tournament or a series of scheduled events in which records are kept of the standing of competitors, awards are given, championships determined, admission fees charged and special publicity made. Professionals and amateurs should be allowed to intermingle promiscuously regardless of past or present practices in such informal recreation where fellowship is the chief incentive. Under an arrangement of this kind we should be concerned with an individual's classification only in organized competitions. In this manner there would be no intermingling of amateurs with professionals except in the most unusual circumstances when special authorization is granted by the federation governing the sport. [47]

The extent of the problems and disagreements about amateurism that had quickly arisen following the 1932 Olympic Games is evident from reading the minutes of the July, 1933, meeting of the executive committee of the International Olympic Committee with delegates of the International Sports Federation. [48] Recommendations from this meeting were then presented to the International Olympic Committee which approved on June 8, 1933, the measure listed below to combat semi-professionalism. The IOC sent these recommendations to the "International Authorities of Sports."*

1. All correspondence and negotiations about competitions and touring of athletes in foreign countries shall be sanctioned and supervised by the National Federation of the competitor's country and the National Federation of the country visited.

2. All payments of the competitor's actual expenses must be made not to the competitor but to the Federation of his own country.

3. Reimbursement for actual travelling and other expenses of the competitor shall be given, as far as possible, not in cash, but in kind, providing tickets, lodging, etc...

4. An amateur must not accept or in any manner receive any money or other pecuniary gain in going to, attending, or returning from a sports-meeting other than his actual outlay for transportation, meals, and lodging. Under no circumstances shall the amount paid or accepted for expenses exceed one second-class railway fare, (including sleeping accommodation) or one first-class steamship accommodation, and one pound (gold) or the equivalent per day for meals and lodgings.

5. The duration of competition in foreign countries shall not ex-

*This term apparently refers to representatives of national and international sport organization affiliated with the International Olympic Committee.

ceed 21 days in all per calendar year. Excluded from this rule shall be the time necessary for taking part in Olympic Games, official championships and international meetings, where countries are officially represented through Federations, whether by individuals or by teams.

6. In the interest of maintianing intact the high moral and sporting force of the Olympic Games — the greatest amateur sporting organization of the world — it seems desirable that the attention of all international and national authorities of sports should be called once again to the importance and high value of the two major formal guarantees for the pure amateurism of the participants; the countersigning of the entries from the amateur point of view and the Olympic Oath to be taken by the competitors.

A — International Federation of Sports, National Olympic Committees and National Associations of Sports are earnestly requested to refuse absolutely to countersign any entry to the Olympic Games if the competitor in question transgresses even in the smallest way the rules of amateurism. They shall disregard all thought of nation and consider solely the high principles of true amateur sport and the honour of the Olympic Games.

B — All National Olympic Committees are requested once again to elucidate to all sportsmen of their country the importance of the Olympic Oath as well as the shamefulness of giving an untrue and false declaration, because a false oath dishounours not only the person giving it but also the Nation, under whose banner he is competing.

7. To improve by all available means physical education in Schools, Colleges, and Universities of the Countries where it has heretofore been neglected, with the idea of making it possible to recruit future Olympic Competitors from among the youth.

8. It is desirable to get the leaders of University Sports to use their own Championships as preparation for the Olympic Games.

9. Amateurs are forbidden to compete with professionals without special permission being given in each case by the National Federation of which they are members and only in a meeting arranged for charitable or patriotic purposes.[49]

This resolution did not change the wording of the official amateur rules for the 1936 Olympic Games in Berlin. Thus, the official rules remained the same as for the 1932 Games.*[50] The IOC statement was essentially an at-

---

*For additional detail regarding the amateur rules used various international sports federations at

tempt to clarify existing rules and to communicate these interpretations to all international sports authorities, National Olympic Committees, and national sports associations. The problem of communicating rules and interpretations must have been as great, if not greater, in 1933, as it was in 1966 when Avery Brundage wrote, "I have been endeavoring to establish a uniform amateur definition for many years, but when you are dealing with 25 to 30 sports in 120 countries, in a score or more languages, it is not easy."[52]

In May, 1934, at a conference comprised of delegates of the International Sports Federations and an IOC sub-committee on amateurism, the following definition of an amateur was unanimously approved.

> An amateur is so called who practices sport solely for the love of it and for his own pleasure, without any intention from a spirit of greed (or) of obtaining any direct or indirect profit. Every International Federation shall regulate and control the application of this fundamental principle.[53]

This was the first attempt to define amateurism in a positive manner by the International Olympic Committee and representatives of the International Sports Federations. The first positive American definition was given in 1910 by a committee of the NCAA. These positive definitions sought to describe an amateur as what he was rather than what he was not. However, this effort over the years only added to the problems surrounding amateurism.

The first significant change in the definition of an amateur since 1925 was the statement that allowed the participation of teachers whose normal duties included elementary instruction in physical education or sport, providing that this was not their principal occupation.[54] It should be noted that this new rule still eliminated teachers who taught elementary level physical education as their principal position. This limited opening-of-the-door-to teachers was a small step in the right direction, but since the step was small, the issue was destined to rise again. In fact, in 1938 the issue rose between the International Skiing Federation and the International Olympic Committee. Apparently the president of the International Skiing Federation felt that skiing instructors* should be allowed to participate in the Olympic Games. The result of this dispute was the elimination of skiing from the Winter Games which were scheduled for Sapparo, Japan in 1940.[55] However, these Games were not held due to World War II.

Looking back at the period following the Olympic Congresses in Prague in 1925 and in Berlin in 1930, it appears that this was a time of relative harmony

the 1936 Olympic Games consult the Handbook, General Rules and Progammes of the Competition: XIth Olympiad Berlin, 1936.[51]

*The level of instruction is not clear from the reference.

concerning interpretations of amateurism. However, as years went by, the pressure to clarify and modify the rules increased. It seems that the International Olympic Committee and the international sports federations were always facing the problem of whether to liberalize or tighten up and enforce the definition of an amateur.

The decision of the International Olympic Committee in 1938 at Warsaw marked the beginning of major changes in the method of defining and clarifying who was eligible to compete in the Olympic Games. The changes approved at this time involved a slight liberalization of Article 2 of the amateur regulations and the addition of answers to ten questions regarding what were acceptable practices for amateurs who anticipated participation in the Olympic Games. From this date until 1970, the eligibility rules of the Olympic Games became progressively more detailed and conservative. The rewording of Article 2 of the amateur regulations in 1938 and the ten interpretive questions and answers which were included in the official rules for the Olympic Games are as follows:

Art. 2.—Must not have received reimbursement or compensation for loss of salary.

Article 2 does not apply: when holidays are taken under normal professional conditions on the occasion of the Olympic Games, provided that they do not constitute a camouflaged reimbursement—direct or indirect—of the salary lost; and when after personal investigation and as a very exceptional permission a payment is made directly to the employer of compensation for the wife, the mother or father of the athlete during his absence if he is the sole support of his family.

RESOLUTIONS REGARDING THE AMATEUR STATUS

1. Examination of the question of the nationalization of sports for political aims.

Reply:

The International Olympic Committee, establishing with much satisfaction that the aim it pursues meets with universal approval, can only rejoice at the emulation which the Olympic Movement has instigated among the different nations, and it extols the Governments which have adopted wide programmes of collective physical education with a view to perfecting popular sport.

Nevertheless, it regards as a danger to the Olympic ideal that by the side of the legitimate development of sports in conformity with the principles of amateurism there can be propagated certain tendencies which envisage above all a national exultation of success achieved rather than realization of the common and harmonious objective which is the essential Olympic Law.

2. Examination of the customary practice of preparing athletes for the Olympic Games in training camps. When this practice is permissible, how much time may it occupy without infringing on Olympic Regulations?
Answer:
The practice of interrupting an athlete's occupation be it studies or employment, in order to submit him to special training in an athletic camp for a period exceeding two weeks is not in accordance with the idea of the Olympic Games.

3. Can Olympic victors who have received presents from their governments be again allowed to participate in the Olympic Games?
Answer:
Participants who have received money presents or advantages of a material character shall not be admitted to the Olympic Games.

4. Is there universal respect paid to the ruling that a professional in one spot cannot be an amateur in another?
Reply
A professional in one sport is generally regarded as a professional in all other sports. In the opinion of the International Olympic Committee it is desirable that this rule be generally observed.

5. Position of professional sporting writers.
Reply:
In some countries athletes, solely due to their sporting achievements, have found positions in branches of journalism, in the theatre, or films, or in broadcasting. Such exploitation of sporting reputation does not accord either with the principles or with the spirit of the Olympic Games.

6. Doping of athletes.
Reply:
The use of drugs or artificial stimulants of any kind must be condemned strongly, and everyone who accepts or offers dope, no matter in what form, should not be allowed to participate in the Olympic Games.

7. Is not the payment of a lump sum to an individual team, with a view to obtaining his or its participation, a most serious detraction of the principle forbidding the making good of lost earnings?
Reply:
An amateur has the right to receive full reimbursement for his travelling, board, and lodging expenses when he takes part in the competition. But the expenses should not exceed one pound per

day, not including the expense of travel by motor car, aeroplane, steamer (saloon), train (second class). Every other recompense is prohibited.

8. What sum may be granted to an athlete as pocketmoney?
Reply:

An athlete can receive reimbursement of his normal expenditures, such as for: washing, bus and tram fares, etc., etc., on conditions that they do not exceed a maximum of three schillings daily.

9. Are the National Federations, National Olympic Committees or clubs authorized to come to a financial arrangement with an employer so as to assure that a participant will be restored to his post after an absence due to his taking part in an international competition?
Reply:

Participation in the Olympic Games should be regarded as a very high honour. This is the view of most employers, who are proud to have an Olympic athlete among their workers. Thus, there is no necessity to make financial arrangements for them. Supplementary grants paid in excess of the usual salary constitute a breach of the Olympic qualification regulation.

10. Can an indemnity be paid during his absence to the wife, mother or father of an athlete, if he is the sole support of his family.?
Reply:

The payment of such indemnity as a very special exception, after individual enquiry and in the form of a payment direct to the employer, is not regarded as reimbursement for lost salary.[56] [57]

POST-WORLD WAR II ERA: 1946-1952

World War II caused the cancellation of the Olympic Games scheduled for 1940 and 1944, and no meetings of the International Olympic Committee were held between 1939 and 1946. Since concerns about amateurism were relatively unimportant to everyone in this wartime period, the definition of an amateur issued in 1938 remained intact until 1946. In 1946 the International Olympic Committee resumed its meetings, and comments about amateurism appeared in the minutes as usual.

The main item on the agenda at the first post-war meeting was the election of a new president and vice-president of the IOC. Count de Baillet-Latour had died during the war years. The committee elected J. Sigfrid Edstrom from Sweden as president and Avery Brundage from the United States as vice-president.[58] Brundage was destined to exert considerable influence on amateurism during the next twenty-eight years.

During the first year of the renewed meetings of the International Olympic Committee, Avery Brundage was appointed chairman of a commission on amaterism.[59] In June 1947 this commission made its final report at the meeting at the IOC in Stockholm. At this time the IOC approved the following new statement that athletes participating in the Olympic Games had to sign.

> I, the undersigned, declare on my honor, that I am an amateur according to the rules of the International Federation governing my sport, that I have participated in sport solely for pleasure and for the physical, mental, and social benefits that I derive therefrom; that sport to me is nothing more than a recreation without material gain of any kind, direct or indirect, and that I am eligible in all respects for participation in the Olymic Games.[60] [61]

Some new interpretive statements about amateurism were also approved at this time. These statements were, in essence, the same as the first six questions and answers approved in 1938 and listed earlier in this chapter.[62] [63]

In spite of the fact that the International Olympic Committee appeared to have reaffirmed its position against "broken-time" payments then, the Committee made an exception for football (soccer) at the 1948 Olympic Games. Athletes under the jurisdiction of the International Football Federation were allowed to be reimbursed for the loss of salary.[64] This decision is of special interest because Avery Brundage, who, as indicated earlier, was vice-president of the International Olympic Committee and chairman of the special commission on amateurism in 1946-1947, wrote a strongly worded article against payment for "broken-time" in 1948.[65] The pressure to keep football in the Olympic Games must have been siginificant.

In the *Olympic Rules* booklet published in 1949* the new definition of an amateur devised in 1947 became paragraph 38 in the rules and read as follows:

> An amateur is one who participates and always has participated in sports solely for the pleasure and the physical, mental, or social benefits he derives therefrom, and to whom participation in sport is nothing more than recreation without material gain of any kind direct or indirect and in accordance with the rules of the International Federation concerned.[66]

With the placement of this definition in paragraph 38, the statement par-

---

*For the reader who may be interested in a compilation of definitions of amateurism for most Canadian amateur sports organizations in 1949 see the Proceeding: Second National Conference of Sports Governing Bodies.[67]

ticipants in the Olympic Games had to sign was reduced to the following: I the undesigned, declare on my honor that I am an amateur and fulfill the conditions stipulated by the Olympic rules."[68] These changes did not alter the definition or the significance of what each athlete signed.

In 1950 at the meeting of the International Olympic Committee in Copenhagen, two definitions of an amateur were proposed which would have given various international sports federations the responsibility for defining an amateur in their respective sports. The proposal by Mr. Fearnley was as follows:

> An amateur must fulfill the conditions of the amateur rules of the international (sic) Federation which governs his sport. If an International Federation adopts or practices amateur rules which are not in accordance with the Olympic spirit, the International Olympic Committee can withhold recognition of such International Federation or exclude same from participation in the Olympic Games.[69]

The second proposal by Mr. Ditlev Simonsen, Jr. was briefer and read as follows:

> An amateur is one who participates in sport in accordance with the rules of the International Federation which governs his sport. Said Federation must be recognized by the International Olympic Committee.[70]

These proposals are of interest because they are so similar to the rule of the International Olympic Committee in 1921. However the Committee was not ready to go this route, especially after a lengthy counter agrument by Avery Brundage.[71]

In 1951 a second exception to the Olympic Games amateur rules was approved. This time it was with the International Skiing Federation which had disagreed with the International Olympic Committee back in 1938 because ski instructors were not considered amateurs. The agreement approved by the International Skiing Federation and the Executive Committee of the International Olympic Committee was as follows:

> Ski teachers shall not be eligible unless:
> a. they teach as an incident to their main vocation or employment in a purely part-time manner,
> b. they teach elemetary skiing not including any kind of competitive skiing or coaching for competition,
> c. their reward differs in no way from that earned by their non-competing colleagues, that means that they capitalize under no circumstances of (on) their athletic fame or ability,
> d. that such teaching be discontinued at least 90 days before the

beginning of the Games.[72]

This rule differs from the 1938 rule which allowed participation by teachers whose regular duties included elementary instruction in physical education or sport, providing this was not their principal occupation. The new agreement with the International Skiing Federation allowed skiers whose main vocation was not teaching but did teach elementary skiing as a part-time job to participate in the Games.

AMATEURISM AND THE OLYMPIC MOVEMENT: 1952-1970

During the 1952 Olympic Games in Helsinki, Avery Brundage was elected president of the international Olympic Committee, a position he held for twenty years. During this period he became known throughout the world as the leading spokesman for amateurism.

One issue regarding amateurism that emerged during the 1950's was the amateur status of athletes in communist countries. The entry of such athletes into international competition resulted in the birth of the term "state amateurs." Whether the privileges of athletes in communist countries should cause them to be classified as professionals rather than amateurs has remained an issue until this time. The status of students in the United States who were receiving financial aid primarily because of their athletic ability and of soldiers who were receiving special privileges in the armed forces was also being questioned at this time. To clarify the rules regarding these types of abuses, the following interpretive paragraph was added to the official rules for the Olympic Games in 1956.

PSEUDO AMATEURS

Individuals subsidized by governments, educational institutions, or business concerns because of their athletic ability are not amateurs. Business or industrial concerns sometimes employ athletes or sponsor athletic teams for their advertising value. The athletes are given paid employment with little work to do and are free to practice and compete at all times. For national aggrandizement, governments occasionally adopt the same methods and give athletes positions in the Army, on the police force or in a government office. They also operate training camps for extended periods. Some colleges and universities offer outstanding athletes scholarships, and inducements of various kinds. Recipients of these favours which are granted only because of athletic ability are not amateurs.[73]

Another controversial change in the rules for the 1956 Games involved the wording of a new statement which participating athletes had to sign. This statement said:

I, the undersigned, declare on my honour that I am and intend to *remain* an amateur and fulfill the conditions stipulated by the Olympic Rules."*[74] [75]

The phrase "and intend to remain" was added because some people were unhappy over the fact that so many athletes were using the Olympic Games as a springboard to lucrative professional careers. People such as Brundage beleived that this was wrong and hypocritical if one had stated that he "...always participated in sport solely for pleasure and for the physical, mental, and social benefits he derives therefrom, and to whom participation is nothing more than a recreation without material gain of any kind, direct or indirect."[76] However, this effort to question athletes' motives and goals was soon found to be unenforcible, impractical, and subject to considerable misunderstanding. Therefore the phrase "and intends to remain" was eliminated in 1956.[77]

In 1957 the following statements, regarding the meaning of the famous Rule Number 26* on amateurism, were added as Item Number 6 to the other interpretive statements about the Rule.

THE FOLLOWING ARE NOT ELIGIBLE FOR OLYMPIC COMPETITIONS:

a. Those who have participated for money, for merchandise prizes easily converted into money or, without the permission of the National Federation under general approval of the International Federation concerned, for prizes exceeding 40 dollars in value.

b. Those who have been paid for training or coaching others for organized competitions.

c. Those who have capitalized in any way on their athletic fame by profiting commercially therefrom or by accepting special inducements of any kind to participate.

d. Those who have accepted for expenses reimbursement in excess of the actual outlay.

e. Those who have decided to become professional athletes and are participating to enhance their professional value.

f. Those who have neglected their usual vocation or employment for competitive sport whether at home or abroad.[78]

The wording of the other interpretive statements in the rules at this time was as follows:

1. Making capital out of sports for political purposes.

The International Olympic Committee notes with great satisfac-

---

*Underscoring added by author.

**Since 1949 paragraph or rule no. 38 contained the definition of an amateur.

tion that its efforts are universally approved, it rejoices in the enthusiasm which the Olympic Movement has encouraged among the different nations and it congratulates those which, with a different view of encouraging popular sports, have adopted vast programs of physical education.

It considers, however, as dangerous to the Olympic ideals that besides the proper development of sports in accordance with the principles of amateurism, certain tendencies exist which aim primarily at national exaltation of the results gained instead of the realization that the sharing of friendly effort and rivalry is the essential aim of the Olympic Games.

2. Training Camps

The practice of interrupting the occupation of an athlete (studies or employment) to put him in a camp for athletes for over two weeks of special training is not in accord with the ideals of the Olympic Games.

3. Professionals

A professional in one sport is considered a professional in all other sports. In the opinion of the International Olympic Committee, this rule should have general observance.

4. Doping of athletes

The use of drugs or artificial stimulants of any kind is condemned and any person offering or accepting dope, in any form whatsoever, cannot participate in the Olympic Games.

5. National Olympic Committees are reminded that, while the Olympic Games welcome the Youth of the World, it is a physical impossibility to accomodate all that Youth, and are asked to use discretion and send to the Games only competitors of Olympic caliber.

7. If a competitor is paid for the use of his name or picture, or for a radio or television appearance, in connection with commercial advertising, it is capitalization of athletic fame as described above. Even if no payment is made, such practices are to be deplored, since in the minds of many, particularly the young, they undermine the exalted position rightly held by amateur champions.[79]

The newly stated rules and clarifying statements did not solve the problems. This had always been the experience of attempts to define amateurism. The numerous violations of the amateur rules at the Olympic Games were obvious to everyone.[80] Therefore, another commission was established in 1960 to study the problem.[81] As the concerns about amateurism mounted at this time. Brundage stated that "One reason our rules have not always been followed is that they have been interpreted differently in different places."[82] This view led to a more detailed statement on amateurism which was approved in June, 1962, at the meetings of the International Olympic Committee in Moscow. The new wording of Article 26 and its official interpretations were:

ARTICLE 26

An amateur is one who participates and always has participated in sport as an avocation without material gain of any kind. One does not qualify:

a. If he has not a basic occupation designed to insure his present and future livelihood;

b. If he receives or has received remuneration for participation in sport;

c. If he does not comply with the Rules of the International Federation concerned, and the official interpretations of this Rule number 26.

OFFICIAL INTERPRETATIONS

The official interpretations referred to in Rule 26 follow.

It is the intention that additional interpretation will be issued from time to time as required. Violations of the regulations will be referred to a special committee appointed by the Executive Board of the International Olympic Committee for investigations and report with a view to action.

AMONG OTHERS THE FOLLOWING ARE NOT ELIGIBLE FOR OLYMPIC COMPETITIONS

Those who have participated for money or who have converted prizes into money or, without permission of the National Federation within the rules of the International Federation concerned, have received prizes exceeding 50 dollars in value, and those who have received presents which can be converted into money or other material advantages.

Those who have capitalized in any way on their athletic fame or success, profited commercially therefrom or have accepted special inducements of any kind to participate, or those who have secured employment or promotion by reason of their sports performances rather than their ability, whether in the commercial or industrial enterprises, the Service or any branch of the Press, Theatre, Television, Cinema, Radio or any other paid activity.

Any employment must be bona fide and not cover for excessive opportunities for training and competition in sport.

If an athlete is paid for the use of his name or picture or for a radio or television appearance, it is capitalization of athletic fame as described above.

*

An athlete who becomes a professional in any sport or who indicates his intention of becoming a professional or who plays in [on] a professional team with a view to become [sic] a professional.

*

Those who are paid for teaching or coaching others for competition in sport.

*

Anyone awarded a scholarship mainly for his athletic ability.

*

An athlete who demands payment or expense money for a manager, coach, relative, or friend.

*

Those who have received payment of expenses in excess actual outlay.

*

Those whose occupation (studies or employment) has been interrupted for special training in a camp for over three weeks

A COMPETITOR IS PERMITTED TO RECEIVE

Travelling and living expenses corresponding to the actual outlay during a very limited period of training (no more than three weeks) and during the Olympic Games subject to the approval of his National Olympic Committee.

*

Clothing and equipment as required for practicing his sport from his amateur sport organization.

*

Pocket money to cover petty daily expenses during the Games but only from his National Olympic Committee.

CONTRIBUTION BECAUSE OF SALARY LOSS

The International Olympic Committee in principle is opposed to payments for broken-time which it considers an infraction of Olympic amateurism.

However, when a competitor can prove that his dependants are suffering hardship because of his (or her) loss of salary or wages while attending the Olympic Games, his National Olympic Com-

mittee may take a contribution to his dependents, but under no circumstances may it exceed the sum which he (or she) would have earned during his (or her) actual period of absence, which in turn must not exceed 30 days.

OTHER DECISIONS

An athlete paid for teaching elementary sport (beginners or school children) on a temporary basis without abandoning his usual occupation remains eligible.

*

An athlete may be a full-time professional journalist, radio or television reporter or a full-time manager of or worker in an athletic facility without forfeiting his amateur status.

*

The use of drugs or artificial stimulants of any kind is condemned and any persons offering or accepting dope, in any form whatsoever, cannot participate in the Olympics.

*

So far as the Olympic Games are concerned these rules must be complied with, even if they appear in conflict with the rules of any other bodies.

PSEUDO AMATEURS

Individuals subsidized by governments, educational institutions, or business concerns because of their athletic ability are not amateurs. Business and industrial concerns sometimes employ athletes for their advertising value. The athletes are given paid employment with little work to do and are free to practise and compete at all times. For national aggrandizement, governments occasionally adopt the same methods and give athletes positions in the army and police force or in a government office. They also operate training camps for extended periods. Some colleges and universities offer outstanding athletic scholarships and inducements of various kinds. Recipients of these special favors which are granted only because of athletic ability are not amateurs.[83]

These rules with minor changes remained the eligibility rules of the Olympic Games until April, 1971. The only change of any significance was the extension of the time allowed in special training camps from three to four weeks in about 1967,[84] Because of the concern by athletes and coaches about the effect on performance of the high altitude at Mexico City, the site of the 1968 Games, the IOC made a special allowance for that year by extending the time allowed in special training camps to six weeks. But not more than four of these weeks were to be during the three months preceding the opening of the Games in October.[85]

As of 1967, and perhaps as of 1962, the participants had to sign the following statement: "I, the undesigned, declare on my honour that I am an amateur and that I have read and comply with the Eligibility Code of the Olympic Games as specified on this form."[86]

INTERNATIONAL SPORTS FEDERATION RULES IN THE LATE 1960'S

The definition of amateur used by different organizations during the late 1960's ranged from no statement on the matter, which was the case of the International Jai-Alai Federation[87] and the Water Ski Union,[88] to detailed definitions of an amateur by the International Amateur Athletic Federation[89] and the International Swimming Federation.[90] Three organizations—the International Archery Federation,[91] and the International Amateur Cyclist Federation,[92] and the International Union for the Modern Pentathlon[93] used the Eligibility Code of the International Olympic Committee as their complete definition or as the major part of their definition.*

Some other differences in the definitions at that time were as follows: the International Amateur Athletic Federation included the statement that "An amateur is one who competes for the love of the sport and as a means of recreation, without any motive of securing any material gain."[95] This same emphasis appeared in the definitions of some other federations. The rules of several federations stated that a person is ineligible who has become a professional in another sport, but some federations were silent on the issue, and the International Equestrian Federation specifically stated that "a professional at some sport other than riding can be recognized as an amateur rider."[96] The International Ice Hockey Federation allowed broken-time payments up to thirty days of the year.[97] This was illegal in most other federations. The International Rowing Federation ruled out people that earned money as trainers, instructors, or coaches, not only from competing, but also from serving as umpires, or as members of a national association, club or race committee.[98] Most of the other federations, though, allowed professionals to serve as umpires and as members of committees.

The only organization that allowed cash prizes was the International Shooting Union. They allowed prizes of one hundred dollars for contests covering several days. Such prizes were considered as compensation for costs.[99] Some other differences in definitions were limitations on the number of days in a year that an athlete could receive expense money, limitations on the daily allowance for out-of-pocket expenses, and differences in the procedure for reinstatement as an amateur. The most unusual description of an organization's distinction of who was an amateur was by the Federation In-

*For a complete compilation of the amateur rules for the late 1960's of almost all the International Sports Federations affiliated with IOC consult "A Study of Amateurism in Sport" by Eugene A. Glader.[94]

157

ternationale De Boules (lawn bowling). This organization does not define an amateur; it just assumes professionals do not exist.[100] All the above mentioned organizations in 1967 were either affiliated with the International Olympic Committee or had notified the IOC that they were operating under Olympic Standards.[101] Although differences existed in the definitions of amateur by the various federations, the primary emphasis in the definitions by most federations affiliated with the IOC was on eliminating athletes that had earned money directly or indirectly by participating in the sport.

CHANGES IN THE OLYMPIC RULES AFTER 1971

The rules and interpretations devised during the 1960's for the Olympic Games came under severe criticism seemingly as soon as they were made official. Many felt that the rules were so rigid, restrictive, and aristocratic that there were in actuality very few, if any, amateurs participating in the Olympic Games during that period. Even Brundage in 1969 recognized the dilemma when he said, "We are trying to do the impossible. It's about time to recognize that some sports and events cannot be kept amateur at international levels."[102] Due to the widespread discontent with the existing eligibility statement, a new Rule Number 26 was approved in April 1971, after at least a year of studying the problem. The new rule stated:

I. To be eligible for participation in the Olympic Games, a competitor must observe the traditional Olympic Spirit and ethic and have always participated in sport as an avocation without having received any remumeration for his participation.

His livelihood must not be derived from or be dependent upon income from sport and he must be engaged in a basic occupation to provide for his present and future.

He must not be, or have been, a professional, semi-professional or so-called "non-amateur" in any sport. He must not have coached, taught or trained sports competitors for personal gain. Physical education teachers who instruct beginners are eligible.

II. A competitor must observe and abide by the rules of the International Federation that controls the sport in which he participates, even if these rules should be stricter than those imposed by the International Olympic Committee.

He must comply with his Federation's directives and those issued by the International Olympic Committee. *

*NOTE: The International Olympic Committee's directives are:

a/ He must not have directly or indirectly allowed his name, his photgraph or his sports performance to be used individually for advertising purposes.

b/ He may not write or sign any publication or allow any to be signed on his behalf, nor may he

III. A competitor is permitted to accept:

1. Assistance via his National Olympic Committee or National Sports Federation during the recognized periods for training and participations in competition including the Olympic Games. Such assistance shall include only: lodging in training, food, transport, sports equipment, and installations, coaching, medical care, as well as pocket money to cover incidental expenses within the limits agreed by his respective International Sports Federation or by his National Olympic Committee.

The recognized period for full time training, where agreed by the International Federations or National Olympic Committees, must not normally exceed an aggregate of 30 days and in no case exceed 60 days in one calendar year.

2. Insurance coverage in respect of accidents or illness in connection with training or competition.

3. Scholarships granted in accordance with academic and technical standards, dependent upon the fulfillment of scholastic obligations and not athletic prowess.

4. Prizes won in competition within the limits of the Rules established by the respective International Federations and approved by the IOC

5. The IOC is opposed to payment for broken-time except that compensation in deserving cases may be authorized by the National Olympic Committees or International Federations to cover only the loss of salary or wages resulting from the competitor's absence from work on account of participation in the Olympic Games and important international sports meetings approved by the International Federations.

Under no circumstances may payment made under this provision exceed the sum which the competitor would have earned in his occupation over the same period.

IV. It is intended to eliminate those who are interested in sport for financial reasons and to confine the Olympic Games to those eligible according to this rule and a Committee will be established to consult and co-operate with International Federations and National Olympic Committee in its enforcement.

V. Eligibility Code-As regards pages 44-48 of the English version of

appear on radio or television during the Olympic Games in which he is participating without the permission of his chef de mission.

c/ Advertising resulting from any equipment contracts by National Federations shall be strictly controlled by the International Federations, and copies of such contracts shall be lodged with and approved by the International Olympic Committee.[103]

the IOC Rules 1971, the following is suggested:
ALL TO BE DELETED EXCEPT:
Women's participation-will be amended following the advice of the Medical Commission of the IOC and included in Rule 27 on participation of women.
Doping-to be included following the advice of the Medical Commission in main rules.
Penalties in the case of fraud — to remain unaltered
Non-amateurs and semi-professionals — as at present for pseudo-amateurs.

The statements on penalties in case of fraud and statements about non-amateurs and semi-professionals or pseudo-amateurs which were in the earlier rule books and quoted previously in this chapter were also retained with the new rule.[104] This new wording of Rule Number 26 marked a small change toward a more liberal interpretation of amateurism by the International Olympic Committee.

POST-BRUNDAGE ERA

Following the 1972 Olympic Games in Munich, Avery Brundage resigned as president of the International Olympic Committee and Lord Killian of Ireland was elected as new president. During his twenty years as head of the International Olympic Committee, Brundage was the standard-bearer for a detailed and strict interpretation of amateurism. Brundage was a man of integrity and ethics, and he believed that the solution to the problems of amateurism could be accomplished by clarifying and enforcing the rules. His ideas may have been theoretically sound, but in the pragmatic world of international athletics during the 1960's and 1970's, his views were unworkable. Consequently, the IOC approved another Eligibility Code for the Olympic Games in October, 1974. The new Code said:

ELIGIBILITY CODE
To be eligible for participation in the Olympic Games, a competitor must:
A. Observe and abide by the Rules and Regulations of the IOC and in addition the Rules and Regulations of his or her International Federation, as approved by the IOC, even if the federation rules are more strict than those of the IOC.
B. Not have received any financial rewards or material benefit in connection with his or her sport participation, except as permitted in the bye-laws to this rule.
BYE-LAWS TO RULE 26
A. A competitor may:

1. Be a physical education or sports teacher who gives elementary instruction

2. Accept, during the period of preparation and actual competition which shall be limited by the rules of each International Federation:

a. Assistance administered through his or her National Olympic Committee or National Federation for: lodging, food, cost of transport, pocket money to cover incidental expenses, insurance cover in respect of accidents, illness, personal property, and disability, personal sports equipment and clothing, cost of medical treatment, physiotherapy, and authorized coaches.

b. Compensation, authorized by his or her National Olympic Committee or National Federation, in case of necessity, to cover financial loss resulting from his or her absence from work or basic occupation, on account of preparation for, or participation in the Olympic Games and international sports competitions. In no circumstances shall payment made under this provision exceed the sum which the competitor would have earned in the same periods. The compensation may be paid with the approval of the National Olympic Committee at their descretion.

3. Accept prizes won in competition within the limits of the rules established by the respective International Federations.

4. Accept academic and technical scholarships.

B. A Competitor must not:

1. Be or have been a professional athlete in any sport, or contracted to be so before the official closing of the Games.

2. Have allowed his person, name, picture or sports performance to be used for advertising, except when his or her International Federation, National Olympic Committee, or National Federation enters into a contract for sponsorship of equipment. All payments must be made to the International Federation, National Olympic Committee or National Federation concerned, and not made to the individual.

3. Carry advertising material on his person or clothing in the Olympic Games, World or Continental Championships and Games under patronage of the IOC, other than trade marks on technical equipment or clothing as agreed by the IOC with the International Federations.

4. Have acted as a professional coach or trainer in any sport.[105]

The new rule marked another major step toward liberalizing the concept of amateurism, and it deals in a positive way with the modern practices in sports. The new rule, for the first time, makes a clear statement allowing compensation to an athlete for financial loss due to time spent training for or participating in international competition. Another feature of the new rule is that it eliminates for the first time since 1925 the restrictions on the length of time an athlete can spend away from home for training and competing. It also appears that the new rule absolves the "state amateur" and the college athlete who is receiving financial aid primarily because of his athletic ability. Just how these and other issues will be interpreted in light of the new rules will be of interest.

A basic feature of the new rules is to give to the International Sports Federations more freedom and authority in defining amateurism in their respective sports. The new rules come closer to the rules of 1921 than any rules since the Olympic Congress at Lausanne in that year. During the late sixties and early seventies the rules of many international sports Federations were as conservative and as restrictive as those of the International Olympic Committee.[106] Whether different International Sports Federations will liberalize their rules following the 1974 ruling of the IOC is a decision that is of great interest to sportsmen throughout the world.

SUMMARY

This chapter has reviewed amateurism from 1894 to the present through the history of the International Olympic Committee and the International Sports Federations which have worked closely with the IOC during most of these years. In retrospect, this history seems to fall into several periods. The first was the ingenious beginning of the International Committee in 1894. In this period there was a struggle to define amateurism. The end of this period is marked by the start of World War I. The second period was the time between the two World Wars. Then an amateur was defined with a minimum of words. During this period three significant Congresses dealing with amateurism met. The first was the Congress in Lausanne in 1921; the second was the Technical Congress in Prague in 1925; and the third was the Congress in Berlin in 1930.

The third era involving the Olympic Movement and amateurism was from the end of World War II until 1972. This period, in many ways, was dominated by Avery Brundage, who was elected vice-president of the International Olympic Committee in 1946 and president in 1952. This time was noted for its extreme conservatism regarding amateurism and the development of detailed rules as an attempt to purify sports. The final period started when Avery Brundage resigned as president of the IOC following the 1972 Games. This period began with a dramatic shift in emphasis in the rules of amateurism. This shift has been seen in the major changes in Olympic eligibility rules which were approved in 1974.

Amateurism and The Modern Olympic Movement

FOOTNOTES

1   Pierre de Coubertin, *Une Campagne de Trente-Vinght-et-Ans (1887-1908)* (Paris: Librairie de L'Education Physique, 1908 as quoted by John Apostal Lucas, "Baron Pierre De Coubertin and the Formative Years of the Modern International Olympic Movement 1883-1896." Unpublished D. Ed. dissertation, University of Maryland, 1962), pp. 90-91.

2   John Apostal Lucas, "Baron Pierre De Coubertin and the Formative Years of the Modern International Olympic Movement 1883-1896." (Unpublished D. Ed. dissertation, University of Maryland, 1962), p. 96.

3   Pierre de Coubertin, *Memoires Olympique*, p. 193, as reprinted in "Coubertin and Amateurism," *Olympic Review*, No. 91-92 (May-June 1975), p.160.

4   *Bulletin du Comite International des Jeux Olympiques*, I (July 1894) pp. 1-2 as quoted by John Apostal Lucas, "Baron Pierre De Coubertin and the Formative Years of the Modern International Olympic Movement 1883-1896" (Unpublished D. Ed. dissertation, University of Maryland, 1962), pp. 96-97.

5   "The International Athletic Congress," *The Times* (London), June 23, 1894, p. 9.

6   Pierre de Coubertin, *Memoires Olympique*, p. 193, as reprinted in "Coubertin and Amateurism, *Olympic Review*, No. 91-92 (May-June 1975), p. 160.

7   "Questionnaire," *Revue Olympique* (April 1902), p. 20.

8   Op. cit., Pierre de Coubertin, *Memoires Olympic*, p. 193.

9   "The Possible Unification of the Amateur Definition," *Revue Olympique* (September 1910), p. 138.

10   *The Official Report of the Olympic Games of 1908* (London: British Olympic Association, 1909), p. 761.

11   Ibid.

12   "Olympic Games of London," *Revue Olympique* (July 1907), pp. 302-303.

13   *The Official Report of the Olympic Games of 1908*, pp. 761-79.

14   "The Possible Unification of the Amateur Definition," p. 142.

15   Ibid.

16   Op. cit., Pierre de Coubertin, *Memoires Olympique*.

17   Ibid.

18   Pierre de Coubertin, *Memoires Olympique*, p. 193 as reprinted in "Coubertin and Amateurism," *Olympic Review*, No. 91-92 (May-June 1975), p. 160.

19 "Rapport Sur La Question De L'Amateurisme," *Revue Olympique* (August 1909), pp. 115-22.

20 "The Possible Unification of the Amateur Definition," p. 138.

21 *Revue Olympique* (August 1909), p. 128.

22 Pierre de Coubertin, *Memoires Olympique*, p. 193 as reprinted in "Coubertin and Amateurism," *Olympic Review*, No. 91-92 (May-June 1975), pp. 161, 178.

23 Ibid, p. 161.

24 Ibid.

25 Ibid., 178.

26 "The Possible Unification of the Amateur Definition," p. 139.

27 *The Official Report of the Olympic Games in Stockholm 1912*, ed by Erik Bergvall and Trans. by Edward Adams-Ray, (Stockholm: The Swedish Olympic Committee and Wahlstrom and Widstrand, 1913), p. 95.

28 Ibid., p. 96.

29 Ibid., pp. 424-25.

30 Eugene A. Glader, "A Study of Amateurism in Sports," (unpublished Ph.D. dissertation, University of Iowa, 1970), pp. 269-75.

31 *The Official Report of the Olympic Games in Stockholm 1912*, p. 96.

32 Ibid., pp. 95-98, 456.

33 Gustavus T. Kirby, Frederick W. Rubien and Joseph B. Maccabe, "Report of the Committee at the 1921 Lausanne or Geneva Conferences," *Report of the American Olympic Committee* (New York: Olympic Committee, 1920), pp. 424-425.

34 "Speech Delivered at the Opening of the Session of the E. C. Meeting in Paris in August 1927 by Count Baillet-Latour, President of the I.O.C.," *Official Bulletin*, International Olympic Committee, II (September 1927), pp. 10-11.

35 Bill Henry, *An Approved History of the Olympic Games* (New York: G. P. Putnam's Sons, 1948), p. 160.

36 "Decisions Taken by the Technical Congress at Prague," *Official Bulletin*, International Olympic Committee, I (January 1926), p. 15.

37 Ibid.

38 "Minutes of the Meeting of the Executive Committee," *Official Bulletin*, International Olympic Committee, II (December 1927), pp. 2-3.

39 Ibid., p. 3.

40 "The International Olympic Committee and The British Football Association," *Official Bulletin*, International Olympic Committee, III (April 1928), p. 30.

41 *Official Bulletin*, International Olympic Committee, III (October 1928), pp. 17-18.

42 *Official Bulletin*, International Olympic Committee, IV (July 1929), pp. 4-5.

43 *Olympic Bulletin*, International Olympic Committee, VI (July 1931), p. 12.

44 *Olympic Bulletin*, International Olympic Committee, V (July 1930), p. 21.

45 *Official Bulletin*, International Olympic Committee, V (July 1930), p. 22.

46 Henry, *An Approved History of the Olympic Games*, p. 188.

47 *Official Bulletin*, International Olympic Committee, VII (October 1932), pp. 12-13.

48 *Official Bulletin*, International Olympic Committee, VIII (September 1933), pp. 2-6.

49 Ibid., pp. 10-11.

50 *Report of the American Olympic Committee*, ed. by Frederick W. Rubien (New York: American Olympic Committee, 1936), p. 353.

51 *Handbook, General Rules and Programmes of the Competitions: XIth Olympiad Berlin, 1936* (Berlin: Organizationskomitee Fur Die XI Olympiade 1936).

52 Kenneth Doherty, "A Better Future for United States Track and Field," *Quarterly Review* (June 1966), p. 39.

53 "Report of the Conference Held by Delegates of the International Sports Federations with the Committee on Amateurism Nominated in Vienna," *Official Bulletin*, International Olympic Committee, IX (October 1934), p. 3.

54 "Rules of Qualification for the Olympic Games," *Official Bulletin*, International Olympic Committee, XII (October 1937), p. 7.

55 *Olympische Rundschau*, International Olympischen Institute, II (July 1938), pp. 24-25.

56 Ibid., pp. 29-31.

57 *Olympische Gesetz* (Berlin: Schriftenreike Des Internationales Olympisches Instituts), Vol. I, 1938, pp. 52-53, 87-88.

58 Henry, *An Approved History of the Olympic Games*, pp. 268-69.

59 *Bulletin*, Comite International Olympique, I (October 1946), p. 13.

60 *Bulletin*, Comite International Olympique, I (July 1947), pp. 22-23.

61 Henry, *An Approved History of the Olympic Games*, p. 323.

62 Avery Brundage, "Why the Olympic Games," *Report of the United States Committee,* ed. by Asa S. Bushnell, (New York: United States Olympic Association, 1948), p. 25.

63 *The International Olympic Committee and the Modern Olympic Games* (Lausanne, Switzerland: International Olympic Committee, 1950), pp. 22-23.

64 *Bulletin*, Comite International Olympique, (May 1948), p. 22.

65 *Bulletin*, Comite International Olympique, (February 1954), pp. 20-21.

66 *Olympic Rules* (Lausanne, Switzerland: International Olympic Committee, 1949), p. 18.

67 *Proceedings: Second National Conference of Sports Governing Bodies* (Ottawa, Canada: The National Council on Physical Fitness, January 6-7, 1950).

68 *Olympic Rules*, 1949, p. 21.

69 *Bulletin*, Comite International Olympique, (June-August 1950), pp. 18-19.

70 Ibid.

71 Avery Brundage, "Stop-Look and Listen," *Bulletin*, Comite International Olympique (June-August 1950), pp. 20-21.

72 *Bulletin*, Comite International Olympique, (September 1951), p. 21.

73 *The Olympic Games, Fundamental Principles, Rules and Regulations, General Information* (Lausanne, Switzerland: International Olympic Committee, 1956), p. 77.

74 Ibid., p. 22.

75 *Bulletin*, Comite International Olympique (October 1956), p. 50.

76 Ibid.

77 *Bulletin*, Comite International Olympique (November 1957), p. 65.

78 *Bulletin*, Comite International Olympique (February 1958), pp. 49-50.

79 *The Olympic Games, Fundamental Principles, Rules and Regulation, General Information* (Lausanne, Switzerland: International Olympic Committee, 1958), pp. 95-97.

80 *Bulletin*, Comite International Olympique (November 1960), pp. 67-69.

81 Ibid., p. 63.

82 *Bulletin*, Comite International Olympique (May 1961), p. 36.

83 *Bulletin*, Comite International Olympique (November 1962), pp. 44-46.

84 *The Olympic Games* (Lausanne, Switzerland: International Olympic Committee, 1967), pp. 43-46.

85 "Lettre d' informations," *Newsletter*, International Olympic Committee, No. 1 (1967).

86 Ibid., p. 25.

87 Robert H. Grossberg, Executive Director of the United States Amateur Jai-Alai Players Association, personal correspondence to the writer on January 22, 1969 and August 1, 1969.

88 Franco Carraro, President of the World Water Ski Union, personal correspondence to the writer on July 2, 1969.

89 *Official Handbook* (46 Victoria Street, London, S.W.I.: International Amateur Athletic Federation, 1965-66), pp. 51-55.

90 *Handbook: 1969-1972*, ed. Harold W. Henning (George St. 247, Sydney, N.N.W., Australia: International Swimming Federation, [1969]), pp. 29-31.

91 *Constitution and Rules 1968* (1, quai des Usines, Bruxelles 2, Belgium: Federation Internationale de tir a l'arc, 1968), p. 10.

92 Rodolfo Magnani, Secretary General of the International Amateur Cyclists Federation, personal correspondence to the writer on May 13, 1969.

93 *Statutes* (Skoldvagen 32, Djurshom, Sweden: Union International de Pentathlon Moderne, [n.d.]), p. 4.

94 Glader, "A Study of Amateurism in Sports," pp. 282-368.

95 *Official Handbook of the Amateur Athletic Union of the United States* (231 West 58th Street, New York: Amateur Athletic Union of the United States, 1969), p. 51.

96 *General Regulations*, 12th ed. (12 Avenue Hamoir, 38, Bruxelles 18, Belgium: International Equestrian Federation, 1967), p.14.

97 *By-Laws* (Empire House 175, Piccadilly, London W. 1: International Ice Hockey Federation, 1967), p. 18.

98 *Statutes: Rules of Racing and Regulations for F. I. S. A. Championship Regattas* (Case Postale 215, 1820 Montreux, Switzerland: International Rowing Federation, 1966), p. 39.

99 "Amateur Rules" (62 Wiesbaden-Klarenthal, West Germany: Union International de Tir, [19690]).

100 Sambuelli, Luigi, President of the Federation Internationale De Boules, personal correspondence of the writer on April 3, 1969.

101 *The Olympic Games*, 1967, pp. 83-84.

102 *Newsletter*, International Olympic Committee, No. 22 (July 1969), p. 364.

103 "The New Rule 26," *Olympic Review*, International Olympic Committee, No. 43 (April 1971), pp. 202-204.

104 Ibid., p. 204.

105 "New Rules," *Olympic Review*, International Olympic Committee, No. 85-86 (November-December 1974), pp. 585-86.

106 Glader, "A Study of Amateurism in Sports," pp. 282-368.

CHAPTER VII

Problems Involving Amateurism

INTRODUCTION

The basic problems involving twentieth century amateurism are identified and discussed in this chapter. These problems relate to basic principles which I believe should form the proper foundation for the development and administration of an acceptable system of athletic competition for the public on the local, national and international level. The problems referred to also involve the general principles of amateurism that have been commonly found in regulations of national and international sports governing bodies at various times throughout the recent history of amateurism. In order to objectify this discussion, the restrictions listed in the Eligibility Code for the Olympic Games during the 1960's will be frequently referred to.*

Two of the important problems in amateurism have been associated with attempts to control the amount of time an athlete spends in training and competition and efforts to prevent an athlete from "capitalizing in any way on [his]...athletic fame or success."[1] Underlying these two problems are three other issues. One is related to the motives of the person who engages in athletics. A second involves the concern for equality of opportunity that should be part of any system of athletics in which competition is open to the public. The last problem is the issue of hypocrisy and deceit in amateur sports.

---

*The 1977 rules on amateurism by the Amateur Athletic Union of the United States which contains many of the same principles are included in Appendix A as a reference for the reader.

PROBLEMS RELATED TO TIME SPENT
IN PRACTICE AND COMPETITION

The principle that an amateur is one who has always participated in sports as an avocation has been generally agreed upon throughout the nineteenth and twentieth centuries. When the rule was stated in this broad, general manner, more latitude was allowed as to what was avocational in contrast to the more recent interpretations which stated that an amateur must have "...a basic occupation designed to ensure his present or future livelihood"[2] and "Any employment must be *bona fide* and not cover excessive opportunities for training or competition in sports."[3] The latter wording was used by the International Olympic Committee from 1962 to 1971. During this period the rules for the Olympic Games also specified that the following people were not eligible to participate:

1. *Those whose occupation (studies or employment) has been interrupted for special training in a camp for more than four weeks in any one calendar year.*[4]*

2. *Those who have received expense money for more than thirty days, exclusive of the time spend [sic] in travelling, in any one calendar year, except when:*
   a. *The National Federation concerned has given an extension to cover competition in the Olympic games, Regional Games, or Championships, or for genuine matches with other countries;*
   b. *The authorities of the International Federation concerned have granted a very limited extension in exceptional circumstances.*[5]

3. *Those who have neglected their usual vocation or employment for competitive sports whether at home or abroad.*[6]

Similar restrictions exist in the rules of some International Sports Federations.

The definition of amateur used by many amateur sports organizations which states that an amateur is "one who engages in sport solely for the pleasure, and physical, mental and social benefits he derives therefrom and to whom the sport is nothing more than recreational" also has implications for the problems related to time spent in practice and competition.

The basic purpose of these restrictions appears to be an attempt to achieve "fair and equal competition," to keep sports as an avocation for

---

*From 1938 to 1962 this period was two weeks; and from 1967 to 1971 the period was four weeks and from 1971 to 1974 the period was 60 days. The rule was eliminated in 1974.

many, and to prevent some athletes from having special advantages over others. The desire to keep sports an avocation is based on the conviction that one's job or training for a job is more important than sports *per se,* and that specializing in athletics is a poor value choice.[7] One of the reasons that a person's so-called vocation or job is considered more important than sports is that a person can excel in sports only during his youth and early adult life, which is a relatively short portion of the normal life span.

If the purposes and the reasons cited for the restrictions on time spent practicing and in competition are valid, then the intent of the restrictions is logical and reasonable. However, because the intent of a rule is reasonable does not, in itself, justify a particular rule that is formulated. The belief that in a modern society a person cannot devote a few months or years of his youth to sports, if he so desires, and still attend high school or college or receive the training necessary for a job or profession is unrealistic. This principle was clearly demonstrated after World War II when thousands of United States military personnel returned to schools and jobs after serving in the Armed Forces for a few years. Today, hundreds of professional athletes attend school and develop job and business skills during the off-season or after their athletic careers are terminated. No longer is the view accepted that people cannot learn the knowledge and develop the skills necessary for a variety of occupations when they are past young adulthood or between sports seasons. In fact, adult education on a part-time and occasionally a full-time basis is now recognized as not only possible, but vital, in this era of rapid change. In addition, a strong case can be made for the view that the discipline, hard work, travel experience, and general maturing, which are part of a champion athlete's experiences, will enable him to return to his studies or vocation with increased motivation and dedication.

In contrast to the spirit and letter of the statements during the 1960's about not neglecting one's usual vocation or employment for practice and competition are the examples of athletes who have participated in the Olympic Games or other high level, international competitions. George Young is an example in track and field. As a middle-distance runner on the 1968 American Olympic Team, he stated that for fourteen months prior to the Olympic Games, he ran more than one hundred miles a week. Each morning he got up at six and ran for two hours; in the afternoon he ran for three additional hours.[8] Ron Clarke of Australia is reported to have moved to the French training site located at Fort Romeu[9] in order to train at high altitudes in preparation for the 1968 Olympic Games. On August 24, Clarke competed in London and on September 2, in White City, England, before travelling to Lake Tahoe, California, for additional training.[10] From these examples, it seems reasonable to believe that schedules such as these at best interfere with one's usual vocation; nevertheless, many such persons competed in the Games in 1968.

171

In the sport of tennis Billie Jean King stated that as an amateur she went to Australia for three months in 1964 and practiced tennis eight hours a day, while being financed by a tennis philanthropist.[11] Mrs. King, who later signed a $80,000 professional contract, stated, "I made my living as an amateur tennis player. Now that I am a pro I just make money, that's all."[12]

The swimming champions also spend similar amounts of time practicing. Rollins reports that Debbie Meyer, a gold medal winner at the 1968 Olympics, swam seven to eight miles a day while training for the Olympics.[13] Another American team member, Catie Ball, similar to her California competitors, had "been swimming four to six hours a day, six days a week, since she was eight years old."[14] In skating, Sonja Henie, a gold medal winner in 1928, 1932, and 1936 is reported to have practiced eight hours a day at the age of seven.[15]

Harold and Olga Connolly, both veteran participants in the Games, wrote, "For an increasing number of competitors, the problem is no longer how to squeeze in sufficient training time after work, but how to fit enough rest into a day that includes three two-hour training sessions."[16]

Not only is a considerable amount of time spent in training, but also a significant amount of time is spent in traveling to and from tournaments and meets. The practice time, plus the travel time, plus the time spent competing in tournaments and meets preparing for the Olympics put a real burden on athletes who wish to go on to the Olympics. For example, any American track and field athlete who had trained sufficiently to perform well enough to win the right to train and compete in the tryouts for the Olympic Games, which were held at the track and field training site at South Lake Tahoe, California, in August and September 1968, and who won the privilege of competing in the Olympic Games in October, certainly had to neglect his "usual vocation or employment." The exception may be someone who had some free lance publicity or journalistic type of position which permitted him to perform his job while at the various sites for training and competition. The high school and college students who participated in the 1968 Olympic Games definitely had to neglect their studies in order to compete. Undoubtedly, many, if not most of them, missed an entire school term.

Perhaps the most obvious violations of the occupational requirement and limitations on the time spent at training sites occurs among skiers who must train where adequate skiing conditions exist. Consequently, they may need to live away from home several months while training in the mountains.[17] The fact that the International Ski Federation in 1969 requested that the International Olympic Committee approve "broken-time" payments for a maximum of nine months supports the opinion that many skiers spent more than the allowable time away from their jobs while training during the 1960's.[18] In 1970 Marc Holder, president of the International Ski Federation, again requested a special training waiver from the International Olympic Committee because he claimed that competitive skiers must spend ten months of the year in training away from home.[19] A record of the time spent in training and in competition for all competitors at recent summer and winter Olympic Games would undoubtedly reveal many violations of the rules pertaining to time limitations for training. To assume that athletes are not neglecting their vocations or employment when competing today in athletics on a national and international level is a naive assumption that would not withstand a close scrutiny. In fact, if the rules concerning neglecting one's employment and the limits on time allowed in special training camps were strictly enforced, few *bona fide* amateur athletes would have been found at the 1968 Olympic Games.

PROBLEMS RELATED TO CAPITALIZING ON ATHLETIC ABILITY

A basic characteristic of most definitions of amateurism since 1972 has been that an amateur did not compete for financial rewards. In spite of this basic point of view, many amateur organizations have authorized rather generous rewards to attract athletes to meets. For example, in 1888, the Amateur Athletic Union of the United States awarded one hundred dollar gold watches for the first place,[20] and a meet promoter in 1969 awarded a color television set for the premier athlete at a meet.[21] Thus we have a situation where amateur sports organizations such as the Amateur Athletic Union of the United States, which as recently as 1977 defined an amateur as "one who engaged in sports solely for the pleasure and physical, mental and social benefits he derives therefrom and to whom sport is nothing more than an avocation,"[22] at times encouraging athletes to participate in events for the reasonably valuable rewards which will be given. The concern about capitalizing on one's athletic ability resulted in a detailed regulation on the issue by the International Olympic Committee between 1962 and 1969. The main statement in the Eligibility Code said that "To be eligible for the Olympic Games a competitor must always have participated in sports as an avocation, without any material gain of any kind"[23] and "...he does not receive or has never received any remumeration for participation in sport."[24] Other interpretive statements included in the code relating to capitalizing on one's athletic ability are listed on previous pages. One interpretation stated that "Anyone awarded a scholarship mainly for his athletic ability"[25] was ineligible.

In the United States the most obvious violation of this aspect of the Eligibility Code was probably commited by college athletes. Hundreds of college athletes in the United States received money in the form of a scholarship, grant-in-aid, payment for board, room, tuition, and cash year after year during this era, primarily or solely on the basis of their athletic ability. These violations were obviously condoned by college officials and overlooked by amateur athletic organizations. Lew Alcindor, a former All-American player on the basketball team of the University of California at Los Angeles, said, "Most Negro athletes are hired to perform at colleges and their education is secondary. He's there first...to win games and secondarily to get an education."[26] Nevertheless, no American college athlete receiving a typical financial aid package because of his athletic ability has been barred from the trials for the Olympic Games. Another statement in the eligibility rules for the Olympic Games between 1962 and 1969 stated that the following persons are ineligible:

> "Those who have participated for money, or who have converted prizes to money or, without permission of the National Federation within the rules of the International Federation concerned, have received prizes exceeding 50 Dollars in value, **and those who have received presents which can be converted into money or other material advantages.** * [27]

In spite of these restrictions and similar rules of the International Amateur Athletic Federation governing awards,[28] Ralph Doubell of Australia was awarded a color television set for being the premier athlete at the Los Angeles Invitational Track Meet in January, 1969. At the same meet the regular award for first place in each event was a portable typewriter; for second place, a clock radio; and for third place, an attache case.[29] At many major athletic events throughout the United States the usual practice is to award wrist watches for first place. These watches can be obtained for a cost under the legal limits (the AAU still allows awards to be given that cost as much as $100) set by the International Federations, but the legitimate retail or whole price of a new color television set would appear to exceed this limit.[30] Furthermore, all such gifts do have an intrinsic value and can be easily converted into cash. This violates the rule against converting awards into cash. Regardless of this fact, this writer is unaware of any action taken by the Amateur Athletic Union, the American Olympic Committee, the International Federation involved or the International Olympic Committee to declare ineligible anyone who received a valuable watch or gifts from the Los Angeles Invitational Track Meet.

Perhaps the reasons these violations have often been overlooked is that they appear so insignificant compared to the other widely known payments to so-called amateur athletes. The most widely publicized situation involves payments in thousands of dollars to skiers.[31] The magnitude of this problem was well known to Avery Brundage and other members of the International

---

*Boldface type by the writer.

Olympic Committee in 1971.[32]

Another statement in the list of official interpretations of the Eligibility Code of the Olympic Games during the 1960's specified that athletes not eligible for the Olympic Games are:

> Those who have capitalized in any way on their athletic fame or success, profited commercially therefrom or have accepted special inducements of any kind to participate, or those who have secured employment or promotion by reason of their sport performances rather than their ability, whether in commercial or industrial enterprises, the armed services or any branches of the Press, Theatre, Television, Cinema, Radio, or any other paid activity.[33]

To believe that champion athletes do not capitalize, intentionally or unintentionally, on their fame as athletes is extremely naive. Athletic fame obviously opens doors and contributes to an athlete's success in almost any trade, profession, or business. The cliche, "It's not what you know, but who you know," is certainly applicable to the famous athletes because athletic fame helps them get to know the right people. In 1928 Brown said that "no man can rise to the top in any form of athletic competition without profiting financially by his prowess."[34] The following statement shows that Kofoed also agrees with this view.

> No man who works for a living can fail to gain indirectly if he becomes a golf or tennis or polo star. If he sells bonds or insurance or automobiles he will find more customers as a champion in any sport than he would as Mr. X. Conceding this to be true, and it is beyond a doubt, then the only absolute amateur champion is the man of independent means.[35]

For example, was it merely a conincidence that Emil Zatopek of Czechoslovakia was promoted to 1) Captain after winning the 10,000 meter race and placing second in the 5,000 meter race at in the 1948 Olympics 2) Major after breaking the record from 1,000 to 20,000 kilometers and 3) Lieutenant Colonel after his victories at the 1952 Olympic Games? He probably did not have the time to expend in military study and affairs normally necessary for such promotions in such a short period of time.[36]

Another item in the Eligibility Code for the Olympic Games, from 1962 to 1971 stated that "an athlete who becomes a professional in any sport or who has decided to become a professional is ineligible."[37] The last half of the rule is completely unenforcable. Undoubtedly, hundreds of amateur athletes have decided to become professionals as soon as they have completed college competition or the Olympic Games. It appears that Peggy Fleming, who won a gold medal in figure skating in the 1968 Olympic Games, was planning to sign a professional contract, prior to the Games. After the Games, Ms. Fleming was reported to have signed a contract for $500,000.[38]

PROBLEMS RELATED TO BOTH MONETARY AND TIME RULES

Both the monetary regulations and the rules related to time spent in practice and competition are violated in the case of some athletes in military services or on championship teams, and by "state amateurs" in communist and socialist countries. For example, the sixteen military personnel who trained at Fort Sam Houston, Texas, for the pentathlon competition for the 1968 Olympic Games were for all practical purposes paid professional athletes. They received regular military pay and benefits while engaged full-time in a training program designed primarily to win the pentathlon competitions rather than to obtain traditional military objectives.[39] Similar benefits and privileges are experienced by athletes in the military services of most, if not all, countries that send athletes to the major international meets.

Another facet of the problem of amateurism in military services involves such sports as target shooting. Since learning to shoot is a basic aspect of military training, it seems logical to conclude that target shooting is a professional sport for military personnel. If fact, military personnel are paid for practicing target shooting. Nevertheless, military personnel are allowed to compete in target shooting competitions in the Olympic Games.

In communist countries, successful athletes are rewarded materially, socially, and with time off from their regular jobs. An example of financial reward given to victorious athletes in Eastern European countires is reported by Olga Fikotova Connally, who competed for Czechoslovakia in the 1956 Olympic Games. She received three thousand Koruna (this equalled approximately $185.70 in 1969) for winning the women's discus throw.[40] In order to camouflage the professional training practices of the Eastern European athletes, most of them are listed as students, teachers, and professional soldiers.[41]*

In capitalistic countries, similar to the treatment of athletes in communist countries, the oustanding players on industrial teams, who often have been hired because of their athletic skills, are rewarded financially and with time off from their jobs.[42] Even if it were true that athletes on industrial teams were not given time off from their jobs with pay because of their athletic skills, few will doubt that the athletic skills of the star athletes are often instrumental in helping them obtain positions which do not conflict with their athletic career. Benefits of this type appear to have conflicted with the Eligibility Code of the Olympic Games prior to 1974.

*For a more complete report on athletes and the issue of the "state amateur" in the Soviet Union see Chapter 5 in Soviet Sport by Henry W. Morton.

THE PROBLEM OF MOTIVE

The motive for participating in athletics can create problems in amateur athletics. As the evidence in Chapter II shows, there is inherent in competitive athletics a drive to excel. This drive conflicts with the idea of an amateur athlete being a person "who engages in sport solely for the pleasure and physical, mental, and social benefits he derives therefrom and to whom sport is nothing more than a recreation."[43]

In a speech made in 1969, Brundage extolled the values and importance of the Olympic Movement. He equated the amateur spirit with "the seeking for perfection." He said that devotion to a task was the secret of success.[44] To equate the amateur spirit with a seeking for perfection is incorrect because amateurism implies pleasure, play, and recreation, and not a striving for excellence or perfection. In athletics, however, a strong striving for excellence and perfection exists. This striving for excellence and perfection, which requires long and arduous training and competition, is necessary in order to win at the Olympic Games or at other international athletic contests. The fact that striving for perfection involves physical "work" is evident in the American term for athletic practice sessions called the "work-out." Certainly the innumerable hours that athletes must "work-out" month after month can hardly be expended "solely for recreation and pleasure." Doherty points out that "only if one finds pleasure in pain and recreation in sweaty hard work can such a term as pleasure be justified"[45] for the effort exerted in athletic training. Athletes may enjoy the results of work—the success, fame, and rewards—but that does not mean that they necessarily enjoy the "work-out." Some athletes say that they enjoy the work, but whether one works or plays at something is strictly determined by the state of mind of the person performing the task. Even if a "work-out" is defined as being enjoyable and pleasurable, it is impossible to determine whether someone else has participated in such an activity solely for pleasure. Therefore, such lofty statements as "an amateur is one who has participated solely for pleasure" should not be included in any eligibility regulations for athletic contests. It is noteworthy that the International Olympic Committee did omit this phrase from its 1961 Eligibility Code[46] but several national and international federations still retain this expression in their code.

THE PROBLEM OF EQUAL OPPORTUNITY

Another problem of contemporary amateurism is the failure of amateurism as a category of competition to treat all men equally, to give all athletes an equal opportunity to be successful in competition. The Declaration of Independence of the United States, the Charter of the United Nations, and the

Universal Declaration of Human Rights by the United Nations General Assembly all state that all men are inherently equal. The first states, "We hold these truths to be self-evident, that all men are created equal."[47] The second declared, "We the peoples of the United Nations determined...to reaffirm the faith in fundamental human rights...in the equal rights of all men and women of nations large and small."[48] The preamble of the third proclaims the recognition "of the inherent dignity and of the equal and inalienable rights of all members of the human family is the foundation of freedom, justice, and peace in the world."[49] Article One of this Declaration states that "all human beings are born free and equal in dignity and rights."[50]

These statements do not mean that all men are born with equal abilities and similar personal characteristics, but they say that everyone should have an equal opportunity to use and develop his talents. These documents imply that the basic worth of an individual's life is equal to that of others regardless of an individual's race, talents, position, social standing, or religion. In spite of the universally held belief that all men are created equal and should be treated that way, and in spite of the stated objective of such organizations as the International Olympic Committee to promote "fair and equal competition," amateur organizations have always discriminated against some groups. In the nineteenth century the social discrimination against laborers, artisans, and workers was evident. Since about 1880 this discrimination has been increasingly indirect and subtle. Two of the major areas of discrimination in amateur athletics during the twentieth century have involved restrictions on time allowed for training and competition and limitations on the financial rewards that an athlete may receive, regardless of his financial or occupational situation.

In discussing the discriminatory aspects of amateur sports organizations, the assumption is made that an acceptable system or framework of athletic competition for the public should provide an equal opportunity for all to achieve success in competition, if worthwhile and important values may be gained through success in competition. However, defining a category of athletic competition that is fair and equal for all the people in a certain group does not necessarily mean the same regulations can be applied to all groups. For example, associations of high schools and colleges in the United States, for the good of students in member institutions, usually have rules and regulations to promote fair and equal competition within their "closed" association, but the rules and regulations governing the schools would not necessarily promote fair and equal competition if applied to non-school groups and associations.

Similarly, rules and regulations that may promote fair and equal competition for people of wealth or for people living in a certain culture may prove unfair and unequal when applied to people of little wealth in a different culture. In this respect, the International Olympic Committee's rule on "broken-time" prior to 1974 was clearly unfair when applied to the hourly wage earner in comparison to its effect on a salaried wage earner whose job was flexible concerning the time and place for performing his assignment. In like manner, "broken-time" rules discriminate against hourly wage earners in a capitalistic society when they must compete against a "state amateur" from a communistic society or an athlete with special privileges in a military unit.

In general, the effect of rules that rigidly prevent a person from capitalizing on his athletic fame or that limit travel and living expenses have an unfair or unequal effect on the athlete with little wealth. For example, these restrictions were certainly a handicap to athletes from families in the 23.4% of the United States population who had incomes of less than $3,999.00 in 1965.[51] Most of the people in this income category could not obtain a level of athletic achievement necessary to compete on the national or international level and still fully abide by the Olympic Eligibility Code at that time. Thus, we see that rules that sometimes appear to create equality often actually create inequality, and this, in turn, often does lead to hypocrisy and deceit.

A most recent problem concerning equality of opportunity in athletics on the national and international level involves the unwillingness and/or inability of sports-governing bodies to enforce the amateur rules and declare violators ineligible. Thus, athletes who violate the rules and are not punished have an advantage over the athletes who live according to the letter and spirit of the rules. The frustrations resulting from this type of situation were expressed by one respondent in the survey on amateurism conducted by *Track and Field News* in 1971.

> *I have to put in two or three hours a day, year round, like the next man. I have to neglect my family to the point of tears in the pursuit of a dream...Then after all this to find out that some athletes are making a small fortune from sport.*[52]

THE PROBLEM OF HYPOCRISY AND DECEIT

Underlying the problems discussed in the preceding pages is the problem of hypocrisy and deceit, which is the major problem in contemporary amateur sports. This view is based on the premise that an acceptable system of athletic competition for the public should be conducted with high ideals of sportsmanship and ethics and the system should promote the development of such ideals. Hence, a system of athletic competition should promote respect, good will, and friendship between the participants and the officials of the organizations that control and sponsor athletic competition. In addition, the system should be so structured and administered that hypocritical and deceitful practices are minimized.

When hypocrisy and deceit become common and are accepted by those associated with athletics, the most basic of values—truth—is corrupted. This distortion of values is especially tragic in regard to amateurism because over the years its advocates have identified amateurism with educational objectives, and one of the basic objectives of education is the quest for truth. The importance of this priority of values was expressed by the authors of the Carnegie Foundation Report in 1929, who, after listing some of the potential evils of professionalism in college athletics, wrote: "All this would be true if professionalism were practiced frankly and openly. Where, however its practice [professionalism] is concealed, an even deadlier blow is struck at spiritual values."[53] In other words, to have eligibility statements that are openly disregarded by athletes, coaches, promoters, leaders of sports federations, and members of Olympic Committees creates an attitude that scoffs not only at the idea of amateurism but also at truth itself.

The extent to which eligibility rules are disregarded today is difficult to prove, but the questionnaire survey sent to a broad sampling of coaches, athletes, writers, meet directors, equipment suppliers and amateur and Olympic officials in 1971 by *Track and Field* does shed some light on the subject. The extent of the violations of the amateur code in Europe and in the United States which were reported in this study was alarming. According to the author, the following comments by one meet promoter seem to sum up accurately the situation in the United States:

> *...illegal payments are being given to key athletes at many of the major meets in this country. I know very few indoor meets that don't look after key athletes. That is, very few of the quality indoor meets that depend on the open, world-class athletes for their appeal. Frankly, it is terribly hard to compete with the pro sports, such as football and basketball, considering their TV and radio networks and powerful publicity and advertising compaigns. Unless a track meet has a glamor attraction, it is probably likely to lose money and, therefore be out of business the following year... Those receiving payments are pretty well confined to the top 10 or 12 athletes in a meet, the athletes who will provide the drawing power. There is simply not enough money in track to go deeper in taking care of athletes. At that, many of the meets are only a break-even situation... The amounts are generally quite small, perhaps only enough to allow the athlete to devote the time needed to train to be a world-class performer... I would say it would take a phenomenal attraction to rate a $500 payment for a meet. Most would simply get $200, or maybe just a little extra per diem help, often not amounting to $100.[54]*

Further evidence of the widespread acceptance or awareness of the violations of amateur and Olympic eligibility rules is apparent from a reported observation made by Willi Daume, president of the German Olympic Committee, about eligibility rules sent out in 1967 for the Olympic Games. Mr. Daume is reported to have said, "Nobody will pay any attention to the rules."[55]

Consequently, the potential evils that might result from professionalism are greater than the erosion or decay of values that are resulting from many of the current definitions of amateurism in athletics. This decay in values stems from two sources. One is the nature of contemporary athletics which has as its primary goal the desire to win. The second is the failure of many formulators of the current amateur codes to accept this fact. As a result, the amateur category of athletic competition on the national and international level is often composed of psuedo-amateurs (professionals) who, when they know they are not being honest, are forced to lie by signing amateur statements or eligibility codes in order to compete. In recognition of this fact, Umminger in 1962 wrote that "Under existing conditions the stars must either perjure themselves or stand in suspicion of perjury if they are to avoid being hounded out by the IOC."[56]

It must be recognized that it is possible to have an organization with high and nobel ideals, values and purposes and still have a situation in which the very nature of the organization's rules and regulations breed hypocrisy and deceit. For example, an organization may sincerely desire fair play and equal opportunity for the public, but unintentionally discourage participation in its activities by rules which may handicap or limit opportunities for participation and success by people in certain jobs, social levels, or economic circumstances. The rule in opposition to "broken-time" payments is considered by some to be an example of this situation.[57]

Another aspect of the contemporary athletic scene, which many people view as hypocritical, is the practice of accepting as amateurs: 1) student athletes on athletic scholarships, 2) athletes who receive special privileges or industrial or military teams, and 3) athletes who receive special privileges under various socialistic, communistic, and capitalistic forms of government.

Acceptance of these athletes has not been consistent with the essential emphases and purposes of amateurism. The inevitable result of this contradiction is hypocrisy. Furthermore, whenever a rule favors one group, other groups will tend to lose respect for the system and strive for equality by circumventing the letter, if not the spirit, of the law.

Another example of hypocrisy and deceit in sports is the scandal concerning the payoffs made to athletes for wearing certain brands of track shoes in the Olympic Games in 1968. According to Horst Dassler, an executive of

Adidas Shoe Company, officials of the Amateur Athletic Union of the United States were aware that payments were being made to athletes prior to the Games, but they said they could do nothing about it.[58] Underwood's comment about this incident was that: "They (Puma and Adidas Shoe Manufacturing Companies) discovered that amateur athletes, conditioned by deceit and by outdated rules and comatose amateur ruling bodies like the AAU, were no more loth to compromise than a child is reluctant to open a candy wrapper."[59] Receiving money for running in a certain brand of shoes in and of itself is not hypocritical or deceitful, but to sign the Eligibility Code of the International Olympic Committee, which for track and field athletes demands conformance to the rules of the Amateur Athletic Federation, and then to accept money for wearing such track shoes is hypocritical and deceitful.

The current world amateur system often maximizes rather than minimizes hypocritical and deceitful practices. In fact, because of the obvious disregard by officials and athletes, the Olympic Games at times may have done more to destroy morals than to develop moral qualities, which is one of the objectives of the Olympic Games. In a similar vein, McIntosh, commenting on the moral development of sport, stated in 1963 that "the charge of corruption might now be laid more justly at the door of the amateur than the professional."[60] Hughes and Williams in 1944 came to the conclusion that amateurism in sports was corrupt and said that "There is no need to emphasize the fact ...that the whole amateur code, surrounded by legalistic definitions is rotten to the core."[61] Certainly hypocritical and deceitful practices are anathemas to the spirit of fair play and equality.

In light of the rules of national sports organizations, international sports federations, and the International Olympic Committee, in my opinion there have been few world-class competitors since 1952 who could truthfully claim to be amateurs; that is, having not violated some amateur rule along their way to success. John B. Kelly, Jr., former president of the AAU, said in February, 1972, that as many as two-thirds of the athletes signing the Olympic Oath are committing perjury. He went on to say, "What does not seem to have even concerned us is the extent to which we damage the character of a young competitor when we validate the lies, the cheating, and the deceit he practices trying to abide by a thoroughly outmoded amateur code. Instead of teaching the great lessons of sport—honesty, integrity, and fair play—we are sanctioning the worst. It is worse than hypocrisy. It is dishonorable, disreputable, and disgusting."[62]

Perhaps Gallico was correct when he wrote "Amateurs? There ain't none."[63] If this is true, then amateur sports is truly saturated with hypocrisy. Rene Mahen, Director General of UNESCO, in 1963 effectively summarized the situation concerning amateur sports with the following statement:

It is no longer true...that the champion can emerge, train, establish himself and give full measure of his potentialities — which is properly not his individual role in society — in that state of independence of, and indifference to the economic contingencies — or rather necessities — of ordinary life which confers what is called amateur status...To try to make amateur status obligatory for the elite of the sport world means...imposing falsehood on that elite... Why should we feel reluctant to admit that the champion athlete is a professional?...We deny the obvious fact that the champion is obliged to live the life of a professional athlete.[64]

Just because rules are broken does not make them bad. Nor does the inability to catch rule-breakers make rules bad. However, this type of reasoning is unacceptable for defending all definitions of amateurism in light of all the other problems associated with amateurism. If the problems associated with amateurism could be isolated to one period of time such as a decade or two, or to one culture or to one sport or to one attempt at defining amateurism, there would be less to criticize. Unfortunately, problems of equality of opportunity and/or deceit and hypocrisy/have been associated with amateurism since its first written definition in 1866.

SUMMARY

In this chapter the problems of amateurism have been indentified and discussed. The rules on the limitation on time that an athlete may spend in practice and competition and the prohibition against his capitalizing on his athletic achievements are responsible for many of the problems. Underlying the rules is the problem concerning the motives for competing and the issue of equality of opportunity. The final problem discussed was the issue of hypocrisy and deceit.

One of the primary reasons these problems exist is the fact that sports-governing bodies have defined amateurism with a "sport" or recreational emphasis, whereas, in reality, the competition is conducted with an "athletic" emphasis. In addition, the governing bodies have been inconsistent in their interpretations of amateurism when applied to athletes in colleges, in communistic countries, on industrial teams, and in military services.

This led to the conclusion that the very nature of contemporary amateur athletics leads to professionalism and that amateur sports are saturated with hyprocrisy. Consequently, many amateur sports organizations need to revise their rules to solve these problems. In the next chapter some solutions to these problems are proposed.

FOOTNOTES

1 *The Olympic Games* (Lausanne, Switzerland: International Olympic Committee, 1967), p. 44.

2 Ibid., p. 43.

3 Ibid., p. 44.

4 Ibid.

5 Ibid., pp. 44-45.

6 Ibid., p. 45.

7 "The Athletic Research Society," *Mind and Body* 17 (February 1911), p. 363.

8 William F. Reed., Jr., "Warmup for the Canyon Run," *Sports Illustrated* 30 (January 27, 1969), p. 19.

9 James Coote, *Olympic Report: 1968* (London: Robert Hale, 1968), p. 14.

10 *Track and Field News*, September 1968, pp. 11, 41.

11 Kim Chapin, "Center Courts Is Her Domain," *Sports Illustrated* 28 (June 24, 1968), p. 47.

12 Ibid., p. 49.

13 Richard Rollins, "The Only Year of Their Lives," *Sports Illustrated* 29 (August 12 1968), pp. 18-19.

14 Ibid., p. 21.

15 Walter Umminger, *Supermen, Heroes and Gods*, trans. and adapted by James Clark (New York: McGraw Hill Book Company, Inc., 1963), pp. 242-43.

16 Harold and Olga Connolly, " 'Olympic Purpose and Friendship Spoiled by Phony Professionalism,' " *St. Paul Sunday Pioneer Press*, October 27, 1968, section four, p. 8.

17 Coate, *Olympic Report: 1968*, p. 154.

18 "Scorecard," *Sports Illustrated* 30 (June 23, 1969), p. 9.

19 William Johnson, "The Name is the Name of the Game," *Sports Illustrated* (March 9, 1970), p. 14.

20 *The Spirit of the Times*, December 15, 1888, p. 738.

21 Reed, "Warm-up For the Canyon Run," p. 16.

22 *1975 Official Handbook of the AAU Code* (AAU House, Indianapolis, Ind.: AAU of the U.S., 1975), p. 14.

23 *The Olympic Games*, 1967, p. 43.

24 Ibid.

25 Ibid., pp. 43-44.

26 *Des Moines Sunday Register*, July 21, 1968, p. 3-S.

27 *The Olympic Games*, 1967, p. 44.

28 *Official Handbook* (46 Victoria Street, London, S.W.I.: International Amateur Athletic Federation, 1965-66), pp. 51-52.

29 Reed, "Warm-up the Canyon Run," p. 16.

30 *1975 Official Handbook of the AAU Code*, p. 98.

31 Johnson, "The Name is the Name of the Game," pp. 12-17.

32 *Olympic Review*, International Olympic Committee, No. 52 (January 1972), pp. 13-14.

33 *The Olympic Games*, 1967, p. 44.

34 Heywood Brown, "Simon-pure Athletes," *Forum*, 69 (March 1928), p. 406.

35 John C. Kofoed, "Sport and Snobbery," *The American Mercury*, 15 (December 1928), p. 432.

36 Umminger, *Supermen, Heroes and Gods*, pp. 228-29.

37 *The Olympic Games*, 1967, p. 44.

38 "Sweet Life of an Olympic Doll," *Sports Illustrated*, 29 (November 11, 1968), p. 26.

39 John Sayre, "Pentathlon, the Sport of the Versatile Man," *Pace* 4 (April 1968) pp. 20-25.

40 Olga Connolly, *The Rings of Destiny* (New York: David McKay Company, Inc., 1968), p. 203.

41 Henry W. Morton, *Soviet Sport: Mirror of Soviet Society* (New York: Collier Books, 1963), pp. 133-34.

42 Jack Newcombe, "Athletes Tell How Illicit Payoffs Destroy the Amateur Code," *Life* 40 (April 30, 1965), p. 118.

43 *Handbook: 1969-1972*, ed. Harold W. Henning. (George St. 247, Sydney, N.N.W., Australia: International Swimming Federation, [1969]), p. 29.

44   Avery Brundage, "Address at 68th Session of the International Olympic Committee in Warsaw," *Newsletter*, International Olympic Committee, No. 22 (July 1969), p. 362.

45   Kenneth Doherty, "Modern Amateurism," *Health and Fitness in the Modern World* (Chicago: Athletics Institute, 1961), p. 232.

46   *The Olympic Games*, 1967.

47   Harry J. Carman and Harold C. Syrett, *A History of the American People to 1865* Vol. I of *A History of the American People* (New York: Alfred A. Knopf, 1957), p. 653.

48   *The United Nations Conference on International Organizations*, Publications of the United States Department of State, No. 2490 (Washington, D. C.: Government Printing Office, 1946), p. 943.

49   Arthur P. Mendel, ed., *The Twentieth Century 1914-1964* (New York: The Free Press, 1965), p. 170.

50   Ibid., p. 171.

51   Bureau of Census, *Statistical Abstract of the United States, 1967* (Washington, D. C.: Government Printing Office, 1967), p. 333.

52   Bob Hersh, "Trach and Field's Payoffs--the Amateur Code is Outmoded," *Track and Field News*, 24 (December 1971), p. 4.

53   Howard J. Savage, *et al., American College Athletics*, "Bulletin" No. 23, (New York: The Carnegie Foundation for the Advancement of Teaching, 1929), p. 302.

54   Bob Hersh, "Track and Field's Payoffs—Take the Money and Run," *Track and Field News*, 24 (November 1971), p. 4.

55   "The Olympics," *Time*, 90 (July 28, 1967), p. 70.

56   Umminger, *Supermen, Heroes and Gods*, p. 223.

57   Nadejda LeKarska, "An Extraordinary Record," *Bulletin of the Bulgarian Olympic Committee* [1966] , p. 20.

58   John Underwood, "No Goody Two-Shoes," *Sports Illustrated*, 30 (March 10, 1969) p. 22.

59   Ibid., p. 17.

60   Peter C. McIntosh, *Sport in Society* (London: C. A. Watt and Company, Ltd., 1963), p. 182.

61   William Leonard Hughes and Jesse Fairing Williams, *Sports Their Organization and Administration* (New York: A. S. Barnes and Company, 1944), p. 379.

62 John B. Kelly, Jr., "Amateurism in Sport as a Viable Ideal in the 1970's," *Athletics in America*, ed. by Arnold Flath (Corvallis, Oregon: Oregon State University Press, 1972), p. 76.

63 Paul Gallico, *Farewell to Sport* (New York: Alfred A. Knopf, 1938), p. 108.

64 David Cort, "The Olympics: Myth of the Amateur," *The Nation*, 199 (September 28, 1964), p. 159.

CHAPTER VIII

Proposed Solutions to the Problems of Amateurism

INTRODUCTION

If the supposition is true that amateurism has serious problems, those responsible for contemporary amateur athletics should carefully examine the current rules governing amateur athletics in their associations. During recent years there has been considerable pressure to revise the definitions of amateurism used by the International Olympic Committee and other major sports organizations. Amid this pressure, several people have proposed changes and possible solutions to the problems of amateur sports. The revisions in the Eligibility Code for the Olympic Games in 1974 were a big step in the right direction. Whether the international sports federations will revise their amateur codes to conform better with the contemporary society remains a large question in most cases.

The purpose of this chapter is to suggest specific solutions to the problems of amateur athletics that we discussed in the preceding chapter. The first part of the chapter includes a review of some observations about the development and problems of amateurism. The second part of the chapter discusses some proposals by others for solving these problems. In the last part of the chapter, I give my own suggestions for solving the problems of amateurism. These suggestions emerged from observations and conclusions reported in the previous chapters and are based on certain basic principles set forth in Chapter VII.

PRIOR OBSERVATIONS AND CONCLUSIONS

Two of the basic principles set forth in Chapter VII for an acceptable system of amateur athletic competition for the public were 1) that everyone should have an equal opportunity to participate and succeed, and 2) that the system should minimize the opportunity for hypocritical and deceitful practices. In that chapter it was also concluded that legalistic attempts 1) to control the time spent in practice, 2) to prevent a person's capitalizing on athletics, and 3) to control or determine an athlete's motive for participating in athletics were major sources of conflict with the two principles listed above and still are the major causes of problems involving amateurism.

The history of sports was reviewed in Chapters III through IV. This review began with athletics in ancient Greece.

Although many lessons of value concerning athletic practices can be learned from the methods and customs of the ancient Greeks, athletics in ancient Greece are not a perfect model for an acceptable system of athletics for the twentieth century public. There was no one cause for the growth of athletics in Greece, and there was no one cause for its decline. The factors in both cases were varied. Political, social, economic, military, and religious factors all played a part in the growth and demise of athletics in ancient Greece. Perhaps the major shortcoming of the Greek athletic system was that the opportunity to compete and succeed was limited to a small minority of the population.

Contrary to the implications of the regulations in the eligibility rules of the modern Olympic Games which limits awards, lucrative awards did not destroy athletics in ancient Greece. The awards, which attracted athletes willing to train the year around, ultimately made it difficult for the part-time athlete to succeed in major athletic events, but the awards originally enabled people from a larger cross-section of society to participate in athletics. In addition, participation in athletics was often discouraged by rules which allowed excessive brutality and by the absence in some events of weight classifications, which encouraged specialization. These factors and others need to be carefully considered when using conditions in ancient Greece for a model for contemporary amateur athletics.

In Chapter IV through VI the historical developments of selected sports and the development of amateurism were reviewed. This review showed that the major purposes of amateurism were 1) to make a distinction between the social classes, 2) to serve as a means of declaring ineligible those thought to have some special advantages in competition, and 3) to eliminate those who competed in sports for ulterior motives. In addition, the importance of the distinction between "sports" and "athletics" was noted. "Sport" was characterized as an activity in which a person engaged solely for pleasure and physical, mental, and social benefits that could be derived from the activity, and "athletics" was characterisized as an activity in which a person engaged with a seriousness of purpose and a desire to win.

The evidence presented in the preceding chapter clearly indicated that amateurism has been and still is defined with a "sport" emphasis, but has been and continues to be promoted and conducted with an "athletic" or professional emphasis. For example, the promotion of local, national, and international championship competition creates a stress on excellence and professionalism which is the antithesis of sport and amateurism as defined by most contemporary amateur sports federations. Consequently, the major problem of amateur sports results—hypocrisy deceit.

SOLUTIONS PROPOSED BY OTHERS

Keating's Proposal

Dr. James Keating, a professor at DePaul University, has demonstrated a special scholarly interest in the problems of amateurism in sports. He has suggested that the amateur or sporting spirit could be attained in athletics if the following "simple steps were taken:"

1. Abolish all methods of compensation and reward, together with all trophies, cups, and other statuary of any substantial value. The prize should only have symbolic value—its cash value should never exceed say, one dollar.

2. Prohibit all expense accounts and expect each competitor to pay his own expenses, including his entrance fee. If sport is a pastime, a diversion an amusement, then there is no reason to pay a man's expenses to and from the place of his amusement.

3. Make no effort of any kind to secure publicity—no press releases, no free tickets or special arrangements for reporters, no advertising beyond perhaps the simple announcement of the competition. The glory and public acclaim, the business advantage and social prestige which accompany newspaper headlines, and attract professionals, would be missing.

4. Do not charge admission or employ any strategem for the purpose of profiting from the tournament or competition. The cost of competition would be defrayed entirely from the entrance fee or borne by the sponsoring organization. [9]

Implementing these steps would certainly make competition a recreational and sporting experience, with no great pressure to win, and this would certainly create the true spirit of amateur athletics as this spirit has been traditionally defined. In addition, the consequences of such a situation would be the elimination of many, if not all, major regional, national, and international championships and tournaments. This is obviously not the goal or emphasis of current amateur organizations that are promoting tournaments and athletic meetings.

Keating realizes that his facetious proposal, if implemented, would eliminate amateur athletics as they are currently conducted and promoted. He also realizes that the nature of competitive athletics makes it difficult, if not impossible, to implement these "few simple steps." Although this proposal is theoretically one way to solve the problem, it offers an impractical, if not impossible, solution. However, the extreme viewpoint of this proposal does help illustrate, as Keating intended it, the inevitable dilemma involving amateur sports; that is, that comtemporary amateur sports on the national and international level are promoted and administered with a professional and "athletic" philosophy, but are governed by rules that emphasize an amateur and "sport" or recreational philosphy.

While considering Keating's proposal, it is of interest to note that in 1930 Count de Baillet-Latour, a former president of the International Olympic Committee, expressed his concern about the growing conflict between the increasing number of international contests and the rules of amateurism.[2] For example, he felt it was impossible to exclude "broken-time" payments or compensation paid in some indirect or underhanded way and continue to increase the number of international contests. His view was not heeded and the number of major national and international contests increased with the growing developments in transportation and communication. The International Olympic Committee remained opposed to "broken-time" payments until 1971. Consistent with the view of Count de Baillet-Latour the National Federation of State High School Athletic Association voted in 1934 to "...refuse to sanction any meet or tournament which is in the nature of a contest to determine a national high school championship."[3] Since this ruling was passed, there have been no national high school championships. I believe this regulation has helped maintain high school athletics as an enjoyable, popular and educational experience for students.

Doherty's Proposal

In 1960, Dr. Kenneth Doherty, a former professor of physical education at the University of Pennsylvannia, proposed that amateurism in sports be defined as a working agreement between two sportsmen:

> 1. who act in good faith to assure both fair competition in sports and equality of oppurtunity for preparation for such competition,
> 2. who participate in sports on an avocational basis only, that is, within the time and energy limitations required by a full-time vocation not directly related to their sport: in school, industry, armed

services or other social service work,
3. who, to further and assure these basic ends, act in accordance
with the limitations of material, social and personal benefits estab-
lished by the International Sports Federation concerned.[4]

One of Doherty's concerns is that the full-time sports professional be re-stricted from competing in a category composed of people who cannot or choose not to devote themselves full-time to athletic training and competi-tion. Theoretically, Doherty's proposal appears to be sound, but again the problem is how to implement the proposal. Attempts to implement this pro-posal would be confronted with the same problems of inequality that con-front today's athlete who has no regular occupation and athletes on industri-al teams, in military services, and from communistic nations. Furthermore, Doherty states that the "present restrictions on material awards must be maintained."[5] That means the restrictions of the 1960 era. The maintenance of these restrictions causes Doherty's proposal to have the same conflicts and problems as other definitions of amateurism, which were discussed in the previous chapter.

Professional in One Sport; Amateur in Others

Ever since the first meeting of the International Olympic Committee in 1894, the issue of whether or not a person could be a professional in one sport and remain an amateur in other sports has been periodically discussed. The most recent significant decision involving this issue was by the National Collegiate Athletic Association on January 7, 1974. At that time the NCAA voted to declare athletes eligible for intercollegiate competition in sports in which they were not professionals.[6] The implications of this rule for athletes who have professionalized themselves in one or more sports, and for others who knowingly have competed with or against these athletes is unclear at this time. Although the rules on this issue does vary among various national and international sports federations, it appears that most of these athletes would be ineligible for world championships and Olympic competition under existing rules.

The major arguments against allowing professional athletes to participate as amateurs in sports in which they have not become professionals are as follows: 1) the belief that such athletes would have an unfair advantage because they could be training for athletics the year round without regard for earning a living in a non-athletic vocation as is necessary for most ama-teur athletes, 2) the fear that this mixing of professional athletes with non-professionals would be a negative influence on amateurs and violate the spirit of amateurism; that is, the view that participation in sport is an avoca-tional experience and something one does for the educational, physical, mental and social benefits derived therefrom with no regard for financial gain.

Two major arguments for this provision are: 1) it provides a way for a young athlete to become an amateur in some sports, if he had intentionally or with poor counsel professionalized himself at an early age and them shortly afterward quit the professional ranks, desiring to participate in amateur sports, 2) it allows a person to participate on a lower level (amateur) in sports in which the athlete is not as talented or has limited time to devote to the sport. For example, a professional baseball player may enjoy playing handball, basketball, or badminton during the off-season as an avocational and recreational experience. Under this rule such a person would be allowed to compete as an amateur in these sports.

In some respects, this rule could be viewed as a type of reinstatement procedure for many contemporary professional athletes, because it provides a way for them to regain their amateur standing in at least some sports. It is also one way of recognizing the fact that a person may not be professional in spirit or skill during his entire life.

There is considerable merit to this proposal. It should be given serious consideration by national and international sports organizations. It should also be possible for an athlete to be allowed to participate as a non-professional or amateur, in the same sport in which he once participated as a professional after a waiting period of perhaps three to five years since being an active professional.

Open Competition

In 1971 Bob Hersh, writing in *Track and Field News,* headlined two articles with the following statements: "The Amateur Code is Outmoded"[7] and "A Solution; Open Track."[8] This proposal is just one of many expressions that "open" competition, with or without athletes being labeled as professionals or amateurs, is the only solution to the hypocrisy and injustice existing under the contemporary amateur rules. There are two points of view advocated regarding "open" competition. One involves a complete abandonment of the labelling of athletes as amateurs or professionals and allows all athletes to compete without discrimination. A second point of view advocates the retaining of criteria for labelling athletes as amateurs or professionals, but would provide opportunities for amateurs and professionals to compete together. The current "open" professional-amateur tournaments in golf and tennis are examples of this point of view. Under either of these positions, agencies such as high school athletic association could still restrict their athletic programs to "closed" competition among amateurs.

There is considerable merit to both of these points of view. The complete abandonment of the distinction between amateurs and professionals would perhaps be the simplest system to administer, but it also opens the door more widely to all the abuses and problems that advocates of amateurism have traditionally feared about professionalism. The more limited opportunities for competition between amateurs and professionals have fewer risks and appears worthy of further experimentation. For those sports organizations interested in moving toward open competition, the limited approach is the best trial step before completely abandoning the distinctions between amateurs and professionals. The limited approach to "open" competition could be incorporated into the general philosophy and solutions advocated in the following pages.

PROPOSED SOLUTIONS

Discontinue the Use of the Term "Amateurism"

Part of the solution to the problems of contemporary amateurism is to discontinue the use of the word "amateur" as a means of legally defining a category of competition, especially on the national and international level. The basic reason for advocating this is that the term "amateur" as used in national and international athletics is in contrast to the normal meaning of the word. As pointed out in Chapter V, an amateur in all areas except athletics is "...one who follows a pursuit without proficiency [and] ...one practicing an art without mastery of its essentials."[9] To refer to national and world class athletes as amateurs is inconsistent with this meaning and creates unnecessary confusion. The effort of Jack Kelly, the former president of the Amateur Athletic Union, to change the name of the union to the American Athletic Union is consistent with this point of view.[10] The term "eligibility code," which has been used by the International Olympic Committee since about 1967 in defining who can and who cannot participate in the Olympic Games, is also a step in the direction of this proposal. It is interesting to note that in 1965 a proposal was made to the International Olympic Committee that the terms "voluntary" and "paid" be substituted for the terms "amateur" and "professional."[11] The proposal was not approved.

Eliminate Statements About Motives

Since it is extremely difficult, if not impossible, to accurately determine the attitude or motive of another person for competing in sports, amateurism as a category of competition should be established primarily on a skill basis. Attempts to define an amateur by expressions such as "one who competes solely for the love of the sport" have proven to be imprecise, ambiguous, and unworkable since no one can determine with sufficient accuracy the motives or attitudes of another person. To assume that an Olympic champion is competing more for the love of sport or the pleasure and physical, mental, and social benefits than is a professional champion is absurd.

Eliminate Restrictions on Time Spent in Training and Competition

As was pointed out in the two preceding chapters, efforts have been made since 1925 to restrict the time that amateur athletes could spend in training and competition. The fact that these rules have all been unsatisfactory seems to have been a major reason why the International Olympic Committee eliminated all restrictions of this type in 1974. The circumstances of athletes who are 1) in military or police units, 2) on industrial teams, 3) students or teachers, 4) wage earners in capitalistic factories, 5) independently wealthy, or 6) citizens in communist countries, are just too diverse to make such controls meaningful or equitable. Therefore, legalistic restrictions on the amount of time an athlete can spend in training and competition on the national and international level should be eliminated from the rules of all organizations. Discontinuing these restrictions would result in a more honest solution to the problems of amateur athletes, and, at the same time, reduce the possibility of hypocritical and deceitful practices.

In support of this view, the following statement by Mr. Albert Mayer, a member of the International Olympic Committee, is pertinent. "Nowadays (1960)—he says—the participation in Olympic competition requires so much effort on both concentration and training that it is no longer possible to attain any sort of classification, without infringing [on] the present rules of amateurism, since an athlete's preparation requires months of effort."[12]

Age, Skill, and Size Categories Are Necessary

To achieve extensive participation in sports by the public, different categories of athletic competition based on factors such as age, size, and individual ability or skill must be established. An example of competitive categories based on age is the Junior Olympic Program of the Amateur Athletic Union of the United States.[13] The junior high, senior high, or college athletic programs in the United States are another example of a type of age grouping. The currently accepted weight categories in judo, boxing, wrestling, and weightlifting are examples of eligibility requirements based on the size of the competitor. Similar weight categories are common in American youth football programs. Variations in the weight of the implement, such as the shot and the discus, represent another method of making participation in some events more appealing. Perhaps greater use of height categories in basketball or a variation in the height of the basket would increase participation even more in this sport.

Establishing categories of competition in athletics according to ability and skill levels may involve minimum or maximum eligibility standards. An example of an eligibility practice in which athletes with a high degree of skill are ineligible is the common practice of declaring varsity letter winners in a school sport ineligible for intramural sport participation. The reason for this restriction is not that there is something evil or corrupting about being on a varsity team, but that varsity players already have an oppourtunity to participate, and they tend to be better players then intramural participants. Because they are better players, they would diminish the enjoyment of intramurals for the main group of participants who are at a lower skill level. Another example of declaring ineligible a group of athletes of superior skill is the rule of the Amateur Athletic Union of the United States governing junior class competition. This rule makes finalists in any National AAU Senior Championship, or members of World Championship, Pan-American or Olympic teams ineligible for junior class competition.[14]

Following this pattern of reasoning, it may be advisable to declare ineligible for contests such as the Olympic Games, international games such as the Pan-American Games, World Championships by international sports federations, and competition below these levels, athletes who play on major league baseball, basketball, ice hockey, and soccer teams, and top level athletes in individual sports such as boxing and tennis.

Just as the procedure for declaring athletes of high ability ineligible for the lower levels of competition ensures a degree of equality in competition, so would the practice of declaring ineligible those athletes whose abilities fall below the selected standard. The process of eliminating athletes in lower level tournaments and trials is an example of how minimum standards of competency are now achieved for championship athletic contests. In track and field and in several other sports, the practice of declaring minimum standards as an eligibility requirment is common practice for national championship meets.

Limit All Awards by Sponsoring Organizations to Symbolic Items

All awards given to victors by organizations promoting and administering what is currently called amateur or non-professional sports should be limited to something that is inexpensive and symbolic in nature. This policy should apply to all levels of competition, including junior high, senior high, college, and national championships, world federation championships, and the Olympic Games. It should be impossible to become a "pot hunter" who can sell one's trophies. The symbolic value of the crown ought to be the motivating factor and reward, and not the crown itself. Nothing of any significant material value should be used as a reward. The current limit of $100 by the Amateur Athletic Union of the United States is probably too high, because prizes of such high value can be used as recruiting devices by promoters and can result in "pot hunting" by athletes.

The principle that is proposed here is essentially that practiced at ancient Olympic Games, where a crown of olive leaves was the only official award. Furthermore, competing for a symbolic prize is a very effective way fo communicating that the real values in athletic competition are not materialistic. It is this message that the Olympic Movement has been trying so hard to communicate over the years.

Change the Restrictions Pertaining to Capitalizing on Athletics

Another point that is being advocated as a solution to the problems of contemporary amateurism is to make a distinction between athletes that participate in competition for monetary prizes or prizes having a monetary value and those who participate only in competition where symbolic awards are given by sponsoring organizations. This distinction would place in a separate category athletes who have competed in a contest or have been competing in an organization that gives financial rewards to the participants, especially to the winner. To avoid confusion of terms, a term such as "paid athletes" or "mercenaries" should be used instead of "professinals" for athletes that compete in a category where monetary prizes are given. A term such as "unpaid athletes" or "volunteers" should be used for the others. Such a rule would place professional boxers and members of basketball, baseball, football, hockey, soccer, and volleyball leagues where the winners compete for purses or playoff money such as in the football Super-Bowl and baseball World Series, in a special category. The consequences of this procedure would be to effectively set apart athletes on the basis of two important principles. One principle involves the importance of establishing competitive categories on the basis of skill as mentioned before. Concerning this point, the assumption is that athletes who are hired and contracted by owners and promoters to make money for them can legitimately be classified as being in a high skill category. This would not be a perfect judgement of skill, but it does seem reasonable to conclude that the members of the current professional major league teams and those competing for prizes in sports such as boxing, bowling, golf, and tennis are the best athletes in these sports.

The second and most important principle involved in this proposal is that the new classification makes a clear and concise distinction between a contest conducted and promoted for money and one promoted and conducted for the other values inherent in athletic competition.

This proposal in no way limits the benefits materially or otherwise that an athlete may receive as a result of participating in athletic competition. In other words, athletes in the "unpaid" category would be totally free to capitalize in any way on their athletic fame or success and still continue to compete in contests such as the Olympic Games. However, an athlete could not be under contract to perform in an athletic event. An athlete could only capitalize on past achievements and not on future events. This principle would prevent athletes from becoming living billboards with various products advertised on their uniforms while competing. Under this system it is possible that some Olympic Games participants would be able to capitalize on their fame and talent more extensively than some athletes under contracts in the paid category. But this would be acceptable, understood and done without deceit or hypocrisy.

For the organizations controlling and promoting what is currently called amateur sports, this classification method and allowance for benefits would allow for a new and cleaner way to emphasize that it is participation that is important and not the winning of awards. At the same time, it would allow such organizations to honestly admit that there are many kinds of benefits that do come from participating in athletics.

The staunch advocates of nineteenth and twentieth century amateurism will probably argue that the professional spirit or "athletic" spirit will inevitably lead to distorted values under the rules proposed here. The excesses of professionalism in ancient Greece, the fantastic personal contracts of this era, and the obvious power of money are sufficient causes for such concerns. The existence of this risk is part of the reason for separating athletes in the "paid" or "mercenary" category from those in the "unpaid" or "volunteer" category. It should be noted that the separate categories and classifications of athletes proposed involves a separation or classification of sponsors, promoters, and owners, as much as a separation of individual athletes. This is important. When corruption and abuse exist in athletics, whether on a professional or amateur level, it is often the fault of owners and promoters. A recent article on professional hockey in *Sports Illustrated*[15] and earlier articles in *Life* magazine clearly support this view.[16] [17]

No rulebook or organization can eliminate greed or totally control people's values and judgement. Therefore, even under the proposed system, if the rewards for winning become excessive, the possibility for some distortion of values exists. But, it must be rememebered that the potential for corruption and distortion of values is probably greater under contemporary amateurism than if the restrictions on awards were eliminated.[18] [19]

This proposal may be an answer to the problems caused by excessive financial benefits. It is helpful to realize that the resources to generously support professional athletes are not inexhaustible. During the 1960's the tremendous expansion in professional sports in the United States was very impressive, but the folding of an entire World Football League, the demise of some basketball and tennis franchises in 1975, and the shaky financial picture of many other professionals teams have been equally impressive. These more recent developments indicate that there is a limit to what the public and wealthy individuals will spend to support athletics. Furthermore, eliminating the traditional amateur restrictions on materially benefiting from athletics for all national and world-class athletes would provide a very broad base of athletes that could legitimately accept some remuneration for their successes. The end result of this approach may prove to be a tremendous leveling effect on the salaries paid to professionals. Such a change could result in a ground swell of enthusiasm for athletics and a renewed feeling of confidence and support for athletics on all levels.

When one considers the alternatives to current rules, it is worth noting that winning at any price, that is, winning by any means fair or foul, is not limited to circumstances where pecuniary rewards are at stake. For example, for many athletes the fame associated with a gold medal at the Olympic Games may be a greater temptation for them to attempt to win by any means, fair or foul, than temptations of pecuniary rewards. Furthermore, the striving for excellence and the desire to win which are involved in the "athletic" or professional spirit do not necessarily mean winning at any cost. For the athlete, it is important to demonstrate his excellence by winning within the rules of the contest, because winning by cheating, bribery, and any other dishonorable tactic is victory devoid of any value or meaning. The honest athlete asks no favors and gives no favors. Nor does an athlete's desire to win imply conflict with the traditional sportsmanship behavior that is best described by the following "Code of Sportmanship," which was published in 1926 by the Sportsmanship Brotherhood in England.[20]

> *Keep the rules*
> *Keep faith in your comrades*
> *Keep your temper*
> *Keep yourself fit*
> *Keep a stout heart in defeat*
> *Keep your pride under in victory*
> *Keep a sound soul, a clean mind, and a healthy body*

The rules do not mean that the athlete will, when defeated, attempt to convey an attitude of joy because the opponent won; but the rules do imply that an athlete can and should win and lose with self-control and respect for his opponent.

Another traditional fear that advocates of amateurism have expressed concerning professionalism is that it creates a tendency for an athlete to specialize in a certain skill or event.[21] This view developed during the nineteenth century when being a dabbler or amateur at many things was the socially accepted emphasis in England.[22] Also, since amateur athletics has so often been identified with the athletics of ancient Greece, the complaints of the ancient Greeks against specialization by athletes have apparently been a factor in the thinking of nineteenth and twentieth century advocates of amateurism, However, it needs to be emphasized that one of the major reasons given by the Greeks against specializing was that it conflicted with the attributes of a good soldier. This was especially true of the wrestlers and boxers, who put on their excessive bulk in order to win their events for which no weight categories existed.[23] Other reasons why some ancient Greeks complained about the specialization of athletes was because they considered it unhealthy[24] and that the time and energy spent specializing in athletics were not conducive to the proper development of the mind.[25]

These reasons for concern over specialization, which were thought unjustifiable over 2,000 years ago in a different culture, do not mean that specialization per se is bad. Specialization is a relative emphasis which may be detrimental or beneficial. In fact, a degree of specialization in athletics is good if achieving one's maximum potential in an athletic skill is a worthy accomplishment. Certainly, the discipline, sacrifice, work, and concentration that are part of such an experience are of value. In addition, if there are inherent values to be derived from athletics and if one of the aims of education is to help each person develop his abilities to the maximum potential, then it seems reasonable that athletic skills should be part of this developmental goal.

Gardner, when discussing the ideal of individual fulfillment and education, says, "It is expressed in our conviction that every individual should be enabled to achieve the best that is in him."[26] To achieve the best that is in some individuals may mean specializing to the extent of becoming an international champion. Furthermore, in this era it is essntial to specialize in almost every endeavor if one is to achieve much success. This certainly is true in performance areas such as music, drama, and athletics, but it is also true in education, medicine, law, etc. The concern over excessive specialization is essentially a problem for those concerned with the curriculum of educational institutions for young people. Specialization normally is not a problem for adult athletes, because specializing in athletics does not mean that an adult athlete cannot have an interest in educational pursuits, business, government, etc. Present-day professional athletes in the United States are evidenced of the truth of this statement. If specialization in athletics per se is evil or a poor choice of values, then the advocates of amateurism have no choice but to discontinue the Olympic Games and other major tournaments, because these contests encourage specialization. Furthermore, no one can achieve the level of skill necessary to win at the Olympic Games without a high degree of specialization.

Restrictions on Profiting Financially from Athletics
Essential on Lower Competitive Levels

In order to increase the probability that young people will view athletics in a proper perspective, it seems advisable to prohibit young athletes from receiving any direct financial compensations for their performances. This rule seems especially appropiate for athletes that are part of an educational institution. For junior and senior high athletes, the existing amateur or eligibility rules set forth by the National Federation of High School Athletic Associations is a good practical and workable code.[27] The code is workable because it deals with a group of people in essentially the same situation. Competition in such a group is called "closed" because it does not concern itself with the privileges and restrictions of other groups in other situations or cultures. Similar restrictions for local and state-wide non-school programs for athletes high school age and younger seem very appropriate.

This position is not in conflict with the earlier proposal to eliminate restrictions on benefits that national and world-class athletes may receive. This recommendation implies a recognition that important differences do exist between "closed" and "open" competition and between the appropriateness of restrictions on young athletes who are usually living with their parents and older athletes who are financially on their own. To deny that these differences exist is to succumb to the problems that have surrounded international amateur sports for decades.

Necessity of Existential Attitude

The elimination of the legalistic definition of amateurism as a category of competition should be accompanied with a new emphasis on personal freedom and responsibility. In contrast to the current situation in which individuals and organizations are trying to maintain a standard and attain the practice of the spirit of amateurism through legalistic means, responsibility for the attitudes, choices, and consequences should be given to the individual athlete. In essence, what is being proposed is a type of existential emphasis on responsibility for what one will be.[28] This emphasis allows for individual freedom and responsibility. The athlete, especially the adult athlete, should learn to be free—free to make choices, value judgements and decisions— and to recognize that he, and he alone, is responsible for his choices and his actions. If his choices and his actions violate a rule or infringe on another's rights, he should learn to accept the consequence.

The athlete should also learn to accept the responsibility for the joy as well as the anguish that may result from his decisions. The athlete must learn to make decisions that determine how much time, money, and effort he can devote to sports, how badly he wants to win, how important are his job, his family, studies, and other interests, and then be totally responsible for the decisions made. With this emphasis, it becomes the athlete's responsibility to decide whether to participate solely for pleasure or other reasons. He must decide how extensively to specialize. In addition, he must learn to be responsible for his decisions and to be honest in his relations with other men. If he chooses to be dishonest, he alone must bear the responsibility and consequences of his dishonesty. The athlete must learn that in a very real sense he is what he makes himself to be.

This emphasis does not free the leaders in sports, especially the leaders of school-age athletics, from the responsibility of helping athletes to make the right decisions. In fact, it becomes the responsibility of sports leaders to convey to athletes the important values involved in various choices. If sports leaders fail in this responsibility, the athlete cannot use this as a "scapegoat" or excuse for his failure to make proper judgements. He is still responsible for his actions. This philosphy and emphasis would seem to provide the best possibility of helping athletes learn to make the right value judgements and at the same time help eliminate the current problem of hypocrisy surrounding amateurism.

Extensive Participation Should Be Encouraged

A system of athletics for the general public ought to provide numerous opportunities for everyone to compete. This contrasts with the practice in ancient Greece where only a small percentage of the population had an opportunity to compete in athletics. It also contrasts with the practice in England during the nineteenth century when participation in amateur athletics was restricted to those in the upper social classes. These practices can harldy be justified today. What can be justified and what is essential is that a system of athletic competition for the public encourages extensive participation in athletics, especially among the youth, on the local, national, and international levels. The reason that an acceptable system of athletic competition should stimulate participation is based on the premise that all men are created equal and that the worthy physiological, psychological and sociological values inherent in athletics should be available to everyone.

There is some physiological evidence that regular, vigorous exercise benefits the body in several ways, including, 1) an increase in the size and strength of muscles, 2) an improved "precision and economy" of motion, 3) an increased cardiovascular and respiratory efficiency, and 4) an aid to the control of. body weight and shape.[29] Some of the psychological values that may accrue from participation in athletics or training are the development of confidence, emotional stability, poise, and resistance to anxiety,[30] and the satisfying of one's ego.[31] Some of the sociological values that may be derived from athletic competition are development of cooperation, leadership, ability to follow the leader, loyalty to a group, discipline, responsibility, respect for the property of others, and the desire to pursue excellence in performance.[32]

The benefits listed are not isolated physiologically, psychologically, or sociologically. On the contrary, exercise and sports competition have an interrelated effect on the total man.[33] Therefore, assuming that there are inherent worthy values to be derived from athletics and that all men are created equal, it is reasonable to advocate a system of athletic competition that stimulates extensive and perhaps intensive participation by the public, regardless of race, sex, creed, or political views, and social or economic status. And, if there are important values and lessons to be learned from athletic experiences, it is reasonable to encourage participation by young people because the period of youth is universally recognized as the natural and prime time for educating mankind. To encourage youth to participate in sports is also important because young people "...can distinguish themselves in sport to a degree they do [can] not, on the whole attain elsewhere."[34] In fact, in sports a young person can achieve an excellence that cannot be attained by people past their youth.

Open Membership Opportunities to Everyone on National and International Committees

The 1975 rules of the International Olympic Committee state that "The following are not eligible to serve on the National Olympic Committee:

1. a person who has ever competed as a professional;
2. a person engaged in or connected with sport for personal profit (it is not intended to exclude individuals occupying purely administrative positions in connection with amateur sport);
3. a person who has ever coached sports competitors for payment.

Exceptions may be made in the above categories by the Executive Board of the International Olympic Committee in special circumstances on the recommendation of the national committee concerned."[35]

This type of prejudicial view of professionals, especially coaches in educational institutions, is unjustifiable. Almost every athletic director in the United States has coached for pay, and to assume that these men and women, who have been specially trained to administer educational athletic programs, are not qualified to serve on the National Olympic Committees is just another carry-over from the nineteenth century thinking and practice. If rules of this type exist in other amateur sports organizations, it is equally unfortunate. It seems that contemporary amateur sports need more, not fewer, professionally trained sports administrators who understand and believe in the inherent values in athletics. If there are pitfalls to be wary of in professional athletics, it seems that a few intelligent, current or former professional athletes and coaches who have been specially educated in physical education and athletic sports administration and philosophy would be an asset rather than a liability on sports committees that are attempting to promote wholesome athletic programs.

Necessity of Adequately Financing Sports Organizations

In addition to the need to implement the changes proposed in the preceding pages and the need to emphasize the individual's responsibility for his actions as part of the solution to the current problems surrounding amateur sports, are some concerns related to the need to adequately finance amateur sports organizations. It is clear that there should be numerous opportunities for competition in order to have an adequate system of athletics for the public. If there are going to be extensive opportunities to participate in amateur athletics, then adequate leadership must be provided—and such leadership involves finances. In order to have adequate leadership, it is increasingly obvious that more paid professional personnel than presently exist in most amateur organizations must be forthcoming. For exmaple, it is extremely difficult for a volunteer organization such as the Amateur Athletic Union of the United States to succeed in promoting mass participation in the sixteen sports which it governs because of its limited staff and budget. In contrast to organizations like the Amateur Athletic Union of the United States which are essentially volunteer organizations are the high school and the college athletic organizations which operate extensive athletic programs with a significantly greater number of paid personnel on the local, state, and national levels.

The recognition of the need for an increased number of paid professional leaders in amateur sports is directly related to another factor in the solution to the problem of amateur sports in the United States. This factor is the increasing necessity of financing public sports administrative bodies on the local, state, and national level by means of taxes, as well as fees, contributions, gate receipts, and advertising revenue. As long as the sports-governing and-promoting bodies in the United States and elsewhere are financed and controlled by private funds and individuals, open competition will be limited. The athletic programs of the schools, universities, and recreation departments in the United States are proof that "professionals" can promote and control wholesome educational and recreational athletic programs, which are financed by tax money, fees, gate receipts, and contributions.

The stress given by some individuals to the opinion that organizations such as the United States Olympic Committee and the Amateur Athletic Union of the United States should be solely financed by non-governmental sources is basically an aristocratic point of view that is feasible only in relatively wealthy nations. Even if adequate, privately financed, athletic programs could be achieved in the United States, it would not be possible in other countries. The truth of this statement is attested to by the fact that both Great Britain and Canada have begun providing from tax sources some of the finances for their national sports-governing bodies. The Canadian government began giving grants to national sports associations in 1961 with the passage of the Fitness and Amateur Sport Act.[36] The extent of this support is evidenced by the fact that during the fiscal year 1966-67 federal grants amounting to one and a half million dollars were made to various sports organizations.[37]

The British government started giving grants to national sports-governing bodies in 1962 and began to subsidize its Olympic teams in 1964. Prior to 1962 in Great Britain government financial support for sports had been basically only for financing physical education in the schools and colleges and for providing recreational faciliities for the general public. The change in policy was brought about by the importance placed on international competition by the public in Great Britain and by a growing awareness of the limitations of the national sports-governing bodies.[38] Concerning the expenditures for sports by the governments of some other European countries, one authority estimated that in 1967 Sweden was spending five times as much per person as Great Britain; and France, one and a half times as much as Great Britain.[39] The United States is apparently one of the few, if not the only nation in the world that is still trying to finance its national sports-governing bodies and Olympic teams solely from the contributions, fees, gate receipts, and advertisements.

The insistence by some advocates of amateurism that organizations such as the Amateur Athletic Union and the United States Olympic Committee be privately financed is inconsistent with the role played by government schools, college, and military services in financing buildings, coaches, trainers, and athletes. For example, as late as 1948, "the United States Cavalry both furnished and subsidized the equestrian teams that officially represented" the United States, and this practice was discontinued only because the Cavalry became mechanized. The tax-exempt status of the Amateur Athletic Union, the United States Olympic Committee and other sports bodies is also evidence of a type of government support.

Other Aspects of the Solution

The rules of sports and the nature of some events need to be continually reviewed if some sports are to have mass appeal and are to avoid some of the problems often associated with professionalism. This involves the need to consider, in the promotion and creation of events and rules, whether the nature of the event or rule is psychologically, physiologically, and sociologically an asset to the competitors. For example, tossing the 35 pound weight, should not be added to the field events for women because the increase in weight and strength necessary for success in national and international competitions in this event normally would be neither a physical, psychological, nor sociological asset to women competitors. Consequently, women generally would not be attracted to such an event and sports should be appealing to the public.

A second factor concerning the rules which needs to be considered is the possibility of more controls than at present on the use of drugs and food supplements for gaining excessive weight and for increasing endurance. Controls on the use of such drugs and food supplements are important because of the potential health hazards involved and because of the possible unfair or unequal competition which may result until the health hazards and the advantages of these substances are known. The efforts of the International Olympic Committee in this area are very commendable.

A third factor is that the rules of sports must eliminate brutality and minimize the risk of injury in order to attract more participants. For example, boxing should probably evolve to a point system similar to that of fencing where the emphasis is on skill rather than on incapacitating the opponent.[40] The brutality of boxing, wrestling, and the pancration in ancient Greece provides evidence of how the masses become spectators rather than participants when the rules allowed brutality.

A major factor in the proper administration of any competitive athletic situation is the necessity of strict regulations forbidding gambling by any person (players, coaches, promoters, referees, and trainers) associated with a contest or tournament in order to minimize the possibility of any dishonest or hypocritical practices. For a person convicted of gambling on athletic contests in which he is directly or indirectly involved, the penalty must be severe. The stern measures taken at the ancient Olympic Games and by the professional sports leagues in the United States are examples of procedures for minimizing gambling by persons directly involved in a contest.

SUMMARY

Throughout this book and especially in the last two chapters, certain principles or premises have served as the basis for identifying the problems within amateurism and the basis for proposing solutions to the problems. The three basic principles have been the belief 1) that all men are created equal, 2) that there are values inherent in competitive athletics, and 3) that any system of athletics should be conducted with the high ideals of sportmanship and ethics and should promote the development of such ideals. The last principle implies that an acceptable system of athletic competition should minimize the probability of hypocritical and deceitful practices.

Based on these three principles, various solutions to the problem of amateurism were proposed in this chapter. The major aspects of the proposed solutions were to 1) eliminate statements about the motives for competing, 2) eliminate restrictions on time spent in training and competition, 3) continue to establish categories based on age, skill, and size of the participants, 4) limit all awards by sponsoring organizations to symbolic items, 5) change the restrictions pertaining to capitalizing on athletics in the eligibility codes for national and international level competitors. The last item involves making a distinction between those who compete for pay and those who may financially benefit because they have participated. A distinction was also made between promoters and organizers whose basic motives are to make money and those whose basic goals are to encourage participation for other values.

Woven in and out of the proposed solutions was a belief that there are important differences between athletics for school-aged, young people and adults who are competing on the national and international level. Some other dimensions of the proposed solutions were the importance of 1) impressing upon athletes that they are responsible for their own actions, 2) controlling gambling, 3) properly financing athletic organizations, and 4) having rules conducive to safe and extensive mass participation.

To what extent the proposed solutions will make athletics more honest and wholesome, only experimentation and experience will prove. Whether the proposals contained in this chapter will be adequate for the year 2000 is another question. In spite of risks, known and unknown, that would be associated with implementing the proposed solutions, it seems reasonable to do so. In conclusion, amateurism is an attitude or emphasis as well as a level of ability and can be satisfactorily controlled and conducted by following the basic principles proposed in this chapter.

FOOTNOTES

1   James B. Keating,"The Heart of the Problem of Amateur Athletes," *Journal of General Education*, 16 (January 1965), p. 271.

2   *Official Bulletin*, International Olympic Committee, V (July 1930), p. 21.

3   *Official Handbook 1970-1971* (Chicago: National Federation of State High School Athletic Associations, 1971), p. 36.

4   Kenneth Doherty, "Modern Amateurism," *Health and Fitness in the Modern World* (Chicago: Athletic Institute, 1961), p. 234.

5   Ibid., p. 235.

6   *1975-76 NCAA Manual* (Shawnee, Mission, Kansas: National Collegiate Athletic Association, 1975), pp. 6, 210.

7   Bob Hersh "Track and Field Payoffs–The Amateur Code is Outmoded," *Track and Field News* (December 1975), p. 4.

8   Bob Hersh, "A Solution: Open Track," *Track and Field News* (December 1971), pp. 4-5.

9   *Webster's New Collegiate Dictionary*, 2nd. ed. (Springfield, Mass.: G. & C. Merriam Co., publishers, 1949), p. 27.

10 Rich McArthur, "Kelly Offers Six-Point Plan to AAU Convention," *Amateur Athlete*, Amateur Athletic Union of the United States, 42 (February 1971), pp. 4-5.

11 *Bulletin*, du Comite International Olympique, No. 90 (May 1965), p. 56.

12 Nadijda LeKarska, "An Extraordinary Record," *Bulletin of the Bulgarian Olympic Committee*, [1966], p. 19.

13 *1975 Official Handbook of the AAU Code* (Indianapolis, Ind.: Amateur Athletic Union of the United States, 1975), pp. 112-20.

14 Ibid., p. 113.

15 Ray Kennedy, "Wanted: An End to Mayhem," *Sports Illustrated*, 43 (November 17, 1975), pp. 16-21.

16 Wes Sartee, "Names, Places and Pay-offs–Sartee Blows the Whistle," *Life*, 41 (November 19, 1956), pp. 99-100, 103-04, 109-110.

17 Jack Newcombe, "Athletes Tell How Illicit Pay-offs Destroy the Amateur Code," *Life*, 40 (April 30, 1956), pp. 113-14, 116, 118, 120.

18 Peter C. McIntosh, *Sport in Society* (London: C. A. Watt and Company, Ltd., 1963), p. 182.

19 Walter Umminger, *Supermen, Heroes and Gods*, trans. and adapted by James Clark (New York: McGraw Hill Book Company, Inc., 1963), p. 223.

20 "A Sportsmanship Brotherhood," *Literary Digest*, LXXXVIII (March 27, 1926), p. 60.

21 "The Athletic Research Society," *Mind and Body*, 17 (February 1911), p. 363.

22 George C. Brodrick, "A Nation of Amateurs," *The Nineteenth Century*, 284 (October 1900), pp. 521-26.

23 E. Norman Gardiner, *Athletics of the Ancient World* (Oxford: The Clarendon Press, 1967), p. 204.

24 *Plutarch's Lines*, Vol. II, trans. by Bernadotte Perrin, II Vols., The Loeb Classical Library (Cambridge: Harvard University Press, 1914), pp. 101-104.

25 Rachel Sargent Robinson, *Sources for the History of Greek Athletics* (338 Probasco St., Cincinnati: Rachel Sargent Robinson, 1955), pp. 119-20, 137-39.

26 John W. Gardner, *Excellence* (New York: Harper and Brothers, 1961), p. 135.

27 *Official Handbook 1970-71* (Chicago: National Federation of State High School Athletic Associations, 1970), p. 16.

28 Jean-Paul Sartre, *Existentialism*, trans. by Bernard Frechtman (New York: Philosophical Library, 1947), p. 19.

29 Allan J. Ryan, "Contributions of Sports and Athletics to Physical Well-Being," in *Values in Sports*, a report of a national conference. (Washington, D. C.: American Association for Health, Physical Education, and Recreation, 1963), pp. 40-43.

30 Thomas K. Cureton, "Anatomical Physiological, and Psychological Changes Induced by Exercise Programs (Exercises, Sports, Games) in Adults," *Exercise and Fitness* (Chicago: The Athletic Institute, 1959), pp. 177-78.

31 Ryan, "Contributions of Sports and Athletics to Physical Well-Being," p. 44.

32 Leslie F. Malpass, "Competition, Conflict, and Cooperation as Social Values," in *Values in Sports*, report of a National Conference, (Washington, D. C.: American Association for Health, Physical Education, and Recreation, 1963), p. 61.

33 Jesse Feiring Williams, *The Principles of Physical Education*, 8th ed. (Philadelphia: W. B. Saunders Company, 1964), pp. 8-9.

34 Paul Weiss, *Sport: A Philosophic Inquiry* (Carbondale, Illinois: Southern Illinois University Press, 1969), p. 11.

35 *Olympic Rules, Bye-Laws and Instruction* (Lausanne: International Olympic Committee, 1975), p. 15.

36 J. E. Merriam, "Canadian Association of Sports Sciences, a Historical Review," *Journal of the Canadian Association for Health, Physical Education and Recreation*, 33 (August-September 1967), p. 29.

37 "Canada's Fitness and Amateur Sport Program 1966-67," *Journal of the Canadian Association for Health, Physical Education and Recreation*, 34 (February-March 1968), p. 13.

38 Philip Goodhart and Christopher Chatway, *War Without Weapons* (London: W. A. Allen, 1968), pp. 88-90.

39 Ibid., p. 92.

40 Ernest Jokl, *The Medical Aspects of Boxing* (Pretoria, South Africa: J. L. Van Schaik, Ltd., 1941), pp. 216-17.

APPENDIX A

Rules on Amateur from the **1978 Official Handbook of the AAU Code** ʌmateur Athletic Union of the United States.

101.3   **Definitions**.

    (1)   "Amateur" is one who engages in sport solely for the pleasure and physical, mental or social benefits he derives therefrom and to whom sport is nothing more than an avocation.

ARTICLE 54
DISQUALIFICATION

454.1   **Jurisdiction**. A person shall cease to be eligible to compete or exhibit in open or closed events given or sanctioned by the Amateur Athletic Union while disqualified or under suspension of this Union, or any of its Associations or Allied members.

454.2   **Types**. A Person disqualifies himself from competing as an amateur by commiting any of the following acts:

    (a) Fraud.
    (b) Competing for money.
    (c) Coaching, instructing, or preparing any person for competition when other than actual expenses incurred for that specific task are received, beyond established limits. [See 454.6 (h) (2)] .
    (d) Receiving compensation for athletic services.
    (e) Capitalizing on athletic fame.
    (f) Competing with or against ineligible persons.
    (g) Becoming a professional.
    (h) Miscellaneous.

454.3   **Fraud**. Is the participation in any competition or exercise in any sport under an assumed name or by being guilty of any fraud or other grossly unsportsmanlike conduct in connection therewith.

454.4   **Competing for money**. Is directly or indirectly receiving pay or financial benefits in consideration of or as a reward for participating in any public competition or exhibition or, disposing of prizes for personal gain.

454.5   **Coaching, instructing or preparing any person for competition for which compensation is received**. Is directly or indirectly receiving pay or financial benefits in consideration of or as a reward for coaching, instructing or preparing any person in or for any competition or exhibition. The teaching of basic skills in a recreation program, Red Cross Swimming Program, sports camp, or similar type of programs, where such instruction does not prepare for competition, shall not be considered a violation of this rule, and where such activity does not violate the rules of the international body governing that sport.

454.6   **Receiving Compensation for Athletic Services.**

(a) Any person receiving compensation for services performed in any capacity in connection with athletic games, or in any athletic club except as hereinafter provided, will be ineligible to represent such club in games held under the rules of the Amateur Athletic Union until 90 days after the permanent abandonment of such employment, and shall have been ruled eligible to compete by the Registration Committee. The abandonment of such employment shall not entitle a person to compete as an amateur who is not eligible otherwise.

(b) Any person receiving compensation as a lifeguard, bath or playground attendant, who, in the judgment of the Registration Committee is not capitalizing on his or her athletic fame or ability shall be eligible for registration as an amateur.

(c) Any school or college teacher, including physical education teachers whose work is educational or who is not paid more than 20% of their total salary or compensation directly or indirectly, for coaching of athletes for competition is eligible as an amateur, provided such compensation is permitted by the rules of the international body governing that sport.

(d) Any school and college teacher, including physical education teachers whose work is education or who is not paid more than 10% of their total salary or compensation directly or indirectly, for coaching of athletes for competition, are eligible as amateurs in the sport of basketball only.

(e) Any person acting as the personal solicitor for the sale, or as the actual salesman of sporting goods, prizes, trophies or other commodities for use chiefly in or in connection with games or exhibition in any sport, shall be ineligible to compete at any sports given under the sanction of the Amateur Athletic Union and for a period of ninety days after having ceased such employment, unless such person be registered and enrolled as a student at an accredited college, university or high school.

(ii)   His actual expenditure for maintenance, including lodging and meals, up to a total of thirty-five ($35) dollars a day, but not to exceed the reasonable cost of board and lodging in that locality per day for each day, during the time necessarily occupied between going to and returning from the event. Exclusive of necessary travel time, the period for such expenses may be allowed shall not exceed (1) one day before and one (1) day after the event, unless for good reason a longer period is expressly approved by his local Registration Committee.

(iii)   If in any case an athlete has been unable to obtain reasonably suitable hotel accommodations and/or meals at a cost within the amount allowable under (ii) hereof, and if in any one or more days he has actually been required to spend more than such allowable amount therefor, the sponsoring organization and the athlete may jointly apply to the Registration Committee of the District where the event was held, with a copy of such application also sent to the Chairman of the National Registration Committee and to the athlete's local Registration Committee, for permission to pay and accept respectively, a supplemental allowance for expenses equal to the excess amount the athlete has been required to spend in any such day or days, but which supplemental allowance shall in no event exceed five ($5.00) dollars for and one day. Such application must be accompanied by the athlete's detailed statement of all his expenditures for the day or days in question an vouchers or receipts for all such wherever possible. If the Registration Committee shall consider the payment of such supplemental expenses reasonably justified under all circumstances, it may approve such payment. However, the sponsoring organization may not make nor the athlete accept any such supplemental payment as above unless and until the Registration Committee shall have approved the application.

(iv)   No payment of money or other thing of value may be made, directly or indirectly, for expenses or otherwise, to any person other than the athlete, whether friend, relative or otherwise, in any manner connected with or resulting from the entry, appearance or participation by the athlete in any event except that the expenses of the athlete's bona fide coach and/or chaperone who will accompany the athlete to any competition, may be paid. Such expenses, however, must be paid directly to such coach and/or chaperone and may in no event be paid to the athlete, and shall not exceed the amount allowable to the athlete, hereunder, and such coach and/or chaperone shall furnish to the Registration Committee the same statement, vouchers, etc. as required from the athlete herein.

(3) Any athlete proved to have received, or who claims to have received excessive expense money, or any sum in violation of any of the provisions of this rule while competing as an amateur, shall stand disqualified until reinstated to amateur status by the Board of Governors. Any record performance or championship won by such athlete shall be stricken from the record books and all medals or trophies won shall be returned for re-distribution to the athletes entitled to them.

   (i) The receipt of expense money or reasonable per diem expense allowances by amateur athletes in connection with participation in education demonstrations or benefits for civic, charitable, or educational institutions shall not be considered in violation of this rule. However, the approval of the local Registration Committee must be obtained, and all money received must be reported to the Committee.

454.7   **Capitalizing on Athletic Fame.**

(a) Is granting or sanctioning the use of one's name to advertise, recommend, or promote the sale of the goods or apparatus of any person, firm, manufacturer or agent, or by accepting compensation, directly or indirectly, for using the goods or apparatus of any person, firm, manufacturer or agent.

(b) Is engaging for pay or financial benefit in any occupation or business transaction wherein his usefulness or value arises chiefly from the publicity given or to be given to the reputation or fame which he has secured from his performances in any sport rather than from his ability to perform the usual and natural acts and duties incident to such occupation or transaction.

(c) Is accepting pay or material benefits for a display of athletic ability.

(d) Is participating in radio broadcast or telecast either directly or indirectly connected with an advertisement unless special permission in writing is granted by the National Registration Committee. The advertising of any current athletic event or any civic, charitable or educational enterprise by an athlete shall not be considered a violation of the foregoing. However, the approval of the Local Registration Committee must be obtained.

(e) (1) Is allowing his photograph to be taken and used for advertising or motion picture purposes (other than a news picture which may not be used on sponsored programs) whether or not he has received or is to receive compensation of any kind, directly from the use of such photograph, unless special written permission be granted by the National Registration Committee; provided, however, if such photograph or motion picture is in connection with regular gainful employment and not directly related to/or identified with any athletic fame, then it is not a violation of this section, but District Registration Committee should be informed of such occupational intent for record purposes prior to the first acceptance of such employment.

(2) The use of an athlete's photograph in so-called "loop" films or similar films, for training or coaching purposes only, is not prohibited by this section, provided the athlete receives no compensation of any kind, directly or indirectly for or in connection with its use. However, before such films may be sold or offered for sale, written permission must first be obtained from the National Registration Committee.

(f) Is writing, lecturing or broadcasting for payment upon any athletic event, competition or sport without the prior permission of the National Registration Committee. Such permission may be given only to a person who is genuinely making his main career in one or another of such activities; shall not extend to any event, competition, tournament or meet in which the athlete himself participates as a competitor, official or otherwise; and it shall be effective provided the athlete does not violate any of the other provisions of this Article, and is in accordance with the rules and regulations of the International Sports Governing Body of the sport in which the athlete competes.

454.8   **Competing with or Against Ineligible Persons (without having obtained special permission to do so from the National Registration Committee).**

(a) Any person knowingly competing against one who is disqualified under sentence of suspension by this Union, or any of its District

Associations or allied members shall be held to have suspended himself for such period as the Registration Committee of the District Association in whose territory the offense was committed may deem proper.

(b) A person disqualifies himself as an amateur for:

    (1) Participating in any public competition or exhibition as an individual and not merely as a member of a team against one or more persons ineligible to compete as an amateur in the sport in which such participation occurred.

    (2) Participating in any public competition as a member of a team upon which there are one or more members who have received, do receive or who are to receive directly or indirectly, pay or financial benefits for participating. In the case of a college or high school student the National Registration Committee may, with the consent and approval of the Local Registration Committee, delegate authority to grant such consent, to the proper faculty authority of the university, college or high school of which he is at the time of such participation a matriculated student, upon filing such consent with the National Committee.

    (3) Participating in any public competition or exhibition as a member of a team against another team one or more members of which are ineligible to compete as amateurs in the sport in which such participation occurred, unless the team competed against represents a well-established organization and written permission so to participate is obtained from the Association Registration Committee under guidelines established by the National Registration Committee.

(c) The above provisions shall not be deemed to apply to cases where the competitor is a member of a particular school, college, playground or group, and the competition is confined to and in such particular school, college, playground or group.

454.9   Becoming a Professional.

(a) When an athlete receives compensation to compete or participate in any professional competition or exhibition in any sport, he shall thereafter be ineligible to compete as an amateur.

(b) An athlete, who has entered into try-out agreement or contract or participates in a professional training camp and who does not receive any compensation, either directly or indirectly, beyond actual expenses not in excess of the sum permitted by AAU rules, may be reinstated by his Association Registration Committee, upon proper application therefore, at any time after 30 days from the date of his last appearance with the professional group.

(c) When an athlete signs an agreement or contract to compete or participate in any professional competition or exhibition in any sport, he thereafter shall be ineligible to compete as an amateur. However, such athlete may apply for reinstatement by his Association Registration Committee, upon the submission of a written release from such agreement or contract and provided he has not performed pursuant to such agreement, whether or not he has received compensation.

454.10   **Miscellaneous.** The following are other means by which an athlete, official, coach, or club member or other persons can be disqualified from participation in A.A.U activites

(a) Any person who competes or exhibits at games, meets, benefits, exhibitions or entertainments of any kind, unless the same are given under sanction of the Amateur Athletic Union shall thereby disqualify himself from competing at any sports given under sanction of the Amateur Athletic Union. Events held by and on the premises of an organization which is a member of a District Association of this Union, or by an allied member are exempt from the provisions of this rule.

(b) It shall be within the province of the Registration Committee to suspend from competition for such a time as it may deem proper any person guilty of unfair dealing in connection with athletic competition, ungentlemanly or unladylike conduct, or for violation of the rules of the Amateur Athletic Union. The following among other things, shall be considered as unfair dealing and ungentlemanly conduct:

(1) Suppression of true figures from the handicapper.

(2) The use of obscene or profane language in competition area.

(3) The doing of any act which tends to disturb or obstruct a competition or to bring this Union or amateur athletics into disrepute.

(c) Any member of any club of any of the District Association of the Amateur Athletic Union who shall have been expelled from said club for unpaid indebtedness shall not be eligible to compete in any games given by any Association of the Amateur Athletic Union, or by any club or any Association of the Amateur Athletic Union, until such indebtedness is liquidated.

(d) An athlete who permits anyone, other than an officer of the club which he is entitled to represent in competition, to make arrangements for his appearance at any athletic meeting shall thereby render himself ineligible for further competition as an amateur for such period of time as may be decided upon by the Registration Committee.

(e) An athlete who fails to compete after entering an event in a bona fide way, and according to the rules, shall be required to furnish a satisfactory excuse for such failure or render himself liable to censure or suspension by the registration committee of the District Association in which the athlete is registered.

(f) Any person who shall refuse to appear or to testify before any Registration Committee upon any hearing or to answer any question which such Committee shall rule to be proper shall be liable to suspension or such other discipline as the Committee may determine until he has purged himself of such refusal.

(g) Doping is the employment of drugs with the intention of increasing athletic efficiency by their stimulating action upon muscles or nerves or by paralyzing the sense of fatigue. Any athlete who uses drugs as above defined shall be disqualified from the pertinent competition and suspended for a period to be fixed by the Registration Committee. In the case of repeated infringements, the competitor can be suspended permanently.

(h) In all phases of track and field, including race walking and long distance running, an athlete may not accept as a gift, directly or indirectly from a manufacturer, distributor or its representative for use in training or competition equipment, apparatus, implements, or apparel, unless such gift was received with the permission of the Amateur Athletic Union or the national supervising committees for the sports or pursuant to an agreement between the Amateur Athletic Union or the sport supervising committees and the manufacturer, distributor or its representative. Gifts received by an athlete with the approval of the Amateur Athletic Union or the Sports Supervising Committees may not thereafter be given or sold by the athlete or his representative for money or other consideration. An athlete who seeks or receives or disposes of such gift in violation of the provisions herein may be liable to suspension from active participation in amateur athletics.

454.11   **Persons Other Than Athletes**.

(a) Any coach, manger or other person who, directly or indirectly, shall include, or be in any way instrumental in entering or allowing a registered athlete to enter, without a warning of the consequences, any unsanctioned competition, meet, game, exhibition or contest, shall be barred from participating in any capacity in the Amateur Athletic Union program.

(b) Any person aiding or abetting in the use of drugs by athletes shall be permanently excluded from all AAU activities.

(c) Any person aiding or abetting any athlete to disqualify himself in any way as an amateur may be barred from participating in any capacity in the AAU program on the association level by the Board of Managers and on the national level by the Board of Governors.

(d) In all phases of track and field, including race walking and long distance running, a coach, manager, club or other person or organization, who arranges for, accepts or receives on behalf of athletes a gift of equipment, apparatus, implements or apparel for use in training or competition from a manufacturer, distributor or its representative, for the purpose of endorsement may be censured or may be barred from participating in any capacity in the activities of the Amateur Athletic Union.

ARTICLE 55
REINSTATEMENT

455.1   **Not Eligible**.   Persons who are disqualified as amateurs for fraud are indefinitely disbarred from competition as amateurs.

455.2   **Limited**.

(a) Any individual who competes for money or is otherwise professionalized under AAU rules, regardless of age, may apply for limited reinstatement to amateur status and be eligible to participate in amateur competition after (1) year from date of retirement, or unconditional release from the professional sport, or last act of professionalism under the following conditions:

(1) The athlete shall not be eligible to participate in any sport in which he was professionalized.

(2) The athlete shall not be eligible to compete in any national championships, Olympic Games or any international competition.

(3) Any athlete who has been granted limited reinstatement and who is later disbarred for any breach of the rules of the AAU shall never again be eligible for reinstatement.

(4) Any individual professionalized under AAU Rules and whose age puts him in the Master's classifications may revert to amateur status and be eligible as covered in Article 53 of the Code.

218

APPENDIX A

(b) A Basketball player who has been declared professional may, under certain circumstances, be reinstated as an amateur, but with the benefit of limited eligibility only.

In principle, the following are considered as valid circumstances:

    (1) Having signed up as player for a professional club before having reached the twenty-second year of age, and having withdrawn withing the twelve-month period following the signature of contract.

    (2) Having withdrawn from professional basketball in order to follow a recognized professional occupation, and having been engaged regularly in the new occupation for at least one full year.

    (3) Having contracted matrimony.

    (4) Having suffered from severe illness or having been the victim of an incapacitating accident.

By limited eligibility it is understood that such a player may engage only in basketball activities at club level (local, national or international). Under no circumstances may he qualify as a player for a national team, whether for friendly games or for official competitions, such as the Olympic Games, Regional Games, area or continental championships or cups.

Note. The above conditions are applicable only to basketball players in accordance with FIBA rules.

455.3   **For Capitalizing on Athletic Fame.** The Board of Governors is empowered to reinstate to eligibility to compete as an amateur in the sports and exercises over which this Union has jurisdiction one who has capitalized on his athletic fame upon it being shown to the satisfaction of said Board that:

    (a) Such person has ceased to commit any of the acts, or to engage in any of the pursuits or practices set down in said clause.

    (b) Three years have elapsed since the applicant last received pay for a display of his athletic ability or accepted a cash bonus or its equivalent and/or for signing a professional contract, as referred to in 454.9.

    (c) Said person intends never again to commit any of the said acts, or to engage in any of the said pursuits or practices.

455.4   **For Competing Against Ineligible Persons.** The District Registration Committee is empowered to reinstate to eligibility to compete as an amateur in the sports and exercises over which this Union has jurisdiction one who has competed against ineligible persons upon it being shown to the satisfaction of said

Board that:

    (a)   Said competition was not in any of the sports exercises enumerated in 202.2, or if it was, that one year has elapsed since such competition.

    (b)   Such person intends never again to commit such act.

455.5   **For Competing in Unsanctioned Affairs**. The Registration Committee of the Association in whose territory the athlete committing the offense is registered shall have the power to reinstate anyone so disqualified if it shall think fit except that where the offense consists of competing or participating in any competition under the sanction or jurisdiction of any body or group other than the AAU which claims jurisdiction over open competition in the sport in question, such reinstatement shall not become effective until approved by the National Committee.

455.6   **Procedure**. The procedure for reinstatement is as follows:

    (a)   Application in writing shall be made to the Chairman of the local AAU Association Registration Committee stating when and where the last professional act was committed.

    (b)   If the applicant has engaged in more than one sport as a professional, list each sport.

    (c)   This application which must be signed and sworn to before a notary public shall then be sent to the Chairman of the National Registration Committee in care of National AAU Headquarters, together with the recommendation of the local Registration Committee Chairman for approval or disapproval.

    (d)   All such applications must be placed before the National Board of Governors for final action at the next annual convention.

455.7   **By Board of Governors**. Application for reinstatement to full amateur status can be acted upon only at an annual meeting of the Board of Governors. A majority vote shall be necessary for reinstatement.

ARTICLE 56
PROFESSIONAL CONTESTS

456.1   **Forbidden**. No competition may be held between an amateur and a professional unless heretofore provided in the code. A regularly employed instructor, however, may take part with his pupils in group exhibitions only.

(f) Any person receiving compensation for officiating in any sport in which he wishes to compete renders himself ineligible for further amateur competition in that sport. The registration committee of the District Association in which such person is or was registered is empowered to approve registration or reinstatement of such person whose compensation was or is not in excess of allowable expenses under AAU regulations, and who has not otherwise rendered himself ineligible.

(g) An athlete who, for gain, solicits publicly the employment of his athletic services shall automatically disqualify himself from further amateur competition. The Registration Committee of the Association in which such athlete is, or was, registered is empowered to reinstate such offender at the expiration of one year after date of his last offense.

(h) Expenses for competing.

    (1) In all cases where an athlete receives money to cover traveling expenses, whether from his own club or any other organization, he shall immediately upon his return home, send to the Chairman of the Registration Committee of his own district a signed statement showing the amount received and an itemized account of his expenses. When any money is paid to an athlete for traveling expenses, the organization or committee making such payment shall be required to take a receipt therefor in duplicate, containing an itemized statement of such expenses, and forward immediately the copy thereof to the Chairman of the Registration Committee of the District Association in which the athlete is registered, and one copy thereof to the Chairman of the Registration Committee of the Association in whose district the meeting is held, such receipts and statements to be kept on file for a period of three years by said chairman respectively. Any athlete failing to forward promptly the statement, as required above, shall be liable to suspension; and any organization failing to secure and forward the receipt, as above provided, shall be liable to suspension or refusal of sanction as the case may be.

    (2) The maximum expenses which an athlete may request, receive or accept in connection with his competition or participation in any event shall not exceed:

        (i) His actual expenditures for travel up to the cost of first class public transportation fare, including the cost of such transportation to and from airport or railroad terninal; and

456.2   **Tryout.**   Competition with or against professionals during "tryout" shall not be construed as a violation of this rule.

456.3   **Same Program.**   No professional contest or exhibition shall be allowed at any competition, exhibition or other event held or sanctioned by the Amateur Athletic Union, except when requested by the District Association Sports Committee and the Registration Committee of the District Association where the events are to take place, and when recommended by the National Sports Supervising Committee, permission may be granted by the National Registration Committee provided such competition is considered to be in the best interest of the sport concerned or for the benefit of a recognized charity or the Amateur Athletic Union or the US Olympic Committee.

456.4   **Boxing.**   No boxing promoter, manager or any other person shall be allowed to promote or conduct any amateur boxing show solely for personal profit. Appropriate personnel may be employed to direct a program of boxing for the benefit of the sport. All individuals or organizations may receive a proportionate share from an investment made by them, provided the entire conduct of the meet or competition is under the strict control of the Amateur Athletic Union.

INDEX

Index